DOING BUSINESS *in* JAPAN

DOING BUSINESS *in* JAPAN *an* INSIDER'S GUIDE

The CANADIAN CHAMBER *of* COMMERCE *in* JAPAN

JANE WITHEY, *General Editor*

KEY PORTER BOOKS

Please note: All dollar amounts in this book are expressed in U.S. dollars.

The Canadian Chamber of Commerce in Japan
P.O. Box 79, Akasaka Post Office
Minato-Ku, Tokyo 107
Phone: (813) 3408-4311
Fax: (813) 3408-4190

The publisher gratefully acknowledges the assistance of the Canada Council and the Ontario Arts Council.

Canadian Cataloguing in Publication Data

Main entry under title:
Doing business in Japan

Includes bibliographical references and index.
ISBN 1–55013–479–5

1. Canada — Commerce — Japan. 2. Japan — Commerce — Canada.
I. Canadian Chamber of Commerce in Japan.

HF3228.J3B88 1994 382′.0971052 C93–094122–5

Key Porter Books Limited
70 The Esplanade
Toronto, Ontario
Canada M5E 1R2

Design: Scott Richardson
Typesetting: IBEX Graphic Communications Inc.
Printed and bound in Canada

94 95 96 97 98 6 5 4 3 2 1

CONTENTS

The rich mix of cultures that North Americans are born into works to our advantage when we undertake business abroad. The interaction with a variety of ethnic groups and values, which most of us experience in our youth, prepares us to behave properly in our business dealings almost everywhere — except Japan! Unfortunately, North American businesspeople receive little training to prepare them to be effective in Japan. Faced with what appears to be an incomprehensible culture, many do not even attempt to enter the Japanese market.

I believe that this is a tragic mistake — a mistake which this book should help any reader to avoid.

Perhaps the greatest satisfaction I sense when looking back over forty-five years in the international business arena is the knowledge that I made the effort to get to know Japan. And I tasted the rewards. No success in business was ever sweeter to me than what I achieved in Japan. And no customers tried harder than my Japanese customers to stay with me once I had earned their trust.

All of our activities predated the rise of the Asian markets, which have now become the fastest-growing sector of the world economy. My company, Alcan, filled its first export order to Japan in 1903. In 1931, Alcan entered into a joint venture with the Sumitomo Group to form Toyo Aluminium Limited, and in the 1950s we entered into another joint venture with Nippon Light Metal to assist with the postwar reconstruction of Japan's aluminum industry.

This is not to say that the Japanese market is an easy market to enter. To be blunt, Japan is an acquired taste. However, if you make the effort — and last the course — you will accomplish a great deal for your enterprise, for your country, and for yourself.

The turmoil and fire of domestic competition is what prepares an enterprise for successful global competition. From a Canadian perspective, our domestic industrial market is too small to provide the competition necessary to sharpen our enterprises to achieve export success, which leads me to believe that the ultimate benefit of the Free Trade Agreement is that it expands our "domestic" competition base. We could stop there if our ambitions were limited to North America and Europe, but much of the dynamic economic growth of the twenty-first century will take place in Asia. To sharpen your enterprise for success in Asia, you must go after the Japanese market. Once established there, the rest of Asia will come easily. And we badly need the business that is available in Japan.

David Culver

David Culver retired in 1989 as the chairman and chief executive officer of Alcan Aluminium Limited, after forty years with the company. He has been a strong advocate of Canadian interests in Japan, serving as the Canadian chairman of the Canada-Japan Businessmen's Cooperation Committee for eleven years. He is a Companion of the Order of Canada and was awarded the Order of the Sacred Treasure, Grand Cordon, of Japan.

The Canadian Chamber of Commerce in Japan receives many inquiries from businesses seeking to establish footholds in the Japanese market. Over the years, it has become apparent to us that Western businesspeople need to know more about the practical realities of the Japanese way of life and manner of doing business. This is no doubt attributable in part to gaps in our education system, which has been focused on Europe and North America at the expense of most other parts of the world. In addition, Western media coverage of Japan tends to portray it as the economic enemy behind fortress-like trade barriers, ignoring the fact that there are many Western companies that operate profitably here.

Working in Japan, one soon becomes aware of the vast opportunities which exist in this market. Indeed, it is often difficult to contain one's enthusiasm for a country with such economic vitality and dynamism.

Thus, we decided to put together expert advice on doing business in Japan with a twofold aim: to convince Western businesses that the market is one in which they should be operating and, secondly, to pass on concrete information and practical advice that will assist those companies that choose to enter the Japanese market.

There are three reasons why it is crucial that Western companies no longer ignore the Japanese market. The first relates to the opportunities offered by the sheer size of the market itself. The second largest economy in the world, Japan consists of 125 million consumers, each possessing one of the highest per capita incomes in the world. While it is true that the Japanese economy is currently in the throes of the worst downturn of the postwar period, this has followed a long period of unprecedented growth during which the economy and its consumers have matured. Somewhat sheltered in the past, Japanese consumers are more and more aware of, and accordingly have increasing appetites for, the products and services available in other cultures. This has been accompanied by growing demands for openness on many fronts. As Japanese companies struggle to deal with the consequences of the recession, a new questioning is arising in Japanese society, of political structures, corporate personnel policies, agricultural policies, and traditional loyalties, including, most importantly, the social contract under which individual citizens have borne the cost of maintaining Japan Inc. This is creating a demand for freer trade policies and for deregulation of the market to permit the flow of goods within the country at lower costs. Western companies should position themselves to take advantage of these changes as they occur.

The second reason to come to the Japanese market is that Japanese companies are in your markets. Japanese companies have been enormously successful at penetrating global markets and are world leaders in many product areas. Their expenditure on research and development, which as a percentage of GDP outstrips all other countries, means that Japan is on the leading edge in most technologies. By operating here, you will be aware of the changes that are occurring in your industry as they happen and as they determine the changes in global markets. By managing the fierce competition that exists in Japan, your organization will develop the flexibility to allow it to be a first-class competitor in all other markets. The Japanese recession, though longer than most pundits had predicted, is by no means as severe as that suffered by most Western economies. Still, it is raising doubts about the invincibility of Japanese corporations. It is important, however, for the Western corporate world to be aware that the recession is causing a shake-out of certain inefficiencies within the Japanese market, and those companies that do survive will be leaner and more competitive.

Finally, one must consider the position of Japan within the greater region of Asia. It has become almost commonplace to say that the twenty-first century belongs to Asia, and indeed recent growth rates and forecasts for the near term would justify this. With much Western interest now focused on other countries in Asia such as Indonesia, Malaysia, and, most recently, China, many are tempted to forget about Japan and concentrate their energies elsewhere. But, as Dr. James Abegglen has aptly put it, to come to Asia and ignore the Japanese market is like going to North America and ignoring the United States. Japan is now and Asia is tomorrow: Japan is still the only Asian market of any size with income levels remotely comparable to Western nations. Having said that, it is important to note that Japanese investment is pouring into the Asian region, and intraregional trade is rising dramatically. By working with Japanese partners, you can develop another means of access to the Asian engine of economic growth into the future.

This book is divided into three parts. The first sets out answers to the question of why Western companies should come to Japan, looking at economic forecasts and the profile of Japan's imports. The second describes the nature of the Japanese market in terms of its society, market trends and consumer values, and corporate behavior. The final section consists of eight chapters offering practical advice in specific areas on how to penetrate the market successfully.

Our writers have considerable practical experience working in the Japanese market. In many cases, their experience has been gained in advising Western companies on various aspects of the market, whether it be in terms of market entry, public relations, marketing and advertising, or seeking Japanese investment. As such, their insights are invaluable for any potential entrant to the market.

We are indebted to all of the experts we called upon to contribute a chapter to this collection. All have given generously of their time and expertise. In addition, special thanks to Dr. Robert Ballon, who prepared the annotated bibliographies that appear at the end of the book, and to David Culver, who wrote the Foreword.

On behalf of the Chamber, I would like to thank John Treleaven, whose brainchild the book is, and who has supported the project throughout. Thanks also to Judith Johnston-Ueda for her assistance. And finally, thanks to Christopher Evans, executive director of the Chamber, and to the Chamber staff for their support and advice.

Jane Withey
Tokyo
Spring 1994

CHAPTER ONE

Japan in the 1990s: To Still Higher Levels of Performance

KENNETH S. COURTIS

The current recession in Japan has spawned a variety of articles in the Western press about the country's decline as an economic superpower. No one can deny that the high growth the country experienced in the 1980s has slowed, and the economy has now entered a period of transition and structural readjustment. In this chapter, Dr. Kenneth Courtis, strategist and senior economist for the Deutsche Bank Group in Asia, traces the development of the postwar Japanese economy, delineating the policies that engendered that growth. He then discusses why he believes Japan will emerge from the current slowdown stronger than ever, and will continue to outperform the West into the next century.

The role that Japan has begun to play on the international stage still elicits surprise in the West. Yet for much of this century, Japan has been closely involved in many of the key issues on the international agenda — questions of war, recovery in peacetime, and economic prosperity. Considering the trends developing in the world political economy and in Japan itself, it is clear that Japan will play an even greater international role in the future.

For those countries sitting on the Pacific Rim, the importance of Japan will continue to grow. From finance to technology, from trade to economics, the countless microeconomic decisions of corporate Japan, as well as the larger policy thrust of the country's overall economic focus, will act powerfully to shape the Pacific marketplace. Indeed, that is already very much the case; those countries that are more open to the powerful growth dynamics of

Asia have been better able to weather the recent economic recession.

Critical to the transition now occurring in the international environment is a fundamental shift in the balance of power between the United States, the former Soviet Union and its disbanded empire, the European Common Market with a united Germany at its core, and the Pacific, centered on Japan. The transition is being driven both by forces particular to each of these four poles in the world political economy, and by a complex interaction of relationships of cooperation and conflict between them.

Still more profound than these developments is the larger shift in the global balance of economic, financial, industrial, and, increasingly, technological power to the Pacific. Again, Japan is at the very center of this process. In 1960, Japan represented some 3 percent of world GNP, while the United States was just over eleven times larger at 34 percent. By 1990, Japan made up 16 percent of the world economy, and the United States was but one-third larger at 21 percent. Should current trends continue, the gap could well close completely over the next decade.

It is against this broad international background that developments occurring in Japan and its economy can best be put into perspective. What I wish to address here are the forces driving change in Japan. I will highlight the dynamics of that change, which will be critical in shaping Japan's international role through the 1990s. The question that is now at issue is whether the trends of the past three decades are set to remain in place through the decade ahead. If so, what would be the larger international economic and competitive implications? If not, why not?

Many argue, indeed have done so for decades, that Japan is finally about to go over the edge, that the sun is setting on the greatest economic success story of the past half century. Close and careful analysis of the economy reveals a different picture, however. It is that at the end of the 1980s Japan set itself on course to purge the excesses of the previous phase of blistering expansion, to cleanse its economy, and to melt off the fat accumulated during the years of record-smashing growth that followed the G7 decision in 1985 to double the value of the yen. In short, the transition of the early 1990s has been largely policy-induced, and represents phase two of Japan's response to the Plaza Accord.

The Plaza Accord was conceived by Japan's principal North American and European partners as the bitter medicine required to reverse the course of Japan's ever-widening external trade surplus. For most countries, the collapse of their external position would indeed have been the immediate result of such a violent increase in their currency. For Japan, however, the shock served as a powerful stimulus which drove the economy into still another phase of growth. This will later be understood as the opening phase of a cycle of expansion that will take the country through the end of the 1990s.

THE HEISEI CYCLE: THE FIFTEEN YEARS TO THE YEAR 2000

When analyzing Japan's economy, we may come to see the fifteen years from the Plaza Accord until the end of the century as having been composed of three phases. Together, they form what I have termed the Heisei Cycle.

The first phase I call the Heisei Expansion, the period of massive growth that occurred from 1986 through 1991. Those sixty months of expansion were the longest, and the most internationally significant, of any of Japan's previous cycles of expansion since the end of the Second World War.

The second phase is the Transition, predicted to last through the mid-90s. This phase is a purge of the excesses of the 1980s, during which Japan dealt with the side effects of the monetary and fiscal policy measures adopted in response to the Plaza Accord. This transition will leave Japan substantially strengthened from a competitive and financial perspective, for it is resulting in a still more concentrated economy, and has spurred yet another cycle of aggressive rationalization and an increase in competitiveness.

The third phase will be a new period of powerful growth which will carry Japan's economy from mid-decade through the end of the 1990s and will set in place the base for sustainable, long-term growth into the decade beyond. Much of the growth during the second half of the 1990s will come from Japan's increasing integration with and strategic control of the booming mega-markets of East Asia. It is this New Expansion that will position Japan to rival the United States for global economic leadership.

First we will examine the Heisei Expansion. By late 1991, the expansion that began in November 1986 had become the longest in Japan's modern economic history, surpassing even the enormously powerful growth cycle of the 1960s. From an international perspective, the difference between the Heisei Expansion and that of the 1960s is that, three decades ago, Japan's economy was about the size of Canada's relative to the United States. But with an economy now seven times larger than that of Canada, more than two-thirds the size of America's, and two and a quarter times that of Germany, the long-term international competitive and financial implications of the Heisei Expansion are critical.

The effects of this shift have been substantially broadened and reinforced because it has occurred in the context of the collapse of the Soviet Union and a turning inward of the United States, which is hobbled by debt levels reminiscent of the 1930s, with all the attendant financial and economic consequences.

To put the Heisei Expansion into perspective so as to provide some measure of its power, the growth created in the Japanese economy in the five years to the end of 1991 was equal to the annual GNP of France. In other words, Japan's economy was by 1992 one France larger than it was at the time of the Plaza Accord. So powerful was the Heisei Expansion that it will come to be understood as the country's third economic miracle.

Japan's first economic miracle was the cycle of growth that began in 1960. Driven by domestic demand for consumer durables — cars, housing, and household appliances — and capital equipment, and by the expansion of the capital-intensive materials industries, the economy grew almost threefold in the fifteen years to 1975. Take the example of the automotive industry. Japan produced 500,000 cars in 1960 and 5 million in 1970, of which only 18 percent were for export. With a growth rate of 26 percent a year over a decade, Japanese auto producers raced down the cost curve, and so set in place the base for the export surge of the following decade. The same process happened in other sectors such as steel, synthetic fibers, televisions, motorcycles, and audio equipment.

The second miracle was Japan's lightning adaptation to the breakdown of Bretton-Woods, the two Nixon shocks, the double energy crises, and the inflationary blowout of the 1970s. A measure of how quickly Japan adapted to the new conditions is that today Japan produces two and a half times the real output with the same volume of energy input as twenty years ago. Although the country continues to import all of its oil, its ability to absorb a new energy shock is greater today than ever before. Japan's energy imports account today for approximately 1.4 percent of GNP. That is only slightly more than the 1.2 percent recorded for the United States, the world's largest oil producer.

The Heisei Expansion was Japan's third economic miracle. At its core was massive capital investment, driven essentially by strategic and structural forces, and the particular policy mix adopted in response to the Plaza Accord in September 1985. This was reinforced by Japan's policy response to the near meltdown of equity markets in Europe and North America two years later, which was indirectly related to the ripple effects of the Plaza Accord on U.S. interest rates.

STRATEGIC INVESTMENT AND THE INVESTMENT GAP

So powerful was the cycle of capital investment that characterized the Heisei Expansion that in 1988, for the first time in history, Japan invested in absolute terms more than the United States invested. In every year since, the gap has widened.

Take 1991 as an example, a year during which Japan was sliding into recession. In real terms, Japan invested some $725 billion in private sector plant and equipment. These figures exclude all real estate investment and refer only to the domestic economy. In comparison, the United States invested $495 billion, or approximately 11.2 percent of real GNP, in plant and capital investment. During the same period, Japan committed some $100 billion to nonmilitary, civilian research and development, again surpassing the United States and the entire European Community.

These figures are even more striking when analyzed on a per capita basis. In 1991, private sector plant and capital equipment investment in the U.S. domestic economy was $1,960 for every man, woman, and child. For Japan, the comparable figure was $5,491. On the same basis, the United States committed to nonmilitary, civilian research $544 per capita, compared to $822 for Japan.

This investment gap is crippling for America. More importantly, it is not the result of one year's numbers, nor is it limited to the late 1980s. Indeed, not once in more than a quarter of a century has the United States committed more of its GNP to private sector capital investment than has Japan. These trends also have particular impact for Canada, with an economy closely tied to that of the United States.

The investment gap would not matter much if Japan's economy were much smaller. But it matters, and matters a great deal, when such trends occur over a prolonged period between the world's largest economies. On the basis of these capital investment and research trends alone, the momentum is set to continue moving in Japan's favor through the remainder of the decade. In many regards, the Canada–United States Free Trade Agreement was adopted at the very moment that the decline of North America began to accelerate. But more, much more, is at issue than the widening investment gap.

To begin with, as the investment gap has widened, it has put many core industries in North America on the defensive. For Canada, with such a large share of its traded goods sector controlled by American-based firms, these trends are very much at the core of the economic crisis that has been building for more than a decade. Take again the automotive industry as an example.

As the decade began, there were some sixty-nine automotive factories in North America, of which thirty-two were built before 1939, more than half a century ago. Some of these relics of another era are finally being shut down. But think how difficult it has been to introduce flexible manufacturing in such carcasses. Similarly, if you are trying to install a just-in-time delivery system, for example, and your infrastructure is falling apart, it is going to be much more difficult to execute, resulting in higher overall production costs and reduced competitiveness. The recent estimate that one-fifth of all bridges in the United States have become unsafe through lack of maintenance is but a single example of widespread decay.

Similar pressures are forcing the European automotive industry to accept that it has simply too many producers, none of which is a top-level player in all global markets. As the competitive pressure of the Japanese producers builds in the EC market, European industry will be forced into either massive restructuring or massive protectionism. European producers are going to have to use any free cash flow defensively in their home markets.

It is important to note that Japan is not alone in out-investing North America and Europe. Indeed, as a proportion of GNP, all of the rest of East Asia, with Korea and Taiwan leading the way, is out-investing Japan. This is one of the key forces driving the region's booming prosperity, a prosperity which increasingly is linking itself into the growth dynamics at the core of Japan's own performance. For just as Europe and North America are being driven back onto the defensive in sector after sector, Japan is positioning itself to score huge global market-share gains as it aggressively shifts its strategic focus to the booming markets of Asia.

PRODUCTIVITY, INNOVATION, AND NEW CAPACITY

Where did the massive Japanese capital investment of the late 1980s go? It is widely believed that much of it went into capacity expansion and frivolities, such as palatial hotels in Hawaii. While some of the net $3.1 trillion in new private sector domestic plant and equipment investment of the 1986 to 1991 period was indeed not properly invested, analysis reveals that most of it was used to put more muscle into the economy.

Approximately 30 percent of capital investment went directly into rationalization and productivity, into making more for less. Consider again as an example the automotive industry, where the leading Japanese makers have collapsed the development and design cycle to three and a half years, from the five to six years it took in the early 1980s. I have called this process "just-in-time development and design." Although there is much concern about the costs that shorter design times impose on weaker firms, the competitive market effects over the 1990s will be just as powerful as just-in-time delivery has proved to be over the past decade.

Another example of such production-driven investment is "focused production," which is based on integrated global sourcing, supply, production, and distribution. Two other important targets of productivity-enhancing investment are "modular production," which has as its primary objective a reduction in the number of assembly parts for a product, essentially through designing them away, and new generation assembly technologies, for which Japan has established a crushing lead in the critical software that drives the process.

Another 30 percent of capital investment made during the Heisei Expansion went into innovation. Innovation investment has always accounted for a high proportion of Japanese capital investment but, since the mid-1980s, a major difference has occurred. From 1975 to 1985, the period of Japan's export boom, about three-quarters of innovation-related investment was targeted at the development of new products and services designed to penetrate the North American and European markets. Since 1986, however, there has been a complete reversal, with about 80 percent of innovation investment now targeting the domestic market. This means that new products and services will increasingly be introduced in Japan first.

In short, Japan is positioning itself to play a role in the world economy similar to that which the United States played in the 1950s and 1960s. Then, new products were first developed and introduced into the American market, and, as the international product life cycle unfolded, were released in sequence around the world. Over the 1990s, Japan will move to occupy a similar role as the new product laboratory for the world economy.

The evolving balance of innovation across the Pacific becomes apparent through the registration of what are known as "significant patents," that is, patents which are cited in subsequent patent filings. Year after year for the past two decades, the ranking of Japan's firms has improved in all key marketplaces. Nowhere is the trend clearer than in the United States, where Japanese firms lead in patent registrations in various sectors, from automobiles to consumer electronics, from robotics to new materials.

With productivity and innovation having accounted for some 60 percent of capital investment during the Heisei Expansion, the remainder went into new capacity. But even for this type of investment, about half was directed to establishing facilities for providing products and services that did not exist a decade ago.

MORE COMPETITIVE MOMENTUM AND LARGER CAPITAL SURPLUSES

It follows that approximately four-fifths of the investment that occurred in the five years to 1991 was targeted at setting in place the economic base for sustained growth through the 1990s and beyond. This investment in the future gives tremendous long-term momentum to Japan. The divergence in investment behavior between Japan, North America, and to some extent with Europe, sets in place a dynamic that will have far-reaching implications for international economic relations throughout the decade.

It is on the basis of these forces, for example, that the structural dynamics driving Japan's external surpluses were substantially reinforced during the late 1980s. Not only does this contradict the widely accepted view that Japan has structurally "changed" and that imbalances of the past decades are behind us, but also, and still more important, when the West finally realizes what has in fact occurred, Japan's new surpluses will dwarf anything seen previously.

With the issue of jobs set to remain at the very top of the political agendas of Europe and America in the 1990s, Japan's surpluses are sure to trigger even more tension and conflict during the period ahead than anything yet experienced. But the real issue that this politicization begs will be the recycling of Japan's surpluses to the world economy. By mid-decade, once Japan is squarely on the other side of the transition of the early 1990s, it is this question that will come to dominate international economic policy debate.

In a world economy facing a tightening capital shortage through the remainder of the 1990s, these ever larger surpluses under Japan's control will give the country a substantially more favorable position in negotiations with capital-hungry North America and Europe. For Canada, a country still far from coming to terms with its own precarious debt structure and set to remain a significant capital importer through this decade, access to Japan's surpluses will be critical to financing capital shortfall.

As these Pacific imbalances build, tensions between the United States and Japan will continue to intensify. As is already the case for trade, it will be necessary for Japan's other major trading partners to be extremely active and skillful in assuring continued and balanced access to Japanese-controlled surpluses. The best way to assure that access is for the countries of much of Europe and North America to adopt an overall, integrated economic strategy that would allow them to steer away from the difficulties toward which they are currently headed, and that would have the Asia-Pacific as a primary focus of public policy. To do otherwise, or to do less, would be to set a course for even greater difficulties than they have experienced over the past ten years.

THE TRANSITION: 1991–1995

By mid-1989, it had become increasingly clear for those looking closely at Japan's economy that the country was in the process of turning the Plaza Accord to its advantage, as leading exporters were well on the way to being competitive by the mid-1990s at ¥90 to ¥100 to the U.S. dollar. Against this background, and following intense debate among policy-makers, the corporate sector, the opinion press, and influential academics, the Bank of Japan reversed course from mid-1989. It raised interest rates, imposed strict lending controls, and in tandem with the Ministry of Finance, moved to reassert control across the entire financial system. A number of immediate concerns were critical to this reversal. Most important was the upward spiral to ever-higher values in

Japan's equity and real estate prices, which created the risk that an unexpected shock to the world economy would provoke such a violent crash of Japan's markets that it could trigger a global stock market crash.

At the same time, fear grew that in an economy as hot as Japan's was at the time, a spark of inflation from the international economy would have devastating effects. It is of note that some four-fifths of Japanese imports are dollar-denominated, and that this concern was building at the time that the United States had entered a new cycle of inflation.

In addition, the wild speculation of the 1980s had begun to create social inequalities that, left to run their course, would have torn apart the very fabric of Japanese society. That same speculation, and the sparkle of the vast new pools of wealth that it was creating, proved irresistible to the Japanese mob, the yakuza, which began to penetrate ever deeper into the country's financial markets.

Finally, the end of the Cold War, and the liquidity shock created by German unification and the manner in which it was financed, sent interest rates higher around the globe, and so forced the hand of Japanese authorities. Had the side effects of the ultra-easy monetary policy of the 1980s, and the speculation that it permitted, been left to run much longer, Japan's economy would have been deeply destabilized. In the process, much of what had been gained in the five years after the Plaza Accord would have been compromised.

By the time the authorities acted, however, the economy had such a head of steam that it took more than a year and a half before the higher interest rates, lending controls, and regulatory constraints began to slow down the economy. These policies came to be felt with a vengeance from late 1991, as the economy moved into recession.

The recession has been neither short and sharp, nor soft and prolonged. Rather it has been a wrenching purge, particularly bracing for small and middle-sized firms and for the overextended financial sector. But what has occurred through the transition is positive for the economy overall, placing Japan in an even stronger position.

THE DYNAMICS OF RECESSION

The recession has been driven by the overlapping effects of a vicious cycle of asset deflation, a capital stock adjustment, a break in the product cycle in key consumer markets, and the impact on Japan of the recession in Europe and North America, which has itself been driven by the combined process of global debt deflation and the ongoing effects of the monetary and fiscal implications of German unification.

ASSET DEFLATION

The first manifestation of the impact of the policy reversals of mid-1989 was the crash of the equity market from early 1990. It took some thirty months, through the third quarter of 1992, before equity prices stabilized after having lost more than half their value. Although many argued that the purge would be limited to the equity market, such has never been the case elsewhere in similar conditions, and it was difficult to understand why Japan would be an exception.

The second phase of asset deflation occurred in the real estate market. With regard to residential real estate prices, officials continue to issue regular reports indicating that their policy objective is to see average house prices fall to approximately five times annual household income from the level of nine to ten times at the peak of the real estate boom in 1990. That is a dramatic fall, but it is one that can be absorbed, albeit not without great stress, by the household sector.

With still largely full employment and very high household savings rates, only a small portion of the still-to-come losses on residential real estate will be realized. In this regard, Japan is not saddled with the additional difficulties that home equity loans, or their equivalents, create for authorities in North America, Australia, and parts of Europe, economies that have also had to steer residential real estate prices back into balance during recent years.

For commercial real estate, however, the deflation of prices has been a much more problematic process for the simple, but critical, reason that so much of Japan's bank lending is tied to commercial real estate. As a result, were an equivalent shakeout to occur as is in process for the residential property market, it would result in nothing less than a meltdown of the Japanese financial system. The knock-on effect of such developments for the international economy would be to severely increase the risk for financial markets around the world. Although forecasts of such developments continue to haunt the investment community, they are unlikely to occur, at least not as a result of developments in Japan alone.

In the West, commercial real estate continues to be in massive oversupply (for example, close to one-fifth of commercial buildings in the United States were still empty at the beginning of 1993, a full six years after the peak in U.S. real estate prices). This is in marked contrast to the situation in Japan where, four years into the contraction in prices, the occupancy rate for commercial properties has been close to 94.2 percent. That figure will ease further through mid-decade, but not substantially.

Since the peak, yields on commercial property have begun climbing back toward 3.75 to 4.00 percent, a level at which prices could stabilize, given long-term bond yields. In addition, it is important to remember that even at the peak of the crisis, lessees were obliged to deposit, in an interest-free trust for the benefit of the lessor, the equivalent of two years' rent on signature of a lease.

Authorities appear to be working through a combination of rent increases, a further 10 percent drop in property values through mid-decade, and the removal of a significant portion of the resulting bad debt from bank balance sheets. That would put aggregate commercial real estate yields very close to the 3.75 to 4.00 percent target level. While not very attractive from an investment perspective, at that level prices would at least stabilize and signal a bottom for the market.

Should prices begin to move significantly beyond these parameters, authorities would act quickly to increase the net present value of commercial property cash flows by allowing more intensive land use, while at the same time limiting new supply through zoning constraints. In this manner, authorities appear to have worked to engineer a tiered deflation of the real estate market. Although most difficult for the banks to absorb, it is a manageable adjustment, but one which will be completed only by mid-decade.

The programs announced in August 1992 to support Japanese

asset markets — in particular the creation of a Japanese equivalent of the Resolution Trust Corporation in the United States — were directly targeted to addressing the problems resulting from the deflation of real estate market prices, and the larger financial implications for the banks.

The most important of these programs was the decision to create a public corporation to take over a large portion of the bad real estate debt of the banks. In essence, a portion of these debts is being socialized, in a manner that will see much of the losses passed on, one way or another, to the taxpayer. This will be similar to the socialization of the ocean of bad bank debt that resulted from the blowout of the United States savings and loans industry, but with a major difference: In Japan, the authorities moved well before banks began to go bankrupt. In the United States, on the other hand, the authorities began to act only after the fact, which meant that not only was the problem more difficult to resolve, but also the cost to the taxpayer was substantially higher than it needed to be. Whatever the political equity of the Japanese approach, it does rescue the banks at a much lower cost, and much earlier, and so will allow them to start lending earlier than would otherwise have been the case, which is positive for the economy.

CAPITAL STOCK ADJUSTMENT

Central to the Heisei Expansion of the 1980s was the unprecedented investment boom, as we have seen. Over the five years from 1986, net new private sector capital investment, excluding real estate, averaged 21 percent of GNP. The result, however, is that today Japan's net capital stock to GNP is at the highest level ever recorded.

Certainly the economy has become more capital-intensive as a result of the post-Plaza adjustment, and will continue to do so with the current strength of the yen. It remains, however, that not only a pause in the pace, but also a general reduction in the overall level of investment, is required over the short term in order to restore net capital stock balance for the economy as a whole. While Japan will maintain high investment rates during the 1990s, capital investment will be weak through the end of 1994 as a result of the current process of capital stock adjustment.

A PAUSE IN THE PRODUCT CYCLE IN KEY CONSUMER MARKETS

Overlapping waves of new electronic and consumer video products spurred growth through the 1980s. The diffusion of such products reached saturation levels by 1990. Now we are awaiting the next cycle of hot new consumer products.

At the same time, for a variety of regulatory and fiscal reasons, new car registrations hit three successive year-on-year records over the end of the 1980s. As a result, a significant portion of demand in this sector for the first years of the 1990s was brought forward to the end of the 1980s, with the effect that the household sector is at a saturation point for new cars. A new cycle of renewal of the automotive stock is not due to begin until 1994. Thus producers in these sectors are now announcing major new programs of cost reduction and rationalization. Over the intermediate term this process will be positive from both micro- and macroeconomic perspectives, but for the present it is having a dampening effect on growth.

THE IMPACT OF THE RECESSION IN EUROPE AND NORTH AMERICA

Japan's surging trade and current-account surpluses would seem to deny that the recession in Europe and North America has had a depressive effect on the domestic economy.

Think of it. In 1992, the trade surplus was $134 billion, more than three times what it was in 1984 on the eve of the Plaza Accord, which was designed to send the surplus in the other direction. In 1993, the surplus approached $150 billion. In only the first three months of 1993, Japan's current account surplus was $36.1 billion, not only one-third larger than the figure for the same period a year earlier, but more than the surplus generated by Japan in the entire decade of the 1970s.

Where the economic downturn in Europe and North America is having the most damaging effect is on the performance of Japan's overseas subsidiaries operating in those markets. For example, while earnings were down some 20 percent in the domestic economy in 1992, they were down by double that amount for operations of Japanese firms in the United States and in the Common Market.

With the banks having reduced lending because of the difficulties they face, and firms unable to raise substantial volumes of new funds in the equity market, firms have had to generate funds internally in order to cover losses in Europe and North America. These forces have led companies to cut back still further on capital investment, and as rationalization continues, set the labor market on course for difficulties through mid-decade, when these international pressures will have abated. In the interval, massive fiscal stimulus will be the main force to drive the economy ahead.

A NEW PHASE OF RESTRUCTURING

The accumulated effect of the pressures central to the current transition in the economy has been to lead Japan to yet another phase of restructuring and rationalization from which it will emerge still stronger and more competitive than it has been in the past. Critical to this process is the evolution of corporate balance sheets over the past decade.

During the 1980s, a tiering of the corporate sector occurred, based on company size and balance sheets. As the stock market climbed higher and higher, firms listed on Japan's major stock markets were able to raise more funds, through new equity issues, than they required for investment and research in the post-Plaza period. As a result, these listed firms were able to use a portion of this virtually free money to reduce debt, and so to deleverage. As a result, large companies now have the strongest balance sheets they have had since the Second World War.

In contrast, middle-sized and small unlisted firms, which were also forced to raise a massive volume of funds for the post-Plaza restructuring, and which did not have access to the equity markets, were obliged to turn to the banks for assistance. Flooded with excess reserves as the large firms reduced their debt, the banks were only too happy to lend this money to the smaller firms.

While these funds were largely directed to healthy investment, not a negligible portion was used to acquire assets, which were used in turn as collateral for further bank lending. As a result, the small and mid-sized corporate sector found itself highly over-leveraged at precisely the moment policy authorities reversed course to squeeze the excesses out of the economy.

With money supply and bank lending contracting on a real basis during the twenty-four months to the end of 1993, and asset markets having gone through a violent contraction, the over-leveraged small and middle-sized producers have experienced a vicious squeeze. It is for this reason that bankruptcies have climbed to record levels, and that pressures on the banking sector have intensified. It is also against this background that so much fear has emerged in the consumer sector about employment.

But what is occurring beneath the surface is that as the over-leveraged small and middle-sized producer is being pushed to the margin, the overcapitalized *keiretsu* players (*keiretsu* are groups of affiliated companies) have begun to move in to pick up the pieces — the assets, the market share, the employees — on the cheap. As this process continues through mid-decade, it will result in the Japanese economy operating from a still more concentrated and cost-effective base than ever before.

A similar process is in motion for the financial sector. Although more long term in nature, the restructuring of the banking sector will result in the disappearance of one-quarter to one-third of Japan's small and middle-sized banks, precisely those institutions that today have balance sheets overexposed to the riskiest part of the economy and overloaded with assets created at the market peak in the 1980s. Similarly, six to eight of the country's largest twenty-two city, long-term credit and trust banks are likely to disappear through mergers by the end of the decade. As the financial sector is trimmed down, it will also become significantly more efficient and competitive than ever in the past.

GROWING SURPLUSES AND UNDERCONSUMPTION

Although much was made of the brief cyclical decline in Japan's external surpluses in the late 1980s, what was really occurring at the time was that the deeper structural dynamics driving the surpluses were being substantially reinforced. Driven by the further forces of restructuring and rationalization that the phase of transition from 1991 have generated, the structural dynamics central to Japan's surpluses are stronger today than ever in the past. It is against this background that there is today very little prospect that the momentum driving Japan from one record surplus to another will subside any time soon, even with the dollar falling to below ¥100.

The multiple packages of supplementary spending of some ¥37 trillion announced by Japan in the eighteen months from August 1992, while unprecedented in amount, will be of only modest assistance in reducing the surpluses, for the simple reason that the spending is largely focused on the domestic market. Further, the renewed cycle of revaluation of the yen will absorb much of the positive impact of the new spending, such that its net effect in increasing Japan's imports will be at best modest.

A country that has run an external surplus every year for more than thirty years is a country that is structurally underconsuming. A measure of this situation is that consumer spending in Japan represents only 56 percent of GNP, compared to approximately 64 percent for Europe, and more than 68 percent in the United States. This situation is central to North American problems, but it is also central to Japan's external imbalances.

Japan's exploding surpluses are driven by several forces. In the years since the Plaza Accord doubled the value of the yen, corporate Japan has raced to reduce break-even levels on exports to close to current exchange rates, and repositioned with equal speed to produce an ever higher value-added, less price-elastic export product mix. While these forces have been considered above, it is useful to measure more completely their international implications.

In adapting so quickly to the profound changes in its international environment, corporate Japan is more competitive today than ever in the past. As a result, Japan's domestic economy is in the process of becoming still more difficult to penetrate from abroad. A measure of this new strength is that even at a time of recession in the world economy, Japan-based firms have continued to expand their global market share.

Many argued that the rapid expansion of Japan's direct investment abroad in the late 1980s would lead to an equally sharp decline in its exports. However, history provides a different lesson

— that while trade leads to more overseas investment, so more overseas investment leads to still more trade. As was largely predictable, this pattern is repeating itself again. The tidal wave of Japan's direct foreign investment in the late 1980s has led to a massive expansion of production capacity and distribution of Japanese firms abroad. This new strength has in turn generated a powerful new wave of exports of capital goods required to equip these factories, and exports of the strategic, high value-added parts to feed overseas assembly operations.

In this manner, Japanese companies have broadened and deepened their long-term penetration of international markets. In the process, foreign firms have become increasingly locked into a structure of supply relations in which they become first consumers of parts from Japan, and then distributors of these parts in the form of assembled products. In this manner, large segments of the North American automotive and electronics industries are becoming distribution channels of exports from Japan. This deepening relationship of dependence works as a powerful spur to further Japanese exports.

All of East Asia is engaged in an enormous effort toward increased levels of productivity, and to the output of more complex, higher value-added goods and services. To do so, countries of the region must sustain vast capital investment budgets. With two-thirds of the world's top twenty-five machine-tool makers based in Japan, and the country dominating the software that drives industrial robotics, manufacturing and assembly technology, East Asia has little choice but to turn to Japan.

As China is integrated into the world economy through this decade, the push for still higher levels of capital investment in East Asia will intensify as pressure builds on low-end, labor-intensive production throughout the rest of the region.

It is against this background that the pressures driving Japan to larger and larger surpluses continue to build. Low savings and investment rates, ballooning deficits, and the relatively weakened competitive position of much of Europe and North America only work to intensify these pressures. It is also these forces, in the context of the transition from the hothouse growth of the late 1980s, that set Japan on course to play a still more important role in the world economy over the end of the decade. In the interval, Japan will once again be positioned to enter a new phase of growth, which will carry the economy through to the remainder of the 1990s. Let us examine the key forces driving this new phase of growth.

TOWARD A NEW PHASE OF EXPANSION: 1995–2000

For Japan's economy, the current transition will come to an end by 1994, when it will enter a new phase of expansion. This new phase of expansion will be driven by four forces: expanding consumer spending, continuing high investment levels, the rebuilding of Japan's woefully inadequate infrastructure, and the active participation of corporate Japan in the booming growth that is occurring throughout the new mega-markets along the diagonal from Tokyo to Jakarta.

The difference between consumption levels in Japan on one hand, and North America and Europe on the other, constitutes a rough measure of the tremendous ocean of pent-up consumer demand that exists in Japan, and, which, if not released, will lead to enormous political frustrations.

There is a commonly held theory that, through the 1990s, Japan's aging population will cause the savings rate to collapse and the cost of capital to soar. As a result, Japan would no longer be able to maintain the type of virtuous economic development that has propelled growth during the past thirty years. The presumption of collapsing savings rate is at best questionable. Today, about the same portion of the Japanese and American populations are over sixty-five years of age. The country that demographically most resembles what Japan will look like fifteen years from now is Germany, where already approximately 16 percent of the population is over sixty-five years of age.

Although there is much speculation that savings rates decline as a society ages, there is in fact scant research to demonstrate this. Indeed, the contrary appears to be the case. For example, the savings rate of Germans over sixty-five tends to remain very close to what it was when they were in their mid-forties. In a

Confucian culture, like that of Japan, where success is measured not only in providing for your children but also for your grandchildren, it is likely that the savings rate of older people will remain strong.

LIBERATION OF THE URBAN CONSUMER

Over the past four decades, the tax code has been tailored to the particular interests of three groups — farmers, shopkeepers, and the independent medical profession — such that these groups are taxed at a low rate. Not coincidentally, these same groups have also been the key electoral pillars of the Liberal Democratic Party, which ruled Japan until 1993, and continues to play a central role in the government.

But demographics are fast running against these groups today. The average age of Japanese farmers is over fifty-eight years. Within a decade, two-fifths of the country's farms will disappear. The same dynamics are at work for the small shopkeepers and the country's general practitioners, whose average age is sixty years. Together with international pressure, these demographic changes will force the government to adopt policies that cater to urban Japan in a manner that has not previously been the case. The revision of the large-store law in 1991 is an early example of a much broader wave of change to come.

LAND AND TAX REFORMS ARE URGENT

What is now urgent is reform of the tax code and the land system. Both should be modified in a way that allows the urban consumer more fully to enjoy the fruits of Japan's success. Indeed, the government has already begun to move in this direction, albeit at a snail's pace. It will be necessary to increase the speed and breadth of reform through the mid-1990s to create a stable, urban electoral base.

As these reforms are instituted, a whole new wave of healthy, noninflationary consumer spending will begin that will extend well into the next decade. Were consumer spending in Japan to climb to European levels by the end of the decade, some $500 billion (¥62 trillion) in new spending annually would be released, or the equivalent of the current GNP of Canada.

Should this process of change not occur, Japan's surpluses would explode well beyond current levels and the country would find itself dangerously isolated in the international community. Its domestic political system would also become volatile, fragile, and divisive as the country became increasingly paralyzed, unable to adapt to change.

THE PUBLIC SECTOR: MASSIVE SPENDING CAPACITY IN RESERVE

Japan has agreed in negotiations with the United States to increase government spending on infrastructure by ¥430 trillion through the end of the 1990s. That accord was based on the assumption that Japan's external surplus would steadily decline through the 1990s, and the opposite is very much the case. The brief fall in the surplus in the late 1980s was largely cyclical. Indeed, as noted above, the structural dynamics driving the surplus higher have been substantially reinforced by the investment boom that was central to the Heisei Expansion. As a result, strong international pressures will build on Japan to increase still further its commitment to infrastructure investment.

There is no question that Japan is in dire need of dramatic upgrading in the quality of its social infrastructure. For example, only 42 percent of Japanese houses have access to public sewage; airports are collapsing under the weight of cargo and passengers for which they were never planned; and national highways frequently resemble serpentine parking lots. The country needs to build, and very quickly, its social infrastructure: day-care centers, commuter transportation, airports, roads, and parks.

Although investment will not return to the levels of the late 1980s, the continuing move to a more information and research-intensive economy, together with a long-term labor shortage, will work to keep capital spending at 17 to 19 percent of GNP. Such levels of spending will continue to provide an underlying dynamic for growth in the economy, and to maintain Japan's competitiveness.

JAPAN AND THE MEGA-MARKET OF EAST ASIA

Along the diagonal from Tokyo to Jakarta — including Japan, Korea, Taiwan, Hong Kong, the Chinese provinces of Guangdong and Fujian, Vietnam, Thailand, Malaysia, Singapore, and Indonesia — there will be some 600 million dynamic consumers by the end of the decade. The long-term growth rate for East Asia is 7 to 9 percent, twice that of Japan. On aggregate, North American-based firms are in retreat from the region. European firms, preoccupied with the new challenges they face at home, are not increasing investment in the region at the same pace at which economies are expanding, and so are losing market share.

In contrast, throughout East Asia investment by Japanese firms continues to gallop ahead. Indeed, when the early 1990s are viewed from later in the decade, they will be seen as a period when Japan shifted its international economic focus to Asia.

As a result, by both design and default, Japan-based firms are moving into strategic control of the world's greatest and fastest-growing new markets. That will give to these firms high volume increases, and so allow them to continue sliding down the cost curve faster than their North American and European competitors. Not only will East Asian growth fuel expansion of Japan's economy, but it will also prove to be the trump card that corporate Japan plays in the global competitive game through the end of the decade.

As the world economy moves through the early 1990s, it is in a sense on the verge of a new golden age. While the collapse of the former Soviet Union and its empire in Eastern Europe has led to a whole new agenda of difficult issues, it has relieved the world from the specter of global nuclear war, and growth-smothering defense spending.

At the same time, enormous developments are occurring in the Pacific, of which the most important, from a global perspective, is the acceleration and broadening of the cycle of growth and reform in China. Transition toward the politics of participation appears to be well engaged in Korea, Taiwan, and Thailand. As that process continues, it will give to those economies a broader and more stable base. By the mid-1990s, Taiwan and Korea will be among the world's largest trading nations. Although Japan and Russia have still to resolve issues outstanding from the war, should they do so, that would be still another new and powerful link in the region.

Japan's past continues to cast a shadow on present-day perceptions of the country throughout the rest of East Asia. If Japan were able to perform the acts necessary to close the wounds of the past and set at ease the anxieties of its immediate neighbors, its role in the region and on the world stage would be substantially transformed. Viewed from this perspective, the key issues Japan faces today are more political than they are economic.

In 1993, the combined economies of Japan, China, and the rest of East Asia totaled some $5.5 trillion, while the three economies of Canada, Mexico, and the United States (the region which makes up NAFTA) amounted to some $6 trillion, and the European Community stood at approximately $6.5 trillion. In the decade to 2003, the NAFTA economies are set to create some $1.5 trillion in new wealth, and the EC is aiming toward $1.6 to $1.7 trillion, while Japan, China, and the rest of East Asia are on course to creating some $3.8 trillion in new wealth.

Above all else, it is this divergence in performance that must drive Europe and North America to become more completely engaged in the Asia-Pacific region. In embracing the challenge of developments in the region, North America and Europe would be in a position to restore and renew the basis of their own economic expansion.

But taking up that challenge will require not only a rare exercise of vision, will, and determination, but also the development of a strategy and the mobilization of resources to achieve success. What is fundamentally at issue here is the question of leadership. It is in that challenge, the challenge of leadership, that is to be found the greatest test facing Europe and North America in the developments throughout the Asia Pacific. To do less, or to do otherwise than to fully take up the challenge, would be to allow the opportunity that is now so close at hand to slip forever from our grasp.

CHAPTER TWO

Japan's Changing Marketplace: A Survey of Japan's Major Trading Partners

JAMES M. LAMBERT

第二章

Current media coverage of Japan emphasizes its trade surpluses with the rest of the world, with little focus on the dramatic rise in the value and variety of goods that it now imports. In fact, there is a general failure to recognize the opportunities that exist for exporters to Japan. In the autumn of 1992, the Canadian Embassy in Japan undertook a study of the types of products that Japan is importing and found that structural changes have occurred. Where once Japanese imports were primarily resource products, their composition is rapidly shifting to value-added products, such as machinery and equipment and consumer goods. In this chapter, James Lambert, First Secretary (Economic) at the Canadian Embassy in Tokyo, reports on the findings of that study, and offers his prognosis for Japan's economy and the consequences for its trading partners.

The topic of trade relations with Japan evokes a wide range of responses in the West. As often as not, politically charged rhetoric about Japan's escalating trade surplus has edged out empirical analysis of the growing opportunities in the Japanese marketplace. This has been particularly evident in the approaches to bilateral trade negotiations adopted by two successive American administrations. The Clinton administration's determined efforts in its first year in office to address the trade imbalance, through the establishment of framework trade negotiations, suggest that for the time being the focus of the discussion will remain on market impediments rather than market opportunities.

Political pressure is certainly a legitimate instrument if used in pursuit of trade liberalization. However, it can prove to be a double-edged sword, particularly if the repeated accusation that Japan's market is closed to outsiders becomes a self-fulfilling prophecy, causing export-ready companies to rule out Japan's lucrative and growing economy. Unfortunately, there are signs that this has been the case.

In early 1992, in an attempt to get behind some of the public misapprehensions about trading with Japan and in order to understand better the manner in which economic changes in Japan were affecting prospects for exporters, the Canadian Embassy in Tokyo carried out a review of the impact of economic conditions and structural changes in Japan on trade patterns.

That study made three key findings that still hold true. The first suggests that, far from being a closed economy, the Japanese market for foreign products has grown remarkably, particularly due to the dramatic appreciation of the yen which followed the 1986 Plaza Accord. For example, from 1985 to 1991 the value of non-oil imports[1] grew by 124 percent, close to three times faster than the nominal growth rate of the economy as a whole.

The second observation is that there is keen competition for shares of this expanding trade, even on the part of countries which at the political level question the openness of the Japanese marketplace.

The third finding is that in the face of this dynamic growth in import demand, Canada has been outperformed by all major competitors. If we update the survey to include 1992 data, it can be seen that Canada's share of Japanese non-oil imports dropped from 5.4 percent in 1985 to 3.9 percent in 1992. In Canadian dollar terms, the failure to hold market share meant a loss of $3.5 billion in export revenue in 1992.

In analyzing this relatively poor trade performance, the report concluded that it was due largely to a fundamental mismatch between Canadian export offerings (which remained heavily dependent upon raw and semiprocessed materials) and the dynamic sectors of Japanese import demand. As Japan's import profile shifts to include an ever greater share of value-added products, logic dictates that resource-dependent exporters should lose market share.

In order to confirm this assumption, the trade results of seven competitors in the Japanese marketplace were then compared (Canada, U.S., U.K., France, Germany, Australia, and New Zealand — a group which, taken together, represents roughly 50 percent of Japan's imports). This involved both a statistical comparison of their trade with Japan from 1985 to 1991, and a review of the trade strategies developed by their respective governments in order to position themselves to take advantage of changes in the Japanese market. The latter task was approached by surveying senior trade officials of those countries based in Tokyo.

The statistical appendix at the end of this chapter outlines the trade results of the seven countries examined. Not surprisingly, trade performance within the sample varied considerably between countries (reflecting comparative advantages and marketing skills), and the results of individual countries were far from constant across the six years observed (reflecting discrete economic developments in Japan and abroad). However, one feature stands out — those countries which started with a relatively higher share of value-added exports have made more dramatic gains. Also, to the extent that countries have been successful in raising the proportion of value-added products in their exports to Japan, their trade performance has shown improvement.

Based largely on the analysis contained in this report, this paper reviews:

- The link between structural change in the Japanese economy and the growing demand for higher value-added imports;
- The strategies currently pursued by Japan's major trading partners to take advantage of this shift; and
- The question of whether this import boom and the accompanying upgrading of Japan's import demand was a one-time event associated with the late 1980s' economic bubble, or whether it can be expected to continue in years ahead.

STRUCTURAL CHANGE IN THE JAPANESE MARKET

Midway through the 1980s, stresses in the international exchange rate system were becoming unsustainable. An overvalued U.S. dollar and an undervalued yen conspired to create a trade surplus on the part of Japan which contributed to a deterioration of its bilateral relations with key trading partners. The Plaza Accord reached in 1985 by the finance ministers of the key industrialized countries sought to redress this imbalance. The dramatic realignment of exchange rates which followed facilitated not only an expansion of imports into Japan, but also set in motion a fundamental structural adjustment in the economy, which would change the nature of that country's import requirements.[2]

The virtual doubling of the value of the Japanese currency in 1985–86 had an immediate and significant impact on Japan's international competitiveness. In essence it meant that Japan's unit labor cost went through the roof. As a result, some small, labor-intensive manufacturers simply perished. However, due in great measure to the Japanese government's policy of domestic demand stimulation which prevailed between 1986 and 1989, the vast majority of companies were able to survive.[3] To do so they had to eliminate costly, labor-intensive manufacturing. This was accomplished in two ways — by investing in new technologies, particularly robotics, and by moving labor-intensive activities offshore.[4] As can be seen in Figure 1, as Japan's economy moved into activities which embodied higher intellectual and technological content, its import profile also began to change to incorporate significantly higher value-added content. As a result, resource products, which represented nearly two-thirds of Japanese imports in 1985, had fallen to 50 percent by 1991. Figures for 1992 as well as preliminary figures for 1993 show that the trend identified in the survey continues apace.

In terms of value, Japanese total non-oil imports more than doubled in the six years following the Plaza Accord (see Figure 2). Within this, the shift in the composition of imports meant that the rate of growth for manufactured products was considerably greater than the overall 124 percent growth rate — indeed, between 1985 and 1991 imports of machinery and equipment rose 246.4 percent. The growth of "other" manufactured goods (a generalized category representing all value-added products which fall between resources and machinery and equipment) during this period was also over 200 percent. Conversely, total growth in resource product

Figure 1 Japanese Total Non-Oil Imports

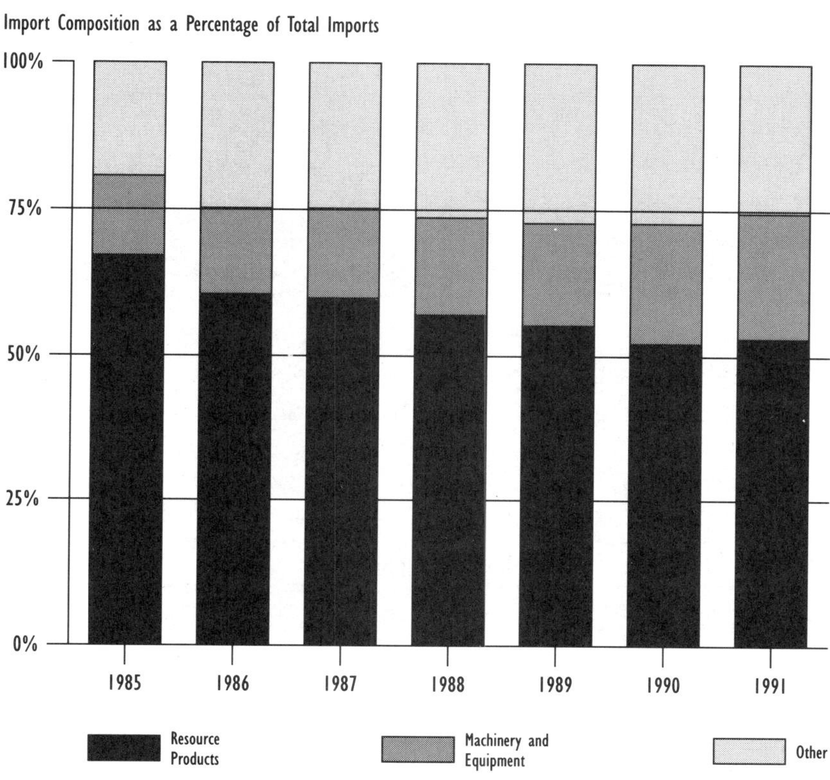

imports in this six-year period was a much slower 75 percent. (See Figure 3 for a breakdown of Japanese imports by country.)

That this would constitute a problem for countries whose trade with Japan was dependent on resource products appears to be self-evident. And, in fact, the four countries which started out with the heaviest proportion of resource products (all 50 percent or more) in their trade lost market share in the six years following the Plaza Accord. While total Japanese non-oil imports grew by 124 percent from 1985 to 1991, imports from Canada grew by only 60 percent, and those of Australia by 78 percent. New Zealand did little better at 95 percent, and imports from the U.S. grew by 110

Figure 2 Value of Japanese Total Non-Oil Imports

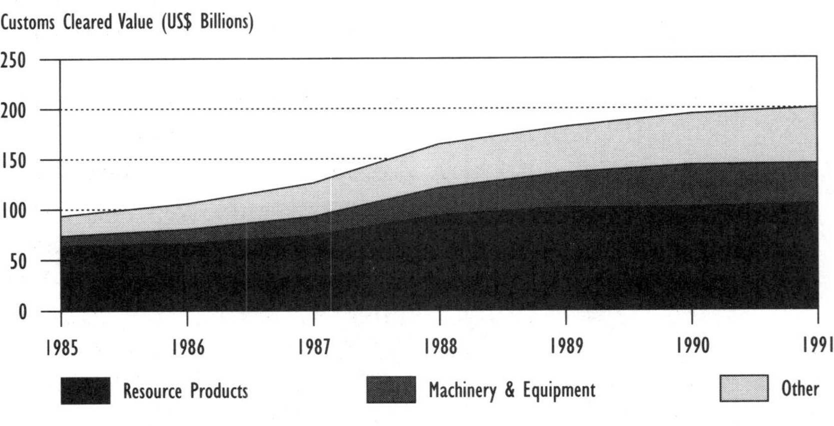

Figure 3 Changes in Japanese Imports by Country

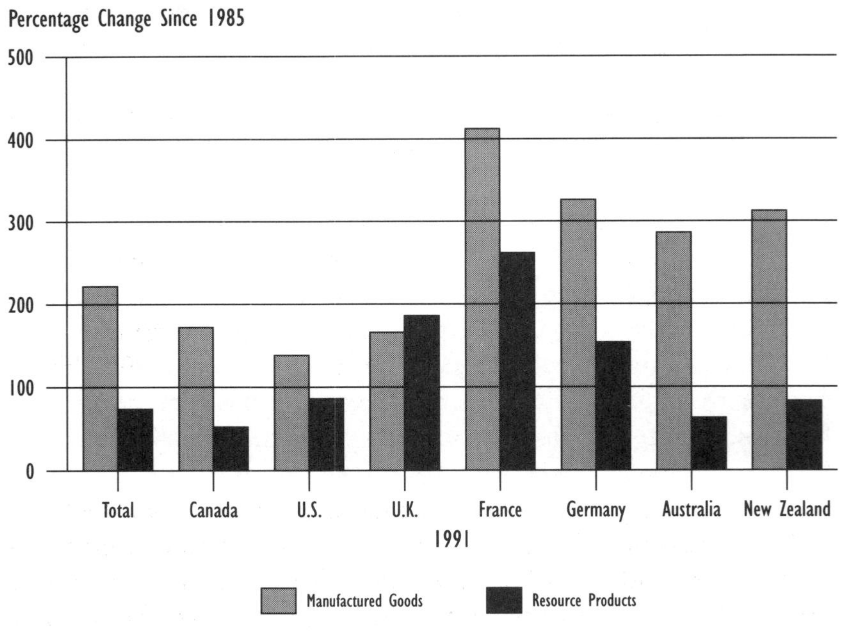

percent. Conversely, imports from the U.K., Germany, and France — countries which started with a higher proportion of high-value exports — gained market share, growing, respectively, at rates of 176, 267, and 339 percent.

This is not to say that traditional markets should be abandoned. Japan's requirements for raw materials remain considerable and, in the medium term, resource exports to Japan will continue to prove lucrative. It must be recognized, however, that they will constitute a declining share of Japan's total import demand. Countries (and companies) that do not begin to work to shift their export offerings into higher value-added categories (for example, by moving from sawn lumber to ready-made window frames and sashes) risk excluding themselves from the most dynamic areas of economic growth in Japan.

NATIONAL TRADE STRATEGIES

As mentioned above, after collating the trade performance of the countries surveyed, senior trade officials were interviewed to see how the countries in question viewed the challenges posed by change in the Japanese market. This section summarizes their comments under two headings: General Views on the Market and Government Trade Promotion Efforts.

GENERAL VIEWS ON THE MARKET

Despite the commonly held view that the Japanese market would continue to expand rapidly, all countries surveyed had some bilateral trade irritants and barriers which they sought to remove. The European countries leave this to the EC, which in 1992 fired a salvo by publishing a list of unfair Japanese trading practices, and which sought to establish a forum similar to the U.S.–Japan Structural Impediments Initiative talks (SII).

American representatives, for their part, believe that the Japanese government still has a long way to go to eliminate discriminatory barriers and attitudes. American officials note that the use of political pressure, whether in the SII (which has now been rolled into the "results-oriented" framework trade talks pursued by the

Clinton administration) or in the Report of the U.S. Trade Representative to Congress, has brought changes which are beneficial to all concerned, including third countries and the Japanese consumer. The reduction of tariff barriers on beef and citrus products and the revision of the Large-scale Retail Store Law to permit the opening of sizable franchises like Toys-R-Us were frequently cited as examples. American officials credit political pressure for the enthusiastic support given by the government of Japan to import promotion schemes such as the establishment of the Office of the Trade Ombudsman, tax and other incentives offered to foreign companies which set up offices in designated "foreign access zones," and the ongoing import promotion activities carried out by the Japan External Trade Organization (JETRO).

Officials of the other countries surveyed suggested almost unanimously that the remaining barriers to participation in the Japanese market are more the result of psychological or cultural factors than direct discriminatory measures. The German official interviewed noted that import barriers are not as important as "the Japanese attitude toward some imports. Japan is an open market, but a closed society." It was also noted that since some alleged barriers, such as the complexity of the distribution system, were as daunting to new Japanese entrants as to foreigners, it was not clear that these obstacles represented discriminatory nontariff barriers.

All officials surveyed were convinced of the market potential of Japan, and were undeterred by the recent slowdown in imports, which was viewed as part of a cyclical economic retrenchment. Indeed, most representatives were confident of the abilities of their respective countries not only to continue expanding exports to Japan, but to move into new sectors embodying higher technological and intellectual content.

These officials stressed the need to tailor strategies and approaches to fit the intricacies of the Japanese market. Expanded participation in the Japanese market is seen to require, on an ongoing basis, a greater level of commitment than in other markets. The demanding specifications of industrial end-users and average consumers alike require close attention to quality, and to the timeliness of delivery and servicing. All agreed, however, that the anticipated gains to those who could adjust their offerings accordingly justified this commitment and the more extensive trade promotion and market-intelligence activities required. Frequently cited as a key benefit to companies able to gear up for the demanding specifications of the Japanese market was the fact that this would improve that company's international competitiveness and profitability in third markets.

GOVERNMENT TRADE PROMOTION EFFORTS

By the late 1980s, Canadian trade officials had become convinced that the massive appreciation of the yen after the Plaza Accord would not, by itself, propel exports to new heights. During the period of soul-searching which ensued, the merits of some traditional methods (large-scale trade shows) and traditional partners (general trading companies)[5] were critically evaluated. This led to two related conclusions: 1) to improve their performance in Japan, companies required better and more detailed intelligence on what was taking place in that market; and, 2) key to this would be an enhanced understanding of Japan's regional sub-markets beyond those in the Tokyo and Osaka regions (which are known as the Kanto and Kansai regions). As this problem was assessed, it became evident that not only are the regional markets of Japan huge (the southern island of Kyushu, for instance, has an economy larger than that of Korea), but their business cycles are different than those of Kanto and Kansai. Thus, if a company could establish itself in the regional markets, it could to some degree insulate itself from cyclical downturns at the center. Moreover, it was seen that importers in these regional markets were developing their own distribution systems to cut out the middlemen in Tokyo and Osaka, and were actively seeking both new products and new sources of traditional imports. As a result, in 1991 the Canadian government took the decision to open several new trade offices throughout Japan starting with Fukuoka and Nagoya, to be backed up by a chain of honorary commercial representatives in Sapporo, Sendai, and Hiroshima.

Of the other countries surveyed, the United States, by virtue of the many offices it operates throughout Japan, is the country with the greatest regional representation. Australia, like Canada, is represented in Tokyo, Osaka, and Fukuoka. They, too, have recently opened offices in Nagoya, Sapporo, and Sendai. The British government sees lucrative opportunities outside the traditional markets in Kanto and Kansai, and is targeting retail chains headquartered in outlying regions. France, however, is concentrating on maximizing the potential of large urban markets, and was not at the time of the survey expanding its regional representation.

Of the countries reviewed, only New Zealand and Germany lack a trade program or strategy specifically tailored for Japan. At the time of the survey, Japan was New Zealand's second largest market (17 percent of exports), of which fully 89 percent were resource exports. Efforts are largely dedicated to consolidating New Zealand's share of this traditional market. Germany is at the other end of the spectrum. Even in 1985, only one-third of German exports were resource related (and this figure was largely composed of exports of chemicals, including value-added medical chemicals). Sales of machinery and equipment received a major boost during the "bubble period," reflecting Germany's position as a premier exporter of luxury vehicles. However, in its approach to the Japanese market, the German government is, in fact, far less concerned with encouraging exports to Japan than with promoting direct investment and local production by German firms.

According to German officials, many firms such as Bayer and Bosch-Siemens established Japanese subsidiaries during the 1930s. These companies have, over time, evolved into mature participants in the economy, acting for all intents and purposes like Japanese businesses. As such, they do not rely on German government support to introduce new products to Japan. These companies are familiar with the demanding specifications of the Japanese purchaser, particularly regarding quality, delivery time, and after-sales service. Their need for government-supplied market intelligence is also negligible.

Thus, Germany adopts a forward-looking approach which views investment by multinational corporations rather than enhanced trade as the key objective to be pursued. Such an approach is consistent with predictions that investment may displace trade as the main engine of international growth in the near future. If this is the case, Germany appears well placed for competition in the twenty-first century. However, from the perspective of trade balances, it should be noted that the German approach may actually dampen the expansion of imports from that country to the extent that they are displaced by products manufactured in Japan by a German subsidiary.

Companies from the remaining countries, lacking such well-developed historical links, require direct assistance from governments to overcome prevailing misapprehensions about the difficulties of penetrating the Japanese market, and to gather the market intelligence necessary to do so. Thus, education and advocacy are major components of the trade-enhancement programs of those countries.

At the time of the survey, the Country Marketing Plan formed the basis for U.S. government trade activities in Japan. According to American trade officials, the Country Marketing Plan highlights four reasons why entering the Japanese market could serve to hone a firm's global strategy. They are: 1) to gather information on Japanese competitors and new technology; 2) to exploit a growing market; 3) to increase international competitiveness by competing with Japanese firms on their home turf; and, 4) to establish relationships, corporate and governmental, which would facilitate access by American firms to projects in third countries financed by the Japanese Overseas Development Agency (ODA). The British "Priority Japan" campaign similarly advises companies not to limit their thinking about the Japanese market to the islands of Japan alone. Companies are instead urged to view the opportunities offered by partnership with Japanese firms from an international perspective. Associations developed in Tokyo can in fact lead to sales in third markets, including sales to Japanese subsidiaries carrying out manufacturing within the EC.

The countries surveyed all had trade development programs intended to introduce prospective exporters to the Japanese market. Incentives to businesses to participate vary by country, but include such items as reimbursement for travel expenses, market research, brochure preparation and translation, and the provision of subsidized exhibition space. Recognizing the fact that getting established in Japan requires a greater investment of time and money than in most other markets, programs developed for Japan tend to be of longer duration, reimburse higher costs, and demand a greater commitment on the part of participating companies, than those developed for other markets. For instance, the American "Japan Corporate Program" provides five years of assistance to eligible companies, but only to selected firms which undertake to: make four or more visits to Japan per year (at least two of which must be at CEO level); participate in trade shows; print literature in Japanese; modify products to Japanese specifications; and guarantee the development of an after-sales service capability.

The U.K. began its program of active education of prospective exporters to Japan in 1988 with an industry-led campaign entitled "Opportunity Japan." It was so successful that it was identified by French officials as a model for their own educational campaign *Le Japon, c'est possible*. The latter had as its stated purpose: "to stop treating Japan as a problem and start treating it as an opportunity." It was also of three years duration, rather than the one-year period which was standard for other French campaigns.

Like Canada, most countries in the survey (U.S., U.K., France, and New Zealand) indicated that they have developed channels for sector-specific market intelligence on Japan. However, unlike the Canadian case where such information is disseminated without charge, the other four countries offer this to potential customers on a fee-for-service basis. Both the information, and the cost, are deemed useful in dissuading companies which are not ready for the Japanese market, or which lacked the necessary commitment to meet high Japanese expectations.

MEDIUM-TERM PROSPECTS FOR THE JAPANESE MARKET

The economic slowdown in Japan has lasted nearly two-and-a-half years, and most analysts now believe that recovery may not be achieved until late 1994. Without question, this slowdown was accompanied, until early 1993, by a deceleration in the rate of import growth. (Total non-oil imports grew by 6.9 percent in 1990, 2.8 percent in 1991, and *fell* by 1.2 percent in 1992.)

This falling off of Japanese imports poses three related

questions: Was the 1992 downturn an isolated event? Can Japanese imports be expected to recapture the rates of growth seen in the late 1990s? When imports recover, will the structural shifts that led to an increase in Japanese demand for value-added imports persist?

Regarding the first question, preliminary results for the first nine months of 1993 show that, in spite of the protracted economic malaise, import growth has once again returned to a positive track. Japan's imports worldwide grew by 3.4 percent compared to the January–September period of 1992, and imports from Canada were up by 6.4 percent. This suggests that the slowdown of imports through the early 1990s may have represented the impact of declining luxury imports associated with the bubble period (exotic cars, *objets d'art,* designer apparel) as much as the cyclical slowdown. However, two other factors have been at play which deserve mention: yen appreciation and the accompanying structural adjustment in the Japanese economy.

YEN APPRECIATION

In the twelve months leading up to October 1993, the value of the Japanese currency increased by 13.2 percent. While the immediate impact of yen appreciation on the value of imports has been somewhat dampened by the so-called "J-curve" effect, its impact on the volume of Japanese trade has been clear, with imports spiking up rapidly over 1993 as Japanese exports suffered clear declines. Normal assumptions about the J-curve effect argue that, after a lag period, we may anticipate an even greater impact on the *value* of trade with Japan.

The Hosokawa administration is committed to passing on the benefits of yen appreciation to the consumer, including through the systematic deregulation of the economy. The success of this strategy is subject to a host of political variables, but any success in this field will amplify the increased tendency to import outlined above.

STRUCTURAL ADJUSTMENT

Opinion is divided on Japan's medium- to long-term prospects. Some have suggested that the onset of structural bottlenecks (including the aging population, impending labor shortages, and a generally inadequate social and economic infrastructure) will hobble Japan's economic progress.[6] While such factors will, no doubt, prevent Japan from recapturing the rates of growth witnessed during recent decades, this should not be confused with economic decline.

Japanese officials for their part do not deny that the rate of the country's GNP growth will fall off somewhat in years ahead, particularly under the impact of labor shortages and tighter environmental regulation. However, they retain the belief that output growth is likely to outpace other G7 countries over the medium term. This, they say, will be achieved by the ongoing efforts of government and business to move out of low-end technologies into industries which represent a higher intellectual and technological component — growth itself may be slower, but the quality of that growth will be significant.

This upbeat view is shared by a number of observers whose findings suggest that Japan, far from being mired in a downward economic spiral, is poised for another breakthrough in which economic growth will be underpinned by a new wave of technological innovation. In such scenarios, Japan will become the test market for leading-edge consumer and industrial technologies — a country to be ignored at risk of being shut out of emerging markets and technologies.[7]

As further rounds of appreciation of the Japanese currency affect the country's level of international competitiveness, the incentive to move low-value production offshore will persist. Indeed, one senior MITI (Ministry of International Trade and Industry) official predicted that the ratio of manufacturing carried out by Japanese corporations offshore (which now stands at about 5 percent) would more than double by the year 2010.

As long as the dictates of international competitiveness force the Japanese economy to upgrade, it stands to reason that the qualitative change in the country's import requirements will persist. A quick review of the sectoral breakdown of Japanese imports in 1992 demonstrates that, even against the backdrop of an overall decline in import quantities, the shift in favor of higher value-added products continued. Machinery and equipment imports into Japan held their own in 1992 in stark contrast to traditional commodity imports such as coal, metal ores, and mineral ores, all of which shrank significantly (by, respectively, 5.0, 9.3, and 7.7 percent). Even within resource imports (which represented 53 percent of non-oil imports in 1992), sub-categories held their own or grew where foreign exporters had been able to increase the value-added component, such as with "other" foodstuffs (15.6 percent growth), fish and shellfish (6.3 percent), meat (18 percent), and wood products (6.8 percent). Senior officials of Japan's Economic Planning Agency have informally confirmed that results to date in 1993 demonstrate that the rapid growth of import volume this year has been led by finished products and foodstuffs, while levels of raw materials, minerals, and fuels have either held steady or declined.

The import boom which took place in the late 1980s created opportunities and opened entirely new markets in Japan to international competition. All signs seem to indicate that the dynamism of this market is far from exhausted. The lesson to be derived from market developments in recent years is that those companies which are able to adapt their offerings to meet the demand for higher-value imports will experience growth levels considerably greater than those of traditional exports. To do so effectively, attention must be paid to the demanding specifications of Japanese consumers, particularly on quality and after-sales service. The process of doing so offers scope to access new Japanese technologies, and to upgrade a company's overall level of international competitiveness, thus enhancing profitability in third markets.

Conversely, those firms which think of Japan solely as a reliable market for traditional resource exports will, in the short term, exclude themselves from the fast-growth sectors of the Japanese economy. In the medium to long term, such an approach will relegate those firms to an increasingly marginal position in the Japanese marketplace.

APPENDIX: TRADE RESULTS OF SEVEN OF JAPAN'S MAJOR TRADING PARTNERS AMONG THE DEVELOPED COUNTRIES

Canada

The value of Japanese non-oil imports from Canada rose only 60.1 percent between 1985 and 1991, less than half the rate from the rest of the world. This was a result of very slow growth (51.4 percent) in imports of resource products from Canada during this period, which fell 11.2 percent over 1990 and 1991. Eight out of Canada's top ten exports to Japan (all ten are resource products) saw Japanese sales decline in 1991. The growth of Canada's principal export item, coal, which in 1991 still accounted for over one-sixth of all Canadian exports to Japan, peaked in 1988 and grew only 13.5 percent between 1985 and 1991. Resource products still make up 88 percent of Japanese non-oil imports from Canada, and chemical products account for only 6.2 percent of that figure. The value-added component of imports has risen much more rapidly, though. Japanese imports of machinery and equipment from Canada rose 232.8 percent during this period and in 1991 grew to 4 percent of total Japanese imports from Canada. Imports of other manufactures from Canada grew by 148.1 percent to form 8 percent of the total. However, the growth in these sectors was insufficient to compensate for the falling off in resource exports, leading to an absolute decline in exports to Japan in 1990, 1991, and 1992.

United States

Japanese non-oil imports from the United States grew 110.4 percent between 1985 and 1991, just below the rate of Japanese imports overall. The United States was able to slightly increase its share of Japanese resource product imports, with above average growth (86.9 percent). While Japanese imports of commodity foodstuffs from the United States have been relatively stagnant during this period, there were items that flourished. Imports of fish and seafood have more than doubled (154.4 percent), and meat imports have more than tripled (239.4 percent). Most striking is the 472.3 percent growth of other foodstuff imports from the

United States, which include fruits and vegetables and prepared food products. This has made Japan the most important destination for U.S. agricultural product exports. On the other hand, the U.S. share of Japanese manufactured goods imports fell between 1985 and 1991. Although manufactured goods imports from the United States more than doubled following the Plaza Accord, the 138.8 percent growth experienced by U.S. manufactured goods between 1985 and 1991 was well below the 223.1 percent growth of total Japanese manufactured goods imports. Last year manufactured goods, including both machinery and equipment and other manufactures, made up just over half of Japanese total non-oil imports from the United States.

United Kingdom

Japanese non-oil imports from the U.K. are fairly evenly divided into resource products (39 percent), machinery and equipment (31 percent), and "other" manufactures (30 percent). Total imports from the U.K. rose 176.2 percent between 1985 and 1991, almost three times the overall rate experienced by Canada. This was a result of the rapid growth (299.1 percent) of machinery and equipment imports. There was also a strong performance (188.6 percent) from the resource product component of British exports to Japan, which generally have high value-added content. "Other foodstuffs," which are composed primarily of whisky and specialty foods, accounted for over one-quarter of resource product imports last year and experienced the most rapid growth (281.4 percent). This was followed by chemical products (186.6 percent), which in 1991 accounted for 47.5 percent of resource product imports from the U.K. Imports of other manufactured goods have been very volatile and their slow growth cannot be solely attributed to the Japanese recession. One reason may be that Japanese imports of luxury goods from the U.K. have been hurt by parallel imports and re-exports from Hong Kong.

France

Non-oil imports from France grew by 339.3 percent between 1985 and 1991, almost three times the growth of Japanese non-oil imports overall. The growth of machinery and equipment imports during the period was particularly strong, growing at a rate of 648.6 percent. The growth of other manufactured goods imports, made up primarily of luxury consumer goods, was even stronger (854.4 percent until 1990, but falling off sharply in 1991 as a result of the economic slowdown). The growth of French resource product imports (265.3 percent) took place at well over three times the rate of Japanese resource product imports overall. It should be noted, however, that raw materials account for less than 10 percent of Japanese "resource product" imports from France. The bulk of French imports which are classified as "resource imports" under the Japanese system are in fact either chemical products (including perfumes and toiletries) or foodstuffs. Wine, not bulk agricultural commodities, accounts for just over 80 percent of French foodstuff imports. The value-added component of Japanese resource product imports from France is thus quite high. It would also appear that the demand for value-added foodstuffs is not as volatile as that for luxury goods. Wine imports from France, for example, slowed due to the recession in Japan but still grew by 24.1 percent between 1990 and 1991.

Germany

The established position of Germany in the Japanese market helped facilitate an increase (266.5 percent) in non-oil imports between 1985 and 1991 that was more than twice the rate of import growth overall. Japanese imports of German machinery and equipment continued to grow at a rapid rate (383.8 percent) during the period, and the growth of passenger vehicle imports, luxury automobiles in particular, became an increasingly important part of this sector. The Japanese recession brought about a sudden decline in demand for German automobiles, however, resulting in a drop in 1991 of Japanese machinery and equipment imports from Germany. Japanese imports of resource products from Germany have very high value-added content. German resource products are 80 percent chemical products, of which over one-third are from the capital- and technology-intensive medical and pharmaceutical sector. German chemical firms are also engaged in substantial local production in Japan.

Australia

Japanese non-oil imports from Australia in 1991 were of a similar composition to Canada's, with resource products making up 86 percent, machinery and equipment at 2 percent, and other manufactures at 12 percent. A further parallel can be drawn from the fact that imports from Australia grew only 77.8 percent between 1985 and 1991 due to slow resource product import growth (62.9 percent). Unlike Canada, however, Japan's principal imports from Australia have generally not stagnated and continue to rise, albeit much more slowly than the rate of increase in Japanese total non-oil imports. Coal, for instance, which in 1991 accounted for over one-quarter of all Japanese imports from Australia, has managed a 42.6 percent growth since 1985. The rapid growth of meat (164.2 percent) and prepared food products (114.6 percent) has also been conspicuous in comparison to Canada's apparent inability to take advantage of the growing Japanese market for these products. The growth of both machinery and equipment (375.5 percent) and other manufactures (274.3 percent) between 1985 and 1991 was well above the rate of Japanese total imports in these sectors, but from a very small initial base.

New Zealand

New Zealand is the only country examined with a higher resource product component (89 percent) of Japanese imports than Canada. The similarity ends there, however, as New Zealand was able to expand its share of Japanese resource product imports between 1985 and 1991 with above average growth (83.2 percent). Resource product import growth from New Zealand was driven mainly by a jump in Japanese imports of raw logs and timber (418.5 percent), resulting from good domestic supply factors. Japanese imports of fish and shellfish from New Zealand also rose rapidly (235.5 percent). Growth has been even faster in the higher value-added sectors, though. In the case of machinery and equipment, Japanese imports from New Zealand grew (662.1 percent) while imports of other manufactures have also risen quickly (293.1 percent). As in the case of Australia, strong growth in Japanese manufactured goods imports started from a very small base. Last year, other manufactures still composed only 10 percent of

Japanese imports from New Zealand, while machinery and equipment formed less than 1 percent of the total.

Statistical Note

In broadly defining three groups of imports (resource products, machinery and equipment, and "other"), this study sought to ensure that, as nearly as possible, "other" represented value-added manufactured goods. This was so that by adding "other" to "machinery and equipment," a bottom-line figure for value-added imports could be derived. To do so, it was necessary to include in the "resource products" category items such as chemicals or foodstuffs which contain imports in both raw and processed form. This meant that figures provided for resource product imports from France were inflated by the inclusion of wine and other specialty foodstuffs. Likewise, resource imports from Germany contained a large amount of highly processed medical chemicals. However, to do otherwise would have, for instance, removed Canadian imports of potash (defined as a chemical) from the resource products group, thus precluding any kind of meaningful conclusion about the overall performance of value-added imports. For the same reason, this formula also understates value-added imports from Canada such as processed foods.

The statistical material in this appendix and the accompanying graphics were compiled by Columbia University graduate student Michael Taylor. The work which he carried out, including the interviews of senior trade officials, provided the substantive backbone for the embassy study, *Penetrating the Japanese Value-Added Marketplace: Strategies and National Approaches of Canada's Competitors*, September 1992.

NOTES

1. *The volatility of international oil prices hampers year-to-year comparisons of Japanese imports. For this reason, this study refers to Japanese non-oil imports.*
2. *The average exchange rate for 1985 stood at ¥238.54 to the U.S. dollar. The average rate the following year had moved to ¥168.51, as the value of the yen nearly doubled.*
3. *In fact, despite the virtual doubling of the value of the Japanese currency in*

1985–86, the number of bankruptcies encountered in Japan actually declined from 1985 to 1990 (Nikkei Database). For an interesting review of Japan's adjustment process after the Plaza Accord, see Hayami Masaru, "Stronger Yen Will Benefit Japan in the Long Run," The Nikkei Weekly *(April 5, 1993).*

4. *The rapid growth in Japanese foreign direct investment after the Plaza Agreement can be seen from these figures, which chart the total value of new foreign direct investment by Japan (in billions of U.S. dollars): 1985, 12.2; 1986, 22.3; 1987, 33.4; 1988, 47.0; 1989, 67.5. Government of Japan, Ministry of Finance,* Zaisei Kinyu Tokei Geppo *476 (December 1991).*
5. *The nineteen largest Japanese trading companies handle 55.6 percent of Japan's total imports (on a contract basis). Broken down by region, reliance on trading companies is as follows: Oceania, 70 percent of exports to Japan; U.S., 60 percent; Canada, 59 percent; Western Europe, 42 percent. The United States has recently added the practices of the general trading companies to the list of grievances it is raising through the SII. It is difficult to empirically demonstrate the degree to which the practices of general trading companies constitute an actual barrier to trade. However, those firms seeking to move to higher value-added product lines may at some point wish to contemplate moving beyond the embrace of the trading companies to establish "hands-on" control of product marketing and distribution in Japan.*
6. *See Bill Emmott,* The Sun Also Sets: The Limits to Japan's Economic Power *(New York: Times Books, 1989), also published in Toronto by General. See also: P. Sanborn and B. Siman,* Thematic Reviews, *Jardine Fleming Securities Ltd. (Autumn 1991).*
7. *See Lester Thurow,* Head to Head: The Coming Economic Battle Among Japan, Europe and America *(New York: William Morrow, 1992); Kenneth S. Courtis, "Japan: The Heisei Cycle," in* Japan Close Up *(September 1992); and "The Japanese Economy: From Miracle to Mid-Life Crisis,"* The Economist *(March 6, 1993).*

CHAPTER THREE

Japanese Culture and Society

GREGORY CLARK

第三章

Japanese society has a reputation for exclusivity, both in the Western press and among Japanese intellectuals who wish to emphasize the "uniqueness" of Japanese society. Examples abound of the seemingly vast differences between Japanese and Western culture, and the contradictory nature of Japanese culture, leading Westerners to despair of ever understanding Japanese society, let alone doing business there. Explanations as to why our cultures have developed differently also abound, in many cases with limited practical utility for the foreign businessperson. Gregory Clark, chancellor of the Institute of Developing Economies Advanced School and professor of Japanese Studies in the Faculty of Comparative Culture at Sophia University in Tokyo, agrees that differences in approach do exist, and offers a theory as to why modern Japan has developed the way it has and how Western businesspeople can use this knowledge to manage their Japanese operations successfully.

The main problem in explaining the Japanese is the fact that almost anything said about them can be easily contradicted. For example, it is often said that the Japanese are a rigidly hierarchical people; yet the essence of good Japanese management is supposed to be its egalitarianism. Many see the Japanese as a highly disciplined people; yet the Japanese see themselves as a highly emotional people given to excessive mutual dependence (*amae*) in their relationships. Indeed, the ease with which emotional moods and "shocks" sweep across the nation is a key characteristic of the Japanese. Some see the Japanese as a highly progressive people; yet it is easy to find examples of extreme conservatism — the Japanese have yet to adopt daylight saving time, for example.

The Japanese can be extraordinarily polite at times. Still, they are reluctant to admit, let alone apologize for, war guilt. The Japanese have a reputation for exclusivist attitudes to foreigners, but in some ways Japan is one of the most open societies in the world. Today, for example, it is not uncommon for foreigners to be asked to join government policy advisory committees, something that would not happen in the West. And when it comes to openness to outside ideas and culture, no other large nation can even begin to match Japan.

And so on. Some say the Japanese lack a proper sense of morality. Yet most foreigners living in Japan for any length of time have stories of lost valuables being returned at great effort by honest citizens. Usually the Japanese are quite hardworking, but at times they can be lazy — university students are renowned for treating their four years of study as a holiday camp. The Japanese like to tell us they are a society which emphasizes *wa* or harmony; yet some very unharmonious farmers have blocked vital construction at Narita airport for more than ten years. Even the one seeming absolute of Japanese society, the strong group instinct, is contradicted by occasional examples of extreme individualism. In 1984, a U.S. academic who was impressed by Japanese enterprise management wrote a paper entitled "Joy on the Factory Floor." A few years later, a foreign researcher here published an article with the headline, "Fear in the Factory." Is it possible that both could be right?

Why are the Japanese the way they are? Assuming that there is something unusual about Japan, then there must be a reason for that something. The standard theories do not help us much — that the Japanese are as they are because they grow rice, because they eat rice, because of the climate, because they live on crowded islands, because they enjoy some allegedly unique homogeneity. Nor can we simply ascribe perceived differences to a broad concept of Oriental culture. Many Westerners who have lived and worked in the East find it easier to relate to Chinese and Koreans than to Japanese. The former are much closer to us in their liking for logic, principles, debate, ideology — the rationalistic approach — than are the Japanese, and they are more individualistic.

Most attempts to define the Japanese concentrate too much on secondary features. It is like trying to say that a fish is fundamentally different from a land animal because it has a particular breathing or blood system, when the primary difference is the fact that it lives in a watery environment and has adjusted to that environment in various ways. Some of those adjustments involve breathing and blood circulation, but there are many others. And ultimately, the fish is not all that different from other animals.

It is not a question of the Japanese having some quality that sets them absolutely apart from all other peoples; as human beings we are all basically the same. Rather, it is a matter of the Japanese operating as human beings in an environment or social dimension different from that in which most Westerners prefer to operate. We non-Japanese prefer a more rationalistic environment, one where principles, universalistic ideologies, and reasons are emphasized. The Japanese prefer something less rationalistic, something similar to the more "instinctive," practical, and emotional values that all of us use in small primary groups: the family, village, team, or tribe, for example.

To put it another way, when we are with our families, we all behave like the Japanese, even if in a much simpler and less refined manner. We are all group-oriented. We have one attitude for those outside our group and another for those inside — the allegedly unique *soto-uchi* phenomenon found in Japan. We employ such "Japanese" techniques as instinctive communication, implicit obligations, situational flexibility, and mutual dependence (*amae*). We do not emphasize such rationalistic tools as law, contract, or scientific planning. We prefer rules to principles, mood to logic, custom and convention to universalistic ideology. We combine arbitrary hierarchy with genuine egalitarianism. We exclude outsiders, but not their ideas. We differentiate sex roles. We cooperate naturally with each other for common goals. We instinctively concern ourselves with the long-term welfare of the group, rather than short-term gains. In short, we behave just as the Japanese do.

However, when we leave our family group and go into the factory, the university, or any other large secondary group, we non-

Japanese do not continue to behave in this familial, instinctive manner. We tend to prefer a more principled, logical approach, what some would call a more rationalistic approach. The Japanese, on the other hand, continue to act as if they were still in a small, primary group situation. To put it more precisely, they refine the more instinctive values and attitudes that we all use in small primary groups and adapt them for use in their secondary groups. To date we have tended to see this as backward and illogical. But some of us are now discovering, via Japan, that this approach has its own practical and emotional logic at times.

Why are the Japanese like this? I prefer to turn the question around and ask why the rest of us prefer the rationalistic approach. Or to go back to the fish analogy, instead of asking why the fish got *into* the water, we should ask why the other animals wanted to get *out* of the water. We all begin by operating in the instinctive dimension. Maybe something happened to the rest of us to push us away from that dimension, something that did not happen to Japan.

Perhaps one clue can be found in the relative lack of war and conflict with foreigners that the Japanese have enjoyed throughout much of their history. As an island nation close to the Chinese mainland but distant from Europe, Japan was in the almost unique situation of being able to absorb the advanced, rationalistic civilizations of China and then the West without being attacked or dominated by either. So Japan was able to evolve without having to change its original "primary group" approach. Or to put it another way, it did not need to move to a more rationalistic approach.

Today, we non-Japanese assume that our more rationalistic approach was the natural result of our desire for progress. In fact, the need to prepare for and survive conflict with foreigners could well have been the main factor forcing the peoples of the Eurasian continent to move quickly to more rationalistic values, including the development of powerful universalistic ideologies. Japan was not put in this position, so it simply retained the values and attitudes of its original tribal-village society. Over its long history, it refined these values to create a feudal society. Up until the middle of the nineteenth century, the Japanese saw no need to take the next step and embrace the more rationalistic values that most other countries used for the creation of the unitary nation state.

Even today, much of what we see in Japan is simply a continuation of the mores of that original village or feudal society. The Japanese refer to their *mura-ishiki* (village consciousness) to explain the closed nature of their groups. Most firms or groups of firms like to think of themselves as familial groups — thus, we see references to the "Matsushita family" and the like. Concepts such as lifetime employment and *keiretsu* (affiliated companies) are basically feudal in nature; the individual or the enterprise "belongs" to the larger group just as in the past the individual and village belonged to the feudal fief or *han*. Some would argue that current Japanese attitudes to women are also feudal.

In the West, many assume that village/feudal attitudes cannot possibly go hand in hand with modern industrial progress, that the Japanese are in effect dissembling when they talk about *mura-ishiki,* and that they will use any pretext to justify their exclusivity and their claims to cultural uniqueness. They are not pretending. What is more, the Protestant ethic of northern European societies — the British Isles, Germany, the Netherlands, Scandinavia, and extending to the United States, Canada, Australia, etc. — owes its origins to a rather similar history of village/feudal development. These societies, like Japan, were for most of their history fairly isolated from the cultural mainstream of the Eurasian continent; they too retained feudal features until quite recently, and were slow to embrace rationalistic values. The early industrial progress in those countries resembled in many ways what we see in Japan today. Like the Japanese, the northern European people have, or rather had, a natural attachment to the workplace, a willingness to cooperate with others in the workplace, and a tradition of craftsmanship. In more rationalistic societies, these qualities do not emerge easily or automatically.

Great Britain, which enjoyed island isolation and was able to adopt aspects of continental European rationalistic civilization at its own pace, comes closest to the Japanese model. Many traditional British attitudes have Japanese equivalents — pragmatism, attention to detail, rules and conventions, and a lack of strong ideological dogmas and convictions, to name a few. This may be why the First Industrial Revolution occurred in Britain and the Second Industrial Revolution is now occurring in Japan, rather than in other countries with much stronger traditions of scientific and other intellectual achievement. This could explain why modern Japanese enterprise management exports so well to the rural areas of Anglo-Saxon societies, and why the management of American firms only a generation ago was so similar to what we see in Japan today.

By contrast, the peoples of the Eurasian continental societies exposed to conflict — China, India, the Middle East, and southern Europe — place more emphasis on principles and ideological absolutes. They would find it hard to accept the ideological looseness of the Japanese. The average Japanese is born into a secular, Westernized world, is educated in a vaguely Confucian morality, has a Shinto wedding (or, perhaps, a Christian ceremony), works in a capitalist enterprise, and is buried with Buddhist rites. Few seem even to be aware of the contradictions involved, a major difference between Japan and the Sinitic cultures of Asia, which are sensitive to ideological inconsistency.

This is not to rule out entirely the role of Chinese Confucian, and to some extent Buddhist, factors in molding the Japanese personality. They may also have contributed to Japan's progress. As an ideology born in feudal China more than two thousand years ago and refined to allow the organization of a large continental civilization, Confucianism may well be superior to many of the more religious or political ideologies that the rest of the world prefers. But it is far from being the deciding factor in Japan. For example, Japanese society plays down the emphasis on blood relations as the principle of group formation found in other Confucian societies. In its place is the assumption that you will cooperate closely with whomsoever happens to be around you in a group situation. This represents a major divergence from the Chinese approach, with obviously favorable implications for enterprise productivity.

The concept of the Japanese operating in a different psychological dimension can also help to explain some of their seeming contradictions. Thus, it is not a matter of them being kinder or crueler, more moral or less moral than the rest of us. Rather, it is a matter of them having much the same qualities as the rest of us, but expressing them differently. For example, when the more "instinctive" morality of the Japanese makes them assume automatically that lost property should be returned to its owner, we are impressed. But when the same morality allows them to ignore principles emphasized by our more rationalistic moralities, we are dismayed — as in their tolerance of political corruption, for example, or their attitude to war crimes. The Japanese are often just as bemused by our contradictions — for example, they cannot understand the scrupulously principled, contractual Western businessman with a take-it-or-leave-it attitude to quality or service.

Or take the hard work versus laziness contradiction. Those of us who prefer the rationalistic dimension rely on what we see as logical incentives to get people to work hard — money and promotion, intellectual challenge, penalties, and so on. When those incentives work properly, productivity can be higher than in Japan. But as we see only too well today, there are also times when they do not work very well. It is not always easy to apply rationalistic incentives effectively in the modern enterprise.

The Japanese rely on more "instinctive" incentives. They start with the natural cooperativeness of the group. They then create emotional challenges, real or artificial, to motivate that group, in the process relying on both joy and fear. This approach may not work well at times — in the universities, for example. But in enterprises, it works very well indeed.

Some see higher education, technology, organization, and skilled management as the keys to Japanese enterprise productivity. But in many cases these are the results, rather than the causes, of that productivity. People who want their group to survive will go out and obtain whatever skills are needed to survive. That, after all, is the way guerrilla armies defeat large conventional armies. Guerrillas, incidentally, are close to the ideal as an example of "instinctive" values in action: Their skills are not developed in universities or management courses; rather, they are the results of practical wisdom growing out of that most powerful of all instincts — survival.

The other strong advantage Japan has in the area of the work ethic is the village/feudal concept of one's work being the main purpose of one's existence. The butcher exists in the society because he is a butcher, the baker because he is a baker. Both take it for granted that they should do their allotted tasks to the best of their ability simply to maintain their place and role in society. This concept survives from an advanced feudal society, one incidentally that northern European societies also had until recently.

Other positive aspects of the more "instinctive," or village/feudal, approach of Japan include political stability, a low rate of crime against the individual, a lack of litigiousness, and pragmatic openness to outside ideas and applied technology. Areas where the Japanese approach works less effectively include intellectual creativity, diplomacy, the rights of women and minorities, service sector productivity (where there is too much emphasis on service and not enough on efficiency), and the scientific as opposed to the practical approach in research and planning. To some, these negatives may outweigh the positives. But when it comes to the creation of a modern industrial society, the Japanese approach would seem to work as well as most. And when it comes to creating powerful manufacturing export industries, it can be argued that the Japanese approach is clearly superior.

How can all this be related to the practical problem of doing business in Japan? Perhaps the most important conclusion is the concept of the Japanese as emotional and nonrationalistic. For example, it is often said that business in Japan revolves around human contacts, to which experienced Western businesspeople reply that when it comes to the bottom line, all business is the same and human contacts become secondary. But Japan really is an exception. Japanese firms may pass up the chance to buy at lower prices or to sell at higher prices in order to maintain long-standing ties with old customers. The emphasis in Japan on *keiretsu* connections, school and university ties, close business-bureaucracy links, factional politics and so on, is not the result of some government policy to create an artificial "system" to run Japan. For the Japanese it is the natural way to do business.

This more emotional, nonrationalistic approach explains many of the other peculiarities of doing business in Japan. For example, in any non-Japanese society, few consumers would succumb to the entreaties of a door-to-door car salesman when they know they can buy the same car more easily, with more choice and almost certainly at a discount, from a nearby showroom. But in

Japan, many consumers will be impressed by the "sincerity" of that salesman and buy the product offered at the price quoted. This lack of price consciousness and weakness to emotional mood was behind the extraordinary popularity until very recently of grossly over-priced European fashion goods in Japan. High price was associated with high quality and scarcity value. As the sales chief for a popular jeans company said when asked why his company's jeans sold in Japan for well above their price overseas: "Japanese do not like cheap prices."

This emotionalism also explains the seeming exclusivity of Japan. The Japanese have a simple "onion-ring" approach to relationships. Individuals see themselves as surrounded by rings of human contact extending outward from the ego center — family and close friends are in the first ring, then work colleagues, school colleagues, industry or regional groups, and so on, with the final and outer ring being the Japanese nation. Almost automatically then, the individual will give priority to someone within a closer ring over someone further out. Thus, the foreigner outside the onion altogether gets lowest priority — a fact well illustrated by the Japanese habit of using the term *gaijin* (literally, "outside person") to describe foreigners.

But the foreigner does not have to remain forever outside the outer ring. A foreigner can move into one of the rings by joining a group within Japan. When that happens, the Japanese within that group will give that foreigner priority over any Japanese outside the group. Those foreigners with long residence in Japan who have been drawn deeply inside the rings may be treated almost as if they were Japanese.

Even without major efforts to break inside one or other of the rings, the foreigner can be favored. Many Western businessmen, confronted by the seemingly tight wall of *keiretsu* groups and ties to long-standing suppliers or buyers, assume that Japan is an impossibly nationalistic country in which to do business. But as with the other contradictions in Japan, the Japanese attitude to foreigners has two sides. It's true that the instinctive approach can at times produce an almost unreasoning rejection of anything that is different (a rejection that applies as much to Japanese who are different as to foreigners, incidentally). But that same instinctive approach can just as easily work in the opposite direction. The Japanese can decide, for example, that foreigners are interesting and important just because they are so different. Emotional, mood-based curiosity has in the past been a major factor in the success of foreign products in Japan. Curiosity about foreigners in general can often help the foreigner businessperson get through doors blocked to Japanese equivalents. At times the desire to avoid angry foreign reactions has also been a factor — the *gaiatsu*, or "foreign pressure," factor — in forcing Japanese concessions on trade.

That said, success in Japan ultimately depends on getting "inside the ring," so to speak. Somehow you have to find a way to make the Japanese regard you as an insider rather than an outsider. Japanese learn very quickly to distinguish between fly-by-night Westerners and those committed to the long haul. Efforts to learn Japanese and a willingness to invest heavily in staff and buildings are seen as firm evidence of "sincerity" and commitment (the Japanese obsession with quality and after-sales service is important for the Japanese not so much in itself but as visible proof of "sincerity" in business relations). In personal relationships, the foreigner who can always maintain a smiling, "sincere" disposition will do better than the so-called *rikutsuppoi* foreigner — someone who is always worrying about principles or trying to argue small points of logic.

The same factors are also important in the handling of staff. Many foreigners assume they cannot hope to get the same loyalty from Japanese employees as Japanese firms can. They are wrong. Obviously anyone setting up business in Japan — Japanese or foreign — has trouble at first in attracting good people. But often foreigners have the advantage of curiosity value; many bright young Japanese are attracted by the foreign image and the chance for foreign experience. Foreigners are also better placed to take advantage of the large pool of intelligent female labor largely overlooked by Japanese firms. Provided foreign employers show the right "sincerity" toward employees, they will earn the same highly productive loyalty that most Japanese firms enjoy.

It is crucial that employers avoid the hire-and-fire approach now so popular in the West. Even if used only in an emergency, it breaks down the familial togetherness of the enterprise group. Foreign managers should also avoid the mistake made by many foreign firms in the past, namely hiring people simply for their ability to speak English and get along with foreigners; these people may not be otherwise suited to the work, and may lack the qualities necessary to get on in Japanese society. Like their Japanese equivalents, foreign employers must try to feel that they are establishing a collective — an *unmei kyodotai*, or a "community bound by the same destiny" — that will work together over the long term, sharing both the failures and the successes of the enterprise.

Many assume that the younger generation of Japanese no longer share the emotional, rather feudalistic, attitudes of the older generation toward employment. And it is true that in some financial sector industries there are young Japanese with a "dry," take-it-or-leave-it rationalism. But most young Japanese still see the workplace in emotional terms. True, they no longer have the feudal attitude that once made loyalty to the workplace automatic, but they still want to see the workplace as a sort of "club" where they can find good friendships, where they can enjoy prestige and bask in the good "image" of the company, and where to some extent they can enjoy paternalistic welfare. Japanese companies now devote enormous resources to "image" creation. Recruitment videos show company jazz bands, trips to Hawaii, evenings out drinking with work colleagues, and so on, with almost no mention of salary or career paths.

The main thing to remember in Japan is this: Beneath the veneer of complexity and sophistication, Japan is really a very simple, emotional, almost naive, society in which straightforward, uncomplicated attributes can be highly effective. Some of the most popular foreigners in Japan are Mormon ex-missionaries who have stayed on in the country.

A brief but true story says it better than I can. It concerns a tough-minded, aggressive American baseball team owner of the 1980s who had ruthlessly hired and fired in a bid to get his New York team to the top. An American television interview with him had been dubbed for broadcast in Japan, and at the end of the interview the owner was asked for his philosophy of life, which was, predictably: "Nice guys finish last." The Japanese translator clearly could not understand this, but assumed it had a positive meaning. In Japanese it came out as: "The nice person struggles through to the very last." Consider that as a philosophy for doing business in Japan.

CHAPTER FOUR

The Japanese Market and Its Consumers

GEORGE FIELDS

第四章

The Japanese market comprises 125 million consumers with high purchasing power and a restless quest for improvement in quality of life. As such, it is a veritable gold mine for Western companies seeking to sell their wares. But the foreign marketer must take the local market into account; consumer values, which are directly derived from prevailing social norms, are difficult to understand in a distant market. In addition, Japanese consumers have undergone dramatic changes in the postwar period, causing further confusion for the foreign company. In this chapter, George Fields, chairman of Survey Research Group Japan, traces the development of the Japanese consumer and presents information about current consumer values that will provide new opportunities for Western businesses in the Japanese market.

Since the 1950s, dramatic growth and the concomitant rise in the standard of living have rapidly transformed the Japanese market, where consumers demand high standards of quality and services based on their distinctive social values. Dramatic changes have occurred in consumer values since the mid-1980s, and the market continues to be in flux. What may seem similar to Western consumer behavior or attitudes is not true Westernization, for that would presuppose that Japanese social values will eventually approach those of the West. Instead, we are witnessing a convergence of many values, but there is no longer a one-way flow from the West to the rest of the world. Japanese and other Asian values are beginning to affect North America and Europe. Just as Canada has not become a clone of the United

States, the Japanese will retain a distinct identity while being affected by global trends.

Japan can no longer be examined as an isolated, unique entity, unaffected by what goes on elsewhere. The traditional Japanese consumer, if there ever was such a species, is nearing extinction. The internationalization of Japan makes the future Japanese market and its consumers ever more difficult to predict or assess.

There are substantial differences in consumer behavior and attitudes between generations — in the broader context, this can be inferred from the evolution of the consumer over recent times. Needless to say, there are also differences between male and female consumers in Japan. Neither of these variations can be covered in one short chapter. In addition, it would be impossible to spot specific opportunities for all readers since the market is composed of numerous product and service categories. However, changes in the market infrastructure and social values should suggest opportunities for the astute marketer.

THE CONSUMER THEN AND NOW

When a social infrastructure is rigid and when government rules and regulations work to protect groups of producers and insulate them from competition, the marketer's options are necessarily limited and the consumer is relegated to a minor role. For this reason, the Japanese consumer was an infant in the 1950s, went to school in the 1960s, got a job in the 1970s, and advanced to senior status in the 1980s. Extending the analogy would suggest maturity in the 1990s and decline in the next century, but the more likely scenario is that, with increased confidence in their own judgment, Japanese consumers will be less reliant on the marketer's corporate or brand image in their purchasing decisions, eroding the latter's power to load the shelves: Corporate authority is being challenged by the new Japanese consumer, who has a greater propensity to search for individual relevance in products, service features, and price. The changes in the market have been rapid, however, measured in mere decades, so it is only to be expected that many of the values of previous generations remain, making the Japanese consumer still staunchly, well — Japanese.

THE SIXTIES: THE QUEST FOR A NEW LIFESTYLE

The mid-1960s was characterized by a new-found access to the advanced economies of the West. Ostensibly, Japanese aspirations were for a lifestyle akin to the West, as seen by the drive for ownership of consumer durables, dubbed "the three C's" — cars, color televisions, and coolers (air conditioners). Initially, catching up with the West was achieved with minimal basic social change; only later did continuing improvements in income introduce changes in consumer attitudes and new values. In the Sixties, the Japanese consumer was enamored with value-added products, regardless of the product's origins. Many foreign brands succeeded — the top soft drink, the top wet or dry razors, the top instant coffee, and the top facial tissues — not because they were foreign per se, but because they offered a glimpse into a new lifestyle which seemed to fulfill consumers' desires for an improved quality of living. In this period, foreign marketers learned, in some cases painfully, not to equate modernization with Westernization.

INTO THE SEVENTIES: THE QUEST FOR QUALITY

When OPEC restricted oil supplies in 1973, causing a sharp increase in prices from 1973 to 1975, the Japanese, who were more dependent on oil imports than any other industrialized nation, considered it a national crisis. Dubbed the "First Oil Shock," it revived memories of the immediate postwar period and raised the prospect of acute inflation, driving a substantial part of the population into a frenzy of buying to hoard such things as detergent and toilet paper. Consumer confidence was seen to be fragile and easily shattered. (Contrast this with the more serious Gulf War in 1991, which had little immediate effect on the Japanese consumer.)

Overcoming the oil shock was a turning point, with Japanese consumer and business confidence reaching new highs. Japan, a resource-scarce country, was felt to have recovered from the crisis much better than the West. Japanese products began to capture increasing shares in, and in some cases came to dominate, overseas markets. Thus, the aspirations of the Sixties turned into earnest quests in the Seventies for improvement in the quality of life, which was becoming increasingly attainable through a growing availability of a variety of higher-quality products. Many Westerners, however, continued to misread these surface changes in consumption behavior as evidence of the increasing Westernization of Japanese society, erroneously linking a preference for jeans or hamburgers with changing fundamental cultural values, forgetting that New Yorkers who eat sushi do so for reasons that have nothing to do with adopting Japanese values.

Beginning in the Seventies, improvement in the quality of life was no longer seen to derive solely from the West. Adaptation rather than transference became the name of the game for many successful Western products that entered the Japanese market during this period. For example, fragrance levels in imported soap had to be lowered, and British chocolates were found to be too sweet for Japanese tastes. In another instance, Avon found that the fact that it was the biggest name in cosmetics in the world was not relevant to the Japanese consumer, and the company adapted a strategy to prove that it was part of the Japanese community.

It was in this period that the marketer was also able to change customs and habits without necessarily offending traditional values. Frugality, for example, considered a key social value in the postwar, developing stages of the Japanese economy, continued to erode with the advancement in material well-being, and enabled the entries of Western products of superior utility. In the 1960s, Japanese commentators had shaken their heads at the extravagance of facial tissues when *chirigami*, inexpensive but rough paper for blowing one's nose, was readily available; although cheap throwaway razors were available and seemed to be adequate for Japanese beards, which are generally not as thick as Westerners' beards, safety razors were thought to provide much better shaves, so the Japanese consumer quickly abandoned throwaways for the superior quality safety razor, despite the higher cost.

The myth of Japanese frugality was exploded by Western marketers in the 1970s. Prior to that, frugality had been promoted as a key Japanese social value, and it was often mistakenly associated with the high levels of savings characteristic of Japanese society. As income levels rose, however, subsequent behavior suggests that frugality had simply been the result of economic necessity, as is common in all societies. The rise of disposable diapers in the Japanese market provides a dramatic example of this. In the late Sixties, paper diapers were of such poor quality that they scarcely existed in the Japanese market. The young mother-to-be received stacks of cloth diapers from her in-laws, enough to last through several generations of babies — an example of alleged frugality. Market research showed that Japanese mothers assiduously changed their baby's diapers, more quickly and more often than in any society for which comparative data were available. With less than two children in the majority of families, the Japanese market might have been dismissed as a limited market for disposable diapers. The first marketing attempts in Japan, which emphasized "convenience" in terms of "disposability," were in fact insufficient as an appeal.

These attitudes and patterns of behavior were fundamental to the culture and daunting obstacles for a single marketer to overcome. However, the American consumer products giant, Procter & Gamble, promoted Pampers as a new type of diaper to suit modern lifestyles, and (most importantly) to provide greater comfort to the baby. Pampers became a generic product as a new type of diaper, not as a disposable diaper. As consumers became familiar with the concept and convinced of the superior satisfaction over existing products, "disposable," as applied to diapers, was no longer equated with waste. Thus, a significant consumer goods category was created by a Western marketer, encouraging the entry of Japanese competition catering to local tastes and resulting in the stimulation of consumer interest.

Nevertheless, some values endured and still endure amidst rapid change. What appeared on the surface to be an innocuous piece of behavioral data — the greater frequency of diaper changes, almost in anticipation of the baby's needs — in fact reflects a deeper difference in social values. Most Japanese babies are in close proximity to their mothers throughout the day, often bathing in the same tub. If the Japanese infant is sleeping on a quilt laid on a tatami (straw mat) floor, he need only crawl across to his mother — she is always close at hand. By contrast, Western babies tend to sleep separately from their parents and must call out for attention on awakening.

This early relationship with authority in Japan — and mother is the first authority one encounters in life — was elucidated in the Sixties' bestseller by Takeo Doi, a Japanese psychiatrist. In the West, no matter how benign, an authority is someone you must ask to receive something — the infant must call for its mother. In the Japanese context, however, authority anticipates the needs of those below, an attitude or process described as *amae*, often inaccurately translated simply as "dependence." *Amae* is based on the assumption that authority in various forms — seniors at school, superiors at work — are responsive to the needs of those ranked below and this, in turn, is reciprocated by a close trust in those above. It explains in part the Japanese consumer's trust in "reputable" manufacturers or establishments. The consequence is that social, rather than legal, pressures are enormous if authority betrays its trust. These concerns continue to be reflected in Japanese quality control, services to achieve customer satisfaction, and corporate identity programs. The flip side of respect and trust in authority is that Japanese consumers traditionally accepted a corporate-driven society, to some extent subjugating their own interests for the good of Japan Inc.

1985: HERALDING THE ARRIVAL OF THE CONSUMER SOCIETY

The word *shokku* ("shock") is used as a suffix to describe traumatic changes in the Japanese system. Until the mid-1980s, most "shocks" resulted from political or macroeconomic pressures coming from outside Japan. Examples include the Nixon Shock in 1971, when the dollar went off the gold standard, prompting the first dramatic rise in the yen; the 1973 oil shock mentioned earlier; and the *endaka shokku* — the rapid rise in the yen after the Plaza Accord of 1985 — which forced Japan to examine its role in the world economy and spawned the buzzwords: *kokusaika* (internationalization) and later, *gurobaruka* (globalization).

While initially the visible effects of these "shocks" were macroeconomic, touching industry and corporate attitudes, irreversible forces were unleashed which rocked the fundamentals of the market. MITI (Ministry of International Trade and Industry) fretted in its 1988 White Paper that if the trade imbalance in favor of Japan persisted, the rest of the world would become so apprehensive of Japan that the prevailing system of free trade would not be sustainable. A little earlier, Prime Minister Nakasone had asked seventeen leaders from various sectors to advise him on the matter. Named the Maekawa Report after the project director, an ex-governor of the Bank of Japan, it set forth now familiar concepts: "stimulation of domestic demand," "restructuring of industry," and "liberalization." The report amounted to a clarion call for the transformation of Japan from a producer- to a consumer-led society, but turned out to be strong in concept and weak in execution.

In 1993, with the long reign of the Liberal Democratic Party over, and with the issues raised in the Maekawa report still largely unresolved, the new government commissioned another study, dubbed the "second Maekawa Report." The Hiraiwa Report raises essentially the same points, but has much stronger support from the business community, now more acutely conscious of the need to come to terms with the business practices of the advanced markets of the West.

In any event, the continuing rise in the value of the yen brought the Japanese consumer more knowledge of other consumer societies — through travel and increased access to foreign luxury items — and, most importantly, the Japanese consumer became aware of the discrepancies in prices at home and abroad. For the consumer, internationalization meant a more rational approach to products, irrespective of their source. This was balanced, however, by the tendency to equate the country's industrial strength with common interests. That is, the consumer accepted a corporate- and institution-driven society, and thus an organized market in effect. Through the 1980s, the Japanese consumer continued to allow sympathy for his fellow countrymen to override economic rationale, and tolerated prices for daily goods, especially food, far in excess of most consumer economies.

Even so, the mid-1980s spawned a whole set of buzz words that related to changes in consumer values. *Shinjinrui*, translated as "new mankind," was the first generation of consumers without fear of the outside world — a fear that Japan, as a small, resource-scarce country, was under threat of being overwhelmed. Japanese who came into adulthood in the 1970s had yet to shed this isolationism and were only just starting to venture out on overseas pleasure travels in the security of group tours. Today, by contrast, the Japanese are the most sought-after group by the travel industry, with some 10 million traveling abroad in 1990. This increased awareness of the world around them bred a new mood of questioning. A letter to a leading daily, the *Asahi Shimbun*, in the spring of 1987, aptly posed the issue:

> We are being attacked from overseas because we have earned an annual trade surplus of $50 billion, but the common soldiers of Japan Inc. are gasping under the weight of housing loans and high taxation, crushed by the solitude of job transfers away from families, and hardly able to breathe on packed trains on which much time has to be spent on commuting. . . . Where did those spectacular sums of money disappear to?

Partly it went back to the United States and other parts of the world as Japanese investment — increasingly in production facilities — to sustain the American consumer's high propensity for spending. The rest caused the so-called "bubble economy."

THE BUBBLE AND ITS IMMEDIATE EFFECTS

After the Plaza Accord of 1985, which triggered a near-doubling in the value of the yen, a supplementary budget was introduced to stimulate domestic demand in a futile gesture toward reducing Japan's mounting trade surplus, and to placate irritated trading partners. The stimulus package was directed at public works projects, with the immediate beneficiary being the construction industry, resulting in a rapid rise in land values. Corporations were able to raise cheap money on the basis of their appreciated asset bases, and their bloated corporate cash war chests led to a speculation binge in land and stocks. In this way, the infamous "bubble" — asset inflation — came into being.

A buzz word, *Nyu Ritchi* (translated as "New Rich") was born, which has connotations among Japanese that are difficult for most outsiders to comprehend. A significant portion of the Japanese population owning real estate not only felt rich, but spent in a manner hitherto unthinkable in a society which had, for so long, promoted saving as an absolute virtue and any deviation as profligacy. With the appearance of the New Rich, the postwar Japanese conviction that theirs is a middle class society par excellence was badly shaken. Between the mid-1950s and the mid-1980s, the average household's assets rose 36-fold, and outstanding consumer loans by more than 116-fold. Easy money, raised from financial institutions willing to lend against inflated land values at low interest rates, created an investment and consumption boom.

The New Rich fed the stock market, bought high-priced imported cars and French Impressionist art, and created a resort boom. Japan became the largest market for Louis Vuitton and Berlitz language teaching, and the overwhelming majority of honeymooners went abroad. There was a surge in experimentation with new foods — *gurume* (gourmet) became a Japanese word used on packages. Italian restaurants sprouted like bamboo shoots after the rain. More than half the married women were now working; consequently, convenience began to take precedence over time-consuming shopping for the sake of optimizing the household budget.

All of these factors led to continually rising costs and no significant short-term reductions in the trade surplus. The continued strength of the yen further accelerated offshore manufacturing; globalization became a concept increasingly grappled with by major Japanese corporations. What this means for the future is that the distinction between local products and imports will become blurred — the Toyota one drives could well be made in Ohio rather than in Nagoya. Perceived value — a mixture, and sometimes a tradeoff, between quality, service, and price — rather than the origin of a product, will determine the winners in the Japanese marketplace from now on.

THE SHAKING OF THE STATUS QUO: THE EFFECTS OF A RAPIDLY AGING SOCIETY

The landscape for the Japanese market was irreversibly changed in several important respects in the 1980s. A new shock — the *1.53 shokku* — was hotly debated in 1987. Unlike earlier "shocks," which had resulted from external political pressures, this one was significant because it was created from within Japanese society. The *1.53 shokku* was registered when statistics revealed that the average number of children a Japanese woman bears had dropped to 1.53. The birth rate in 1992 dropped to 1.5. There are no signs, as yet, of recovery, especially since the average marrying age for women has risen to twenty-six years. From 1993, the number of 18-year-old college entrants will continue to decline.

Of fundamental importance is the resultant shortage of young labor, which accelerated the entry of women into the work force: In 1988, an estimated 60 percent of married women received an income from a job, a large proportion in permanent employment. Older generations of husbands used to refer to their wives as *kanai,* a combination of Chinese characters that means, literally, "inside the home," but most women now spend more time *kagai*, "outside the home." Time has become precious, affecting women's shopping habits — an efficient trip to the supermarket, supplemented by convenience stores, is replacing daily shopping excursions.

One hypothesis for the *1.53 shokku* is that Japanese women have virtually gone on strike, protesting an environment that is not conducive to early marriage and several children, the most obvious factor being the expense of urban housing: A child's natural need for space can put impossible demands upon cramped housing conditions in cities like Tokyo and Osaka. Some Japanese male traditionalists have blamed the entry of women into the workplace as the major reason for the drop in birth rate. It has dawned on many more, however, that what is at issue is not female but male attitudes, and that preventing the equal participation of women in the work force will not increase the birth rate. In fact, the average Japanese woman has shown that, when forced to choose between home and work (most Japanese companies expect women employees to "retire" when they marry), she will postpone marriage, preferring to be socially active for a longer period. Sweden, which earlier suffered a similar decline in birth rate, has proven the trend can be reversed where corporations and society in general provide an infrastructure guaranteeing that women can be active in both work and the home.

In an article that appeared in the authoritative Japanese monthly, *Chuo Koron*, in September 1990, Eiji Suzuki, then the head of Nikkeiren (Japan Federation of Employers Association) and one of Japan's most influential business opinion leaders, linked the denial of equal participation of women in the workplace with the low birth rate. He questioned the so-called Japanese work ethic, which ties the employee's time "unnecessarily" to the company, typically through compulsory customer entertainment in the evenings and golf on weekends. If these are conditions for promotion, then women are clearly denied equal opportunity. In an aging society, corporations require the active participation of young women — an underutilized pool of educated human resources. Suzuki urged "a desperate exploration by both the corporation and the individual to prepare an environment in which women can bring up children" and still continue at work, the individual in this case being the Japanese corporate male.

Suzuki concluded: "It is inconceivable that Japanese women are averse to child care by nature. The cause lies in hounding them into a corner through the corporate-driven culture, making them the sole handlers of problems in housing and education. There is a cry that 'Enough is enough; having children is too much of a financial, physical, and psychological burden.' " With increased independence from household chores, the female consumer is introducing new values — "convenience," "leisure," and "individualization" — to the marketplace.

Japan's population has the most rapid rate of aging in the world, and this is having a ripple effect throughout society, the most obvious being an increased concern for health, and a consequent expansion in demand for health-related products and services. As noted above, it has also created a severe shortage of young workers, who must be attracted by employers with new appeals, such as increased leisure time, in a business environment that overtly discourages competition in terms of wages.

Domestically, the Japanese are being pressured to save less and spend more, preferably on imports, and to work less, at least no more than their counterparts in other advanced economies. The Committee of Economic Councillors (Keizai Shingikai) announced projections in June 1991 that annual working hours will be 1,700 hours by 2010, down from the average of 2,052 hours in 1990. The Japanese consumers will no doubt tackle leisure as earnestly and enthusiastically as they did work in the past. "Leisure" is a new value that will reshape society.

THE SHAKING OF THE STATUS QUO: CONSUMER NEEDS AND A SHIFT TO INFORMATION-BASED DISTRIBUTION

During the bubble, consumers placed more priority on value-added items such as shopping in special environments created in department stores or through the satisfaction of personal attention in a boutique — these being the chief victims of the recession. Price was not an issue; the new values driving the consumer market were "convenience" and "variety." For example, whereas in the past all family members had shared the same shampoo and toothpaste, it became quite common for individual family members to have a brand of their personal preference. The gourmet boom fueled the search for new, interesting foods and a move away from long-established staples. The quest for "variety" created greater opportunities for newcomers and shortened the life cycles of incumbent brands.

Most of the elements of change were in place before the bubble, which merely accelerated the pace. In distribution, for example, the bugbear of foreign entry into the Japanese market, a quiet revolution began in 1985. The market was taken by surprise when Itoh Yokado, then only number three in big-time retailing in terms of number of stores and volume of sales, generated greater profits than Daiei, which had more stores and higher-volume sales. Until that time, a retail chain's performance was assumed to be directly correlated with the number of outlets it had; in other words, market share was the chief performance criterion. Itoh Yokado's greater profits were accredited to the acquisition of the franchise for the 7-Eleven chain, which introduced a new type of retailing based on quality of information rather than increasing numbers of outlets to increase profits.

The irony was that convenience stores became an attractive investment due to the Large-scale Retail Store Law, which was the subject of a U.S. attack during the 1980s. This law was enacted to protect the numerous small stores at the end of the long chain of wholesalers; for every seven food outlets there was one wholesaler, making the entry of foreign products difficult by denying direct access to the consumer. Through a convoluted process of applications and negotiations, approval to open a large store took an average of six years and incurred enormous costs. (The period has been shortened to a year or two through the relaxation of the Act in 1991.) Worst of all, large stores were restricted in trading hours, ostensibly to allow small stores to provide after-hours service.

The West had for a long time contended that the Act was an impediment to free trade. What had not been realized was that this protective wall notwithstanding, the system was being eroded from within. The average age of the "mom and pop" storekeeper, which had been steadily rising, now exceeded sixty years, and many younger family members were not interested in keeping the store, whose return on assets was low. With the leap in real estate values during the bubble, these store sites were sold off to developers, replaced by classy boutiques, or, more importantly, acquired by large corporations such as Daiei and Itoh Yokado and turned into convenience stores. It was this trend that created the convenience store phenomenon — small stores owned by large retail chains, with a much more rational, business-oriented approach than the traditional "mom and pop." Convenience stores became the most profitable retail category in the late 1980s.

Since the definition of a large store was based on floor area, convenience stores were not restricted under the law and could operate on a 24-hour basis, and also could take advantage of the technologies — both in terms of hardware and software — available to a large store. Because the store was often acquired at inflated prices, it had to produce suitable returns on investment. Enter POS — computerized inventory control. Gone were the old forms of trading, which relied on the personal relationships so strongly associated with the Japanese distribution system and the emphasis on capturing shelf space — the latter achieved through the supplier's strength. POS dictated what should be on the shelf through fast information processing at the counter. Slow-moving items, performing below average for their category, were taken off the shelf, a necessity dictated by limited shelf space. This amounted to a revolution in retail marketing, as emphasis shifted from the capture of shelf space to the profit performance of individual items.

With the success of Itoh Yokado came the sudden realization that it was not the product on the shelf that generated profits but information. In the old days, the manufacturer possessed the information before the retailer — through consumer surveys and retail store audits based on the aggregation of a panel of stores' sales invoices. But the situation is now entirely different; with the use of scanners at point of sales, consumer purchases are immediately linked to the chain's centralized computer. Thus the retailer has the information on consumer preferences before the manufacturer. The wholesale sector was not unscathed by this change either, and could no longer continue to be mere deliverers of goods. The small and medium-sized wholesalers banded together with others to invest in hardware and software — with the emphasis on the latter — to service their small store clients with information on what sells or doesn't sell. Power now rests with the ultimate decision maker, the consumer — the ultimate power shift in Japanese retailing.

THE BUBBLE'S AFTERMATH: DESTRUCTION OF THE PRICE MYTH

The bursting of the bubble in 1992 only accelerated the inevitable trends demolishing the many myths concerning the Japanese consumer and market structure. We must be careful, however, to isolate the effects of business cycle conditions from fundamental changes based on new values that have arisen. The recession of the early 1990s offers significant clues.

Despite a decline in other retail categories, most notably department stores and restaurants but even extending to supermarkets, catalogue sales have prospered. Still small in comparison with the United States, this category attained sales of approximately ¥2 trillion (about $17 billion at ¥120 to the U.S. dollar) in 1992 — approximately one-fifth of the sales enjoyed by the huge department store category. One Japanese myth, namely that the majority of Japanese will only shop from retail outlets, is now under siege.

In the 1970s, representations were made to the Ministry of Posts and Telecommunications by a subcommittee of the American Chamber of Commerce in Japan for a reduction in the Japanese bulk postage rate — one of the highest in the world — allowing the foreign marketer more direct, easier access to the Japanese consumer. Given the labyrinthine Japanese distribution system, this would provide, in theory at least, a level playing field for all entrants. Japanese officials told the Americans that direct mail marketing was "un-Japanese." It was reasoned that with the proliferation of stores giving easy access for almost all consumers, Japanese women, who liked personal shopping, would not be interested in buying from a catalogue. The officials overlooked the fact that this was an assumption that had not been put to the test.

It is now obvious that the Japanese female consumer disagrees. The $17 billion question was why catalogue sales grew to this level during a recession, from negligible proportions only a decade previous. First, working women, who now represent the majority of adult females, do not want to spend as much of their precious nonworking hours on shopping; direct marketers give them the option of shopping at their own convenience. Additionally, with the recession, price has become an important factor in the value mix of the Japanese consumer. The traditional view was that of the three principal components that generate perceived value — quality (product and/or image), service, and price — given that quality is a constant, the Japanese consumer tends to be skewed toward service rather than price, the converse of the American case. Japan was like an airline that offered only first and business class seats, without the option of an economy class. Not offering economy fares is fine if everybody can afford the extra cost — if sales are buoyant the supplier will make more money. The point is that when the seats are not filled at the higher prices, economy fares would keep the aircraft afloat. With the bursting of the bubble, there were empty seats and economy fares became the order of the day. For the supplier of products, cutting down on services by reducing the number of store personnel or excessive packaging, or eliminating redundant functions, enables the lowering of the price to the consumer — a new option now offered to the Japanese consumer.

Astute marketers are seizing new opportunities. Cecile, a major Japanese player in the direct mail category that was already successful before the bubble, has further strengthened its position by offering pantyhose at half the price charged in supermarkets. In late 1992, Aoyama Shoji, a discount chain, opened a bargain men's clothing store in the heart of the prestigious shopping area of Ginza, creating a sensation among Japanese retail watchers. On opening day, more than two hundred customers were in line by 7 a.m. Latecomers waited patiently, the line extending around a famous department store, when the overwhelmed new bargain store had to exercise traffic control by periodically closing its doors.

Both Aoyama and Cecile were able to lower costs by avoiding traditional trading houses and accepting the risk of not returning unsold goods to the manufacturer. There are signs that department stores are being forced into changing their traditional trading patterns. (The traditional Japanese system of retailers returning unsold goods to manufacturers keeps costs to the consumer high, as manufacturers set margins to cover their risks.) Until the mid-1980s, the Japanese consumer equated bargains with cheap and inferior, but that tendency (to relate price with quality) is now a thing of the past. Current Japanese consumers no longer easily part with their money just because of a brand name, and must be convinced of the value of the product or service. In a market that was regulated from the top and that had greater concern for stability than the potential disruptions caused by price competition, Japanese consumer goods manufacturers were able to compete largely on quality and service, rather than price. Suppliers are fast being denied such protection, however, under pressures for a free market.

THE BUBBLE'S AFTERMATH: DESTRUCTION OF THE "MODESTY IN ADVERTISING" MYTH

Another myth concerning the Japanese consumer was relegated to the dust heap in the arena of advertising, namely that one does not trumpet one's virtue at the expense of others. Here, too, there was evidence of the arrogance of a business establishment that assumed their behavior correctly reflected consumer values, and a bureaucracy that thought they knew what was best for the consumer.

It had been consistently maintained over the years that comparative advertising, that is directly comparing a product's features with those of a competitor, was culturally offensive in Japan. Comparative advertising in Japan has been slow to come, but one of my early experiences suggests that its emergence is not due to a recent change in consumer values. A commercial for a Japanese vacuum cleaner, which demonstrated that the new model from the manufacturer was superior to its own old model, was tested for consumer reactions before it went on air in the late 1960s. Test results indicated that the ad would be effective, but the commercial had to be withdrawn because of objections within the industry. It was argued that the demonstration covertly suggested superiority over other brands which, indeed, was its aim. Some ten years later, further controversy erupted over some similar attempts, which, while still not directly comparing the product with its competitor, implied a clear link. Research indicated, however, that in some cases the consumer, far from objecting, welcomed the clear communication of the "differences."

Then came the Pepsi challenge commercials, which showed a rock star turning into a balladeer when consuming a Coke and, after switching back to Pepsi, reverting to his proper persona. The Japanese advertising fraternity imposed a compromise by asking that the Coke label be fuzzed, although it was still obvious what the competitive brand was. The entertainment qualities of the commercial delighted the target consumers and even some Japanese advertising pundits. Nevertheless, it was still one foreign advertiser directly challenging another, and the Japanese fraternity could afford to be amused.

In 1992, the matter was brought closer to home when General Motors compared its models with Nissan's. Nissan took the lofty stance that it was "pleased to have been chosen for comparison." The Japanese car industry was evidently not feeling threatened by Detroit on its own turf. In early 1993, an advertising campaign took to the air in which a Japanese manufacturer, NEC, compared its product to that of its U.S. competitor, IBM; a Japanese manufacturer has thus broken the taboo. The Japanese media saw this as a justifiable counter to a foreign invasion, and no objections were raised on cultural grounds. In the course of a few years, we have moved from one foreign brand versus another, to a foreign brand versus a Japanese, to a Japanese brand versus a foreign one. At the time of writing, there are as yet no direct confrontations between Japanese brands, but in all cases there is no evidence of the Japanese consumer objecting to comparative advertising. Irrespective of the traditionalists, never say never!

NEW MALE-FEMALE RELATIONSHIPS

Now for the most important relationship in marketing — that between the sexes. *Manga* are comics that enjoy a large adult readership and account for a significant proportion of publishing in Japan. Female-targeted *manga* have now encroached upon this traditionally male territory. Originally heavy in sexual or romantic content, many more now dramatize women who are tackling professional or career problems. While the fantasy element is still important, the diversity of story lines targeted at the female reflects the changes in her role in society and her expanded areas of activity. Of even greater fundamental importance, since it is not as obvious, is the shift in the relationship between the sexes which is depicted.

That the concern for the opposite sex is an important factor in selecting a brand of cosmetic or male toiletry is common sense to marketers worldwide, although the style of presentation differs by culture. Some have even gone so far as to say that the love element rather than functional appeals determine market share. In Japan, as recently as the 1970s, marriage and motherhood were still the ultimate goals for the female. It is not so long ago that the phrase *tekireiki* — "the appropriate age for marriage" — was in vogue. When a girl reached that age (it used to be around twenty, then was rapidly increased, reaching about twenty-five in the 1970s), she was literally hounded by family and relatives into marriage. If the "Ladies' Comics" are taken as indicators of a greater freedom of choice in lifestyle for women, a fulfilling relationship between the sexes, not necessarily synonymous with marriage, has become the spiritual goal in the 1990s.

However, before we jump to conclusions, the so-called liberation, expressed with a vengeance through the pursuit of leisure activities and the acquisition of fashion goods, may just have been a short-term phenomenon induced by the bubble. Marriage as a goal has hardly been rejected by the majority, and is still preferred over less conventional love relationships. Does this represent a reversion to traditional values relating more to the group and subjugation of individuality? Not so. There has been a fundamental shift in attitudes toward marriage since the 1970s — there is a big difference between the coming together of individuals who are independent, both financially and psychologically, and a marriage forced upon a man and a woman by social pressure and practical considerations. Changes in male-female relationships, especially in marriage, are creating new markets in Japan.

Many contend that there is a global tendency that will make all consumers in advanced market economies similar to their counterparts in the West. As applied to Japan — or anywhere — the answer is "yes" to the general proposition, but "no" when it comes to specific details. For example, home deliveries of pizzas have taken off, as have prepared meals — the equivalent of "TV dinners" in North America. But the fastest-developing product lines in Japan have been traditional Japanese dishes which led KFC to establish a separate division in 1993 under a Japanese name to cater to that market, and McDonald's to introduce rice-based fast foods to defend itself from local competitors — the Big Mac outlet is no longer identical throughout the world.

Price has become an important factor in the assessment of the value of a product or service — a tendency that moves Japanese consumers closer to their Western counterparts — but this does not mean that perceptions of "quality" and the demand for "service" will lose their distinctly Japanese characteristics. Foreign products with price advantages, backed by innovative approaches in communicating to the consumer, will find a potential market here, provided the foreign marketer understands the relevant Japanese consumer expectations and fulfills them as to quality and service.

The Japanese consumer has already become sophisticated in the handling of information. In the past, however, much of the information was controlled by the establishment, including major business and producer organizations. Increasingly, the Japanese consumer will have access to global information, and old-style market nationalism will be difficult to sustain. Married female consumers will play an active role in purchasing decisions; they have traveled more widely overseas and, above all, are no longer tied to the home. With working women now in the majority, women will be more active participants in society, with increased capabilities to absorb information.

All societies aspire to improve the "quality of life," but the definition of "quality" is not a constant. For example, how will environmental issues become part of the Japanese consumer's judgment in selecting products? Environmental control has been targeted as a major industrial category by the Japanese government, creating a potential market for those who produce or service it. Development of this industry will also influence consumer attitudes.

The Japanese have caught up and in many cases surpassed the West in the ownership of consumer durable goods. However, there is still a substantial gap in social capital — in housing, recreational facilities, and services for the elderly. Moves are afoot to reduce work hours to somewhat comparable levels to the West and there will be more leisure time available. The narrowing of these gaps will stimulate many new product and service categories and create opportunities for foreign companies — in modular housing, furniture, do-it-yourself equipment, sporting goods, theme parks, travel and entertainment, and health care items, to mention a few.

There have been important changes in the Japanese distribution system, brought about by a greater need to understand consumer preferences. Rather than shelf space and market share, profit generation based on information technology has emerged as the key criterion. Products are now examined on their individual merits rather than on the fact that they come under the umbrella of a major manufacturer. While not suggesting that the infrastructure based on long-established distribution traditions is going to disappear overnight, this alleviates one of the key difficulties for the entry of a foreign product. There will be a steady erosion of other institutional barriers, presenting opportunities for foreign marketers with the courage to risk entering Japan. But there is no universal model for success — each case will have to be examined on its own merits, and strategies tailored to specific circumstances.

CHAPTER FIVE

The Nature of the Japanese Corporation

JAMES C. ABEGGLEN

第五章

Japanese management techniques are much discussed in Western businesses today. While Western companies may not be able to adopt these methods wholesale, it is essential that they understand the nature of the Japanese corporations they will meet as competitors in the global marketplace, and the reasons for their success. In this chapter, Dr. James Abegglen, chairman of Gemini Consulting (Japan), traces the progression of Japan's industrial successes and examines the challenges posed by the downturn in the Japanese economy.

The decade of the 1990s has posed a rude challenge to Japan's corporations. Japanese companies moved from success to success through the late 1980s, buoyed by a historic increase in the value of the yen and a surging domestic economy. The party ended with the crash of stock and land prices and falling domestic demand. With the bursting of the bubble of dangerous speculation, Japan's corporations have once again entered a period of restructuring, cutting back on growth plans, consolidating product lines, cutting costs, and fighting to regain profitability. Only a few years ago considered invincible, Japan's corporations are suddenly believed to be highly vulnerable.

Some perspective on the problems of the early 1990s is needed in gauging the impact of the adjustment period on Japan's corporations, however. This is by no means the first, nor even the most severe, of the periodic crises that Japan's business firms have experienced. Due in part to the extraordinary rate of growth and change in the economy, the business environment for Japan's firms has periodically undergone periods of turmoil lasting one to three years; the most severe followed the oil price explosion in 1974, when the economy experienced negative annual growth — the only time this has occurred in postwar Japan. Most recently, the sudden and drastic shift in exchange rates in 1985–86 caused a period of adjustment, though not quite so painful nor prolonged as the current one. Earlier crises were widely predicted to bring an end to Japan's economic success and to cripple Japan's companies. Instead, the Japanese economy and its corporations have repeatedly demonstrated both strength and resilience.

This is not to say that these periods of restructuring have been easy. The required adjustments are painful, and not all corporations manage to make the transition to the next stage of growth. However, growth demands change as incomes and wages rise, as the currency appreciates in response to competitive success, as the labor force is ever better educated, and as competition from other developing nations drives Japan's industries forward to more sophisticated products and services. It is the very speed of Japan's growth that forces these crises, and it is the successful response to them that generates continued growth.

THE NATURE OF JAPAN'S SUCCESS

The nature of the modern Japanese corporation is shaped in large part by the highly favorable environment in which it has developed. American corporations were much admired and studied when the U.S. economy was setting the world pace. Attention has shifted to Japan's corporations and their organizational methods and nature. It must be remembered, however, that a good part of the success of the Japanese corporation is attributable to the superb labor force resulting from Japan's family structure and education system, to the low cost of capital resulting from very high levels of savings, to the competence of the government authorities concerned with economic management, and to a generally favorable world environment in terms of raw material supply and trade growth for much of the postwar period. These great advantages enjoyed by the Japanese corporation go far in explain-

Table 1 World Trade in Manufactured Goods

	1960	1970	1980	1990	1992
Japan	3%	7%	12%	14%	17%
Germany	7%	19%	20%	21%	20%
United Kingdom	26%	16%	11%	9%	9%
United States	27%	21%	18%	16%	16%
France	10%	10%	9%	10%	10%
Others	27%	27%	30%	30%	28%

ing their successes and are not attributable to the nature of the corporations themselves.

It must also be kept in mind that Japan's economy has its winners and losers. It is perhaps inevitable that attention focuses on winners — on the highly successful companies in the electronics and auto industries, rather than on the quite undistinguished companies that make up most of Japan's petroleum and chemical industries, for example.

The emphasis by foreign observers on Japan's winners, and a general disregard of losers, is reinforced by the fact that the winners are the companies that march out into world markets to do competitive battle. The losers fall by the domestic wayside, not to be heard of abroad. Honda is well known, and Suzuki, Kawasaki, and Yamaha are familiar brands. But what of the other forty-six motorcycle producers in Japan that went out of the business as Honda moved to the position of world leader? The same forces are presumably at work in the management of Japan's unsuccessful sectors and companies as in the successful ones. One conclusion must be that it is possible to overemphasize management characteristics and overlook other factors that determine competitive outcomes.

Still, the overall story of the economy and its companies is one of great success. One measure is the share of world trade in manufactured goods (see Table 1). Just as the economy of Japan moved from about 2 percent of the world economy in the early 1950s to about 15 percent in the early 1990s, so Japanese companies' shares of world trade have increased, from about 3 percent to about 17 percent. Note that export growth has paralleled the growth of the economy as a whole; Japan is not an unusually large exporter, and

Table 2 Japan's Exports by Industry, 1960–1990

	1960	1970	1980	1990
Textiles	30%	12%	5%	3%
Steel	10%	13%	12%	4%
Electrical Machinery	7%	15%	17%	23%
Motor Vehicles	3%	7%	18%	18%
Other	50%	53%	48%	52%

the growth of the economy and its companies has been driven by the very rapid rise in domestic demand, contrary to conventional wisdom which portrays it as export-driven.

The remarkable fact about this trade increase, and the key implication for understanding Japanese corporations, is the very great and rapid change in the composition of Japan's trade. Japan and the United States have the largest trade interaction ever seen across oceans. Given its scale, it is not surprising that trade tensions are endemic to the relationship, but their focus changes. Not so long ago, in the mid-1960s, the burning issue in trade between Japan and the United States was Japan's textile exports; one-third of Japan's exports then were textile products. Today, Japan is a massive importer of textiles, which now form a very minor part of its export trade (see Table 2). American concerns about Japanese trade now focus on electronic products and machine tools, the most sophisticated of product lines.

CHANGING COMPETITIVE ADVANTAGES

As the trade numbers suggest, the shift in Japan's industrial focus has been remarkable, with each decade having its own leading-edge industry. From generally labor-intensive and low technology textiles, the focus was next capital- and scale-intensive steel, where Japanese firms achieved cost and technology world leadership. But steel, like textiles, is a mature industry, and is energy-intensive into the bargain. As textiles led growth in the 1950s and exports in the 1960s, so steel led domestic growth in the 1960s and yielded its place to autos in the 1970s, with the 1980s the decade of electronics.

At war's end, Japan had a very large, well-educated, and quite inexpensive labor force — Japan's once famous "cheap labor" advantage in trade competition. As wages rose, education levels advanced still further, and a cycle of high growth began. Massive investments in world-scale facilities in heavy industry took center stage, with the toys and textiles of the earlier period losing competitiveness and being imported into Japan. With heavy industry in place and maturing, and wage, education, and technology levels still rising, assembled products — autos, machinery, and consumer electronics — became the focus of investment and growth, yielding more recently to high technology electronics and a focus on research and development. The challenge to Japanese corporations has been to keep pace with these changes.

Of course, most corporations have not managed change of so great a degree. In the 1950s, the largest corporations were textile firms, with Toyobo the largest manufacturing company in Japan. Toyobo remains a large firm, but in real terms has not grown over the past decades. The next leaders in terms of size in manufacturing were the steel firms; Nippon Steel was Japan's largest corporation in the mid-1960s. From basic steel production, the economy shifted to value-added steel production in shipbuilding, with Mitsubishi Heavy Industries the largest firm, succeeded in turn by Toyota in autos in the 1970s. More recently, electronic producers Hitachi and Matsushita Electric have been running close to Toyota in terms of total sales.

In earlier years, this kind of progress to higher levels of economic performance was owed in part to government policy, with investment and trade policies aimed at encouraging the shift to higher value-added sectors in rapid succession. As the economy has increased in terms of size and complexity, however, the capacity of government policy to direct the process has lessened. Instead, the workings of the marketplace are the basic forces for change, and these are supported by government policies aimed at accelerating the market forces. Thus, for example, oil imports worked to close coal mines when the market was given full and free play; energy prices forced the closing down of bauxite smelting; wage increases and competitive imports shrank the textile industry. In all these cases, government policies worked with market forces rather than attempting to counteract them — a frequent policy error in the industrial West.

In summary, the economic and business environment shaping Japanese firms has been one of rapid growth with periodic crises of adjustment, as we are now experiencing in the early 1990s. Whole industries have vanished — coal mining and aluminum smelting, for example — or have greatly diminished in size, as with cotton textiles and shipbuilding. In turn, powerful new industries have more than taken the place of the less productive industries, and the labor force is fully employed in ever more sophisticated and more highly compensated jobs.

JAPANESE FOREIGN INVESTMENT

Overseas investment has come to play an important part in the adjustment to industrial change. Japanese companies have sought to defer the demise of mature, more labor-intensive industries by investing abroad to obtain lower-cost sources of labor, especially in East and Southeast Asia. Investment in the industrial markets of the United States and Europe has been spurred by trade tensions and protectionism, notably in the case of the auto industry. No doubt, Japanese companies would prefer to produce autos and electronic products at home, but they invest abroad to protect and increase overseas market shares.

In addition to seeking lower costs and assured market access, investment abroad has been much accelerated by a rapidly appreciating currency, which in the early 1990s was three times as valuable against the U.S. dollar as it had been in the late 1960s, making the acquisition of foreign assets steadily more attractive. This is introducing an entirely new dimension to the Japanese corporation, however: The need to manage assets, labor forces, and market positions in foreign countries.

FUNDAMENTAL FORCES IN THE JAPANESE ECONOMY

With great wealth, steady movement to economic maturity, and intensified international involvements, Japanese corporations may well begin to change in their nature as we move forward into the twenty-first century. However, the corporations of Japan today have been fundamentally shaped by two great forces. The first is the fact of historically unprecedented economic growth and success over the past four decades. This rapid growth shapes the economy but also works to shape the organization of the corporation and the competitive mind-sets of the men who manage them (they are, still, all men). Fast growth makes for fierce concentration on obtaining market share as the prime corporate objective. It requires a capacity and willingness to change on the part of survivors. Success in high growth situations is gained and measured differently than in low growth economies — differently in Japan, Taiwan, and Korea, than in Great Britain or the United States. Short-term and purely financial measures lose their significance in the context of very high growth.

The second great force is the nature of Japanese society, and its differences from the societies of the West. To appreciate the Japanese corporation's nature, it must be remembered that Japan's is the first non-Western society to industrialize successfully. Japanese society, like societies in most of the world, differs from the industrial West, and its corporate structure reflects this. The Japanese social base and history of development make for relations within and between companies in Japan, and elsewhere in Asia, that are markedly different from those in Western economies.

CAPTURING MARKET SHARE AS A CORPORATE OBJECTIVE

These two forces — a high growth economy and the business relations characteristic of Japanese society — converge in the area of corporate objectives. The Japanese corporation is an institution dedicated to its survival in order to secure the employment and thus the economic well-being of its members. The Japanese corporation does not see as its sole or even main purpose the maximization of returns to shareholders, as in the United States. The corporation is seen as having a number of constituencies, each with a claim on its assets and earnings. It is a primary task of management to adjudicate amongst these claims — the shareholders, banks and other financial institutions as fund suppliers, suppliers and customers, and the ultimate stakeholder in the corporation, its permanent employees. Residual funds, after these claims are met, are held within the company on behalf of the employees, to ensure continued employment and financial security.

Thus, while the legal structure of the Japanese corporation is largely the same as that in Western economies, the Japanese corporation differs, particularly from British and American corporations, in the increased role and power of the employees (including management) and the relatively diminished role of the shareholder. The Japanese common shareholder is more in the position of the preferred shareholder in the West, with a prior claim on a defined return, but with no further claims on assets or earnings. The employee in a real sense is the common shareholder, since the employees are seen as the ultimate holders of the company's assets.

One reflection of the system can be seen in the composition of the board of directors in Japan compared with the West. In the American company in particular, and increasingly in Europe as well, the majority of board members are from outside the company, appointed at the pleasure of the chief executive and with no links to the employees. In nearly all cases in Japan, the board members are executives of the company who have spent their careers in the corporation with few, if any, outside business interests.

JAPANESE CORPORATE FINANCIAL POLICIES

The consequences of this difference in objectives is perhaps most clear in the area of financial policy. Where Western firms — U.S., British, German — have a clear policy of paying out half or more of their after-tax earnings to the shareholder as dividends, the average Japanese dividend payout is between 25 and 30 percent of earnings. In fact, the dividend in Japan is not defined as a percentage of earnings. Rather, it is thought of as a percentage of the par value of the company's shares. The very successful company can pay out as little as 5 or 10 percent of its earnings and meet the expected dividend payment, while the unsuccessful firm must meet the same level of dividend, and therefore pay out most of its earnings to clear the payment hurdle. As a result, dividend policies in Japan severely punish the less successful company, allowing the winner to reinvest heavily, grow faster, and secure the company's position.

The low level of dividend payout is of course another form of savings, in an economy where households are also substantial savers. It is curious to see how the Japanese household and Japanese corporation reflect each other in their tendency to retain funds for savings and reinvestment rather than immediate consumption. Western firms pay out half or more of their earnings, weak and strong companies alike, and indeed if a company is doing very well, it is expected to and almost certainly will pay out an even larger dividend — while the Japanese firm would retain the funds to ensure future growth and thus to secure the future of its employees.

The role of shareholder in the Japanese corporation is greatly affected by the large presence of what are called "stable shareholders." These are institutional holders — banks, insurance companies, suppliers, and customers — who have come to hold the majority of shares of most Japanese companies. Institutional holdings make up the largest group of shareholders in other economies as well, but these shares are usually traded by pension fund and other financial managers. In the Japanese case, however, most institution-owned shares are not traded. Thus, the holders are generally indifferent to short term, or even medium term, changes in share price. This further relieves pressure on the dividend payout. Indeed, it makes it possible for management to accept with some equanimity sharp downturns in earnings, and even very sharp downturns in share price, assuming the downturns are the result of broader economic events and not simple incompetence.

Mention must be made here of the term *keiretsu*, an over-used and not well-defined term that has come to refer, in a generally negative sense, to company groupings in Japan. The "stable shareholders" are other companies or institutions with a long history of relations with the company and among each other, and therefore may be seen as "financial *keiretsu*." It should be noted that these kinds of shareholdings are very prevalent in Germany, Sweden, and elsewhere in Europe, often at levels that would be illegal in Japan.

Under these conditions, Japanese management can take a longer view. Workers need not be discharged, as earnings absorb the shock of downturns. Investments can be continued through difficult times, betting that as the cycle recovers, capacity will be in place to take advantage of renewed growth. In this way, Japanese firms were able to displace U.S. steel and semiconductor firms. Not only did they have the advantage of low cost of capital to help in these capital-intensive sectors, but when these notoriously cyclical industries went through a downturn, the U.S. competitors were forced to cut back on research and development, investment programs, and staffing in a struggle to keep earnings, and thus share price, from dropping. The Japanese competitor, however, could look across the demand valley and continue his investment programs. With recovery, the Japanese firms were well positioned to take market share, and did. The ability to look past current earnings and share price is a powerful advantage that Japanese companies have over most Western competitors.

BIAS TOWARD GROWTH

These financial policies, allowing rapid corporate growth, are a natural development in a business setting where the long-term security of the firm and its employees is the primary objective. However, this objective of security translates in a high-growth economy to a focus on relative competitive position, that is, on market share. Under conditions of high growth, market share is in fact the only relevant measure of performance. If a market is doubling annually over several years — not at all uncommon in a wide range of products during Japan's high growth period — failure to hold share can mean total loss of market in only a few years. The entire generation of current Japanese corporate managers has observed, or has been through the experience of, the disastrous consequences of loss of market share under conditions of high growth. It is no surprise, then, to find Japanese managers focused on competitive position.

Moreover, the structure of the Japanese corporation in much of the postwar period has built in a bias toward growth. High growth required high levels of borrowing, and in turn the cost of borrowing forced continued growth — creating the "bicycle economy," as it has been called. Moreover, as will be discussed shortly, the labor force in Japanese corporations is in good part a fixed cost, since permanent employees are not discharged or laid off; this also introduces a bias toward growth. The growth sectors of the Japanese economy have been highly competitive, with large numbers of producers striving for position. In mature sectors, Japanese corporations, as corporations everywhere, will tend to seek to reduce competition by collusion or "industry statesmanship," because growth is slight and taking market share is costly. But where growth is high, market share can be taken and has high value. Thus, managers trained in Japan's high growth economy look to market share as the critical measure of success.

The special nature of the corporation in its financial aspects in Japan is strikingly illustrated by the general absence of a market for businesses or corporations in Japan. Japanese management is well aware of mergers and acquisitions (M&A), and has considerable, although not always pleasant, experience of them abroad — so-called "in-out M&A," the purchase by Japanese companies of foreign companies. But the purchase or merger of companies in Japan by Japanese companies — "in-in M&A" — is rare, and is nearly always carried out to rescue a failing or deeply troubled corporation. M&A is thus seen as an alternative to bankruptcy, not a device to enrich management or shareholders. The company in a real sense belongs to everyone in it, and its sale is not to be contemplated if the company — or even one business within the total company — is reasonably successful. The exploitation of the corporation by shareholders for their own return is simply not part of Japanese business practice.

JAPANESE CORPORATE PERSONNEL POLICIES

In these respects, the financial and personnel policies of the Japanese firm begin to converge as parts of the nature of the Japanese corporation. When the Japanese refer to "Japanese-style management" as a different system than that of the West, they are generally referring to the system of personnel practices that developed in Japan in the postwar period. The main elements, or "three pillars," of the system are: (1) a mutual commitment between employee and firm to career employment without layoffs or firings or leaving the company; (2) seniority-based pay and promotion; and (3) the "enterprise union," a single bargaining unit comprising all employees eligible for union membership without regard to job classification.

One might view any employment and compensation system as a trade-off between security on one side and opportunity and risk on the other. The Japanese system, which had to be powerfully appealing in the conditions of immediate postwar Japan, maximizes security while minimizing opportunity. This means that the employee will have job tenure with steady income increases, but will not get rich. The company can afford to invest heavily in the employee's training since it is assured of receiving the benefits of that training. Promotions will occur within proper and understood age categories, although the escalator does not carry everyone to the top floor. The employee will not leave for another company, but will risk his lot with the firm he first joins.

The strengths of the system are many: the best young people try hard to identify the best firms; the fast-growing firm hiring larger numbers of young people has the lowest labor costs; the employee's future depends on the company doing well, thus tying the group and individual together in mutual dependence; nor are great numbers of employees thrown out of work by events and decisions over which they have no control and for which they have no responsibility.

The system makes for egalitarianism — "we are all in this together." Thus pay differences in Japanese companies between top and bottom are a fraction — generally about one-tenth — of pay differences in Western companies, making for superior motivation and company identification. Perquisites are numerous, and tend to be distributed in proportion to rank: All get some, and some get more. This is true also with bonuses, paid proportionately across all ranks short of director. And Japan has no system of stock options since treasury shares are not held by companies, thus removing a major source of inequality in compensation by the Western firm.

The enterprise union was once an important factor in the system, but is much less so now. In part, this is due to the fact that the linkage of employee and organization is such that real incomes in Japan have risen very steadily, unlike the situation in the United States, for example. Further, employment security is provided by the corporation and the union is not a necessary component in that part of the employment contract. In addition, key unions in the crisis of the mid-1970s agreed that the rational and proper basis for agreements on wage settlements was an increase equal to inflation, plus a productivity increase. Management could hardly argue, and thus wages largely disappeared from the bargaining table. Finally, in Japan, as in North America, with fast-rising levels of technology in industry, the relevance of the union to professionally trained workers has largely vanished. Thus, unions are not a major issue, even in difficult times such as the early 1990s.

The employment system that developed in Japan in full form in the postwar years has continued in practice to a remarkable degree. It is still the general expectation that employment is for the career, despite increasing variance from the norm. Various forms and degrees of merit compensation have been introduced, but seniority still plays a major part and sets clear limits on the speed of advancement in the organization. The enterprise union remains the basic model of union organization.

It is a powerful system for putting people and organizations together productively. The extent to which the interests of the individual and the organization are tied together is quite exceptional in world corporate management. It is not without its human costs. In fact, the system can be stifling at its worst. But it does not destroy careers heedlessly by mass layoffs and firings to protect earnings and share prices, nor allow a favored few to take enormous economic advantage of the corporate structure. And the employment system, as noted, makes most of labor a fixed cost, thus supporting the bias toward growth.

The Japanese employment system is seen as flawed in part because it does not allow free movement of labor across the economy. This weakness is balanced to a considerable degree by the fact that, within the company, workers can and do move quite freely from job to job and department to department, without the union job classification problems and other intra-company restrictions common in the West. Another weakness is seen as the inability of the company to accommodate business downturns by cutbacks in the labor force. However, leaving aside the question of the economic and social desirability of such labor force reductions, the Japanese corporation does in fact have some flexibility in labor cost management.

First, in times of difficulty as in the early 1990s, subcontracted work, generally of a low skill level, is cut out. Then part-time workers are cut, their numbers varying with the degree of preslump labor shortage in the industry. Next, overtime work is cut — normally a significant addition to the worker's paycheck. Concurrent with this, hiring is curtailed and normal attrition in the Japanese firm will diminish the labor force by about 5 percent per year. Finally, incentives for early retirement are offered. Plant relocations, threatened assignment to undesirable locations, and transfer to meaningless subsidiaries are used to shake out additional workers.

The Japanese government also sees employment stability as a social and economic necessity, and provides employment subsidies to help firms survive slowdowns without having to lay off employees. These subsidies totalled nearly $700 million at the low point of the 1990s recession. Given all of this internal and external effort to support the basic employment relationship, at the low point of the turndown in 1993, fewer than 3 percent of the nearly two thousand firms surveyed indicated they might have to resort to layoffs or temporary leaves. The basic employment system, its strengths largely intact, remains in place.

LEAN PRODUCTION

It was on the basis of the employment system, and the worker motivation it engenders, that the Japanese revolution in product manufacturing occurred. Variously termed the "just-in-time system" and the "flexible manufacturing system," it has lately come to be called "lean production," from the efficiencies in manpower, inventory control, and quality control it makes possible. The development of the system might well have only been possible with Japan's highly disciplined and motivated work force. But, once developed, its methods can be and are being applied throughout the industrial world.

The lean production system, best described in the MIT report on the world auto industry,[1] was developed by Toyota in an effort to deal with a fundamental dilemma. The auto industry's approach to manufacturing required large-scale production volumes to achieve competitive costs. Toyota, while producing only a few thousand autos per year, proposed to compete with the world's largest producers whose single model production runs were in the tens of thousands. Toyota had either to give up the competition or devise a way of taking most of the scale effect out of production. It took nearly two decades to develop a system whereby each unit on the assembly line could be different from all others without major cost disadvantage, and economies of scale no longer a factor.

The system is based on very fast changes in tools and dies on metalworking machines, which allows assembly operations to change from job lot, batch production to nearly continuous process production. In consequence, it nearly does away with work-in-process inventory, makes it possible for one operator to man a number of machines, greatly reduces the space required for production, and, by reduced handling of parts and increased worker control of production, makes high levels of quality output possible. The system does not depend on the use of computers, robots, or special technologies. It simply maximizes the efficiency of seemingly conventional techniques through a new concept of how to apply them.

Lean production methods apply to the whole spectrum of middle-range technology products manufactured by the assembly of metal parts — cameras, autos and trucks, office equipment including copiers and facsimile machines, and electronic consumer goods. These are all mass-produced, assembled, intermediate level technology, cost/price-sensitive products — and are the products in which Japanese corporations achieved world leadership in the 1980s. In the economic crisis of the mid-1970s, the relative success of Toyota was noted by competitors and industry in Japan generally, and was credited largely to just-in-time methods, which were then widely adopted in Japan. It was a decade later before world competitors took notice and began to understand the phenomenon. The system is interesting evidence of Japanese industrial creativity.

EFFECTS OF THE RECESSION

As the success of the 1980s, exaggerated by the asset inflation that occurred late in the decade, gave way to the slowed growth of a Japanese-style recession in the early 1990s, themes familiar from earlier Japanese recessions were voiced once again. In each major downturn, and again in the 1990s, the nature of the Japanese corporation came into question. As in the downturn of 1985–86, there is much discussion of the need to shift corporate objectives from growth and market share to cost reduction and increased profits. This response to recession is inevitable and appropriate, just as a preoccupation with growth and share is the proper objective as the recession ends and growth resumes. The recurrence of these themes with each economic cycle is a case of "deja vu" for observers of the Japanese scene.

So with the much discussed changes in the employment system, as described above. These are transitory issues that take no account of economic or social fundamentals. When growth is rapid in a product or industry, market share is the proper strategic objective, in Japan or anywhere else in the competitive industrial world, just as profit is the proper objective as growth ceases. Japan has more growth, over time, and therefore market share has high value more often than in most economies. This is an economic fundamental.

A comparable social fundamental is the basic social contract in Japan between the individual and the corporation. The corporation in Japan differs from the corporation in the West, just as Japanese society is different. The individual is a member of the corporation, has real ownership in it from his membership, and the corporation is obliged to respect and honor the rights of its members. This is very different — and arguably more sensible — than a system in which all rights belong to the investors in the corporation. In any case, it is unreasonable to assume that an employment system that rests ultimately on social fundamentals and a valued social contract will change quickly or basically under short-term economic pressure. Compensation systems can change, and there is a shift toward compensation based increasingly on merit rather than simple length of service, but the basic social contract remains in force.

There are very real pressures on the Japanese corporation however, and serious challenges that even successful corporations must try to deal with. Just as demand was down in the domestic market as well as in the export markets of North America and Europe, capacity additions of the late 1980s were coming on stream. To add to this pressure, the yen moved sharply upward, increasing relative costs and prices. In past periods of economic problems, whole industries have been impacted upon as economic pressures forced restructuring of industrial sectors. Thus, the crisis of 1974–75 and its consequences on markets and costs forced the shutdown of Japan's bauxite smelting industry and a massive cut in the shipbuilding industry.

It appears now that the pressure will be not on marginal industries as a whole, but rather on marginal companies within various industries. At the industrial level, while Japan's petrochemical industry is weak, a stronger yen reduces input costs and provides some breathing space for companies in that sector. However, a great many of Japan's industries have an unusually large number of competing firms. In general, the industry life cycle occurs in Japan as elsewhere with two or three firms pioneering a product, followed by a surge of entrants as the market takes off, and finishing with a shake-out, leaving a few survivors to reap the benefits of the mature market. In the Japanese case, however, the survivors are more numerous and tenacious than in most industries. Japan's vehicle industry, for example, still has eleven producers making cars and trucks, while three might well be a sufficient number.

In any industry, the dominant producers tend to be lower cost — that is why market share is important. And in a downturn, as the tide rises the smaller firms go under first. In the auto industry, the recession was of no help to Toyota, but with its 1993 cash reserves of more than $9 billion, the company can probably ride it out. So too can Nissan, which is more troubled than Toyota, but has more than $6 billion on hand to fend off hard times. It is the smaller producers that are in trouble: Isuzu is finally retreating from autos, sourcing from Honda, and Mazda is cutting back on product plans and sourcing in part from Nissan. In consumer electronics, Pioneer and Sanyo Electric are in trouble, but Sony and Matsushita are still solid; and in cameras, Minolta is under great pressure but Canon is performing well.

In most other economies, the number of marginal producers would be reduced by mergers. Japan's employment system makes mergers very difficult, and when they have been undertaken on occasion, the economic advantages of the merger are largely lost owing to difficulties in closing redundant facilities and dismissing personnel. The companies made marginal in Japan by economic downturn and exchange rate pressures must slowly and painfully retreat to minor niches in the market on their slow way to oblivion. It is the problems of these companies that make for discussion of changes in the nature of the Japanese corporation. They are a source of economic inefficiency that Japan's corporate system has no quick way of handling.

CREATIVITY IS KEY TO FUTURE JAPANESE SUCCESS

The real challenge to the Japanese corporation is more fundamental than the difficult but temporary problem of dealing with a downturn in the economy. A continuation of relatively high growth in output and incomes in Japan will require a shift to still higher levels of technology. From mining to textiles to steel to autos to consumer electronics — this progression to steadily higher levels of technology and value-added products has driven the increase in output and incomes over the last five decades. This progression was, in a sense, capped by the development of "just-in-time," or lean, production methods. But slowed growth and a strengthening currency put Japan's corporations at still another crossroads —

either to stay at the current plateau, as a prosperous and solid performer in conventional technologies much like Germany today, or to move to still another level, with the increased incomes and economic power that implies.

The issues are those of research and development, and creativity. Can the Japanese corporation make the shift from hard to soft, from product to system? The question can really only be answered in the event. A case can be made that the Japanese corporation can and will make the adjustment. The corporations of Japan have moved over the years from one level of technology to another, with notable success. From the early 1980s, investments in R&D have increased rapidly and are now the highest in the world. Measured by patents issued in the United States, the output has been considerable, with Japanese companies now the largest group receiving U.S. patent approvals. Capital investment remains strong, and the highly literate labor force remains in place. All of these factors argue for success.

Still, Japanese success to date has been in mass-produced semiconductor memories, not in microprocessors; computer operating systems are a U.S. development, not Japanese. The spectacular successes in software have not been initiated in Japan. Japanese firms have been buying into American biotechnology companies to stay at the state of the art in that technology. Is it simply early yet, or is there a creativity shortfall in Japan?

ASIA AS A FOCUS FOR JAPANESE INVESTMENT

The challenge to develop new levels of technology brings as well the challenge to manage major positions abroad. The increasing value of the yen will reinforce the pattern that began with the sharp revaluation in the mid-1980s of Japanese direct investment abroad, as foreign assets are increasingly inexpensive in yen terms and as foreign labor supply for manufacture becomes steadily less costly than domestic labor.

The Japanese move will be into Asia. Major investments in Asia to counter protectionism in autos and electronics in Europe and North America are already in place. Asia is where the growth is; Asia is where Japanese investment has proved profitable; and Asia is where good quality, low cost labor is in ample supply. While only 7 or 8 percent of total Japanese production is now offshore from Japan, compared with 15 to 20 percent of German and U.S. production, the Japanese corporate position abroad, especially in East and Southeast Asia, will continue to grow very rapidly.

The related issues are new to most Japanese companies — recruiting, training, and motivating a foreign labor force; incorporating foreign management into the Japanese corporation; becoming an integrated member of the economies and societies of very different nations; managing a multinational system of research, production, and marketing. The tasks are formidable, and continue to present problems to Western firms with long experience in the area. The Japanese corporation, from an insular background, is finding globalization a very real challenge, and the final results are not yet clear.

IMPLICATIONS FOR WESTERN COMPANIES

It is clear, however, that the transition and restructuring that is taking place in the economy and its corporations in the early 1990s is offering new opportunities for foreign companies in Japan. The industries in which Japan's companies are relatively weak remain, and foreign companies do very well in them — food and beverages, petroleum, chemicals and petrochemicals, and pharmaceuticals. The entire range of luxury goods from autos to cosmetics, apparel, and furniture is dominated by foreign suppliers taking advantage of the strong yen. The pressure on marginal Japanese corporations in many industries provides opportunities for alliances to offshore suppliers of price-competitive goods. Acquisition of these companies remains difficult and in any case very expensive, but alliances with them can provide the foreign company with needed market access. Each of these transitions in Japan provides opportunities; the issue is a willingness on the part of the foreign firm to invest funds and effort at a level commensurate with Japan's current and future importance in the global marketplace.

NOTES

1. *James Womack, D.T. Jones, and D. Ross,* The Machine That Changed the World *(New York: Rawson, 1990).*

CHAPTER SIX

Routes into Japan

KEVIN K. JONES

第六章

One of the first decisions for a company considering the Japanese market is the point of entry. The possible routes — start-up operations, joint venture, acquisition — do not differ greatly from those for other countries, but the characteristics of the Japanese market work to influence the final decision. For small to medium-sized companies, if competitive conditions permit, the entry should be a small step with the goal of gaining experience in the market before making a major commitment. Kevin Jones, a partner at Booz-Allen & Hamilton, outlines the various options open to the foreign company entering the Japanese market, evaluates their respective merits and disadvantages, and discusses how the choice of an entry route can enable the company to avoid the corporate midlife crisis that has afflicted many in Japan.

Japan is a major strategic market for Western businesses. It is the second largest national market in the world and, notwithstanding the recession, is likely to remain so for many years. It is also the country from which Western companies most need to learn: It is the home of cutting-edge technologies and capabilities, and of global competitors; indeed, for many industries, Japan is the world's most demanding market. This mixture of opportunity and challenge makes Japan a focus for companies both large and small.

Building a business in Japan is, however, no easy task. Foreign companies find it difficult to master the customer requirements, distribution methods and channels, and pricing and promotional tactics unique to Japan. Further, the style of competition employed by many Japanese companies makes them difficult adversaries.

Their abilities in "product churning" — rapidly replacing their product range — are legendary, and, although the rate of replacement has slowed in recent years, this capability remains a potent competitive weapon. At the same time, many Japanese companies are masters of distribution channel management, successfully restricting other companies' access to the customer.[1] The process of coming to grips with this unfamiliar and highly competitive environment is prolonged by the difficulty of hiring and integrating good Japanese staff. As one Japanese executive in a foreign company put it, "We hire second-class people and turn them into third-class managers." The net result is that progress is slow and, given the costs in Japan, expensive.

These challenges vitally affect the choice of routes into Japan. The decision should not be made merely with the aim of creating an initial position — making some sales next year, for example. Rather, it should be made bearing in mind the challenges the company is likely to meet over the coming years and how it can best prepare itself to overcome them. For a small to medium-sized company, with limited management time and finances, the first step, if competition permits, should be designed to gain experience in the market, with the expectation that the business will progress to greater commitments as it can better manage them.

THE CHALLENGES

For many foreign companies operating in Japan, the greatest challenge has lain in sustaining business momentum and, frequently, in surviving a corporate midlife crisis (see Figure 1). Although much of Japanese economic life has been modelled on the Western approach and was introduced by Western companies, foreign companies have found it difficult to sustain their position as the source of Western concepts and products. The overall share of business held by Western companies in Japan, excluding imports by Japanese companies, is around 5 percent. The average size of the Japanese operations of a Fortune 500 company is only some three hundred employees. This amounts, typically, to under 1 percent of the company's worldwide staff, yet Japan's share of the world

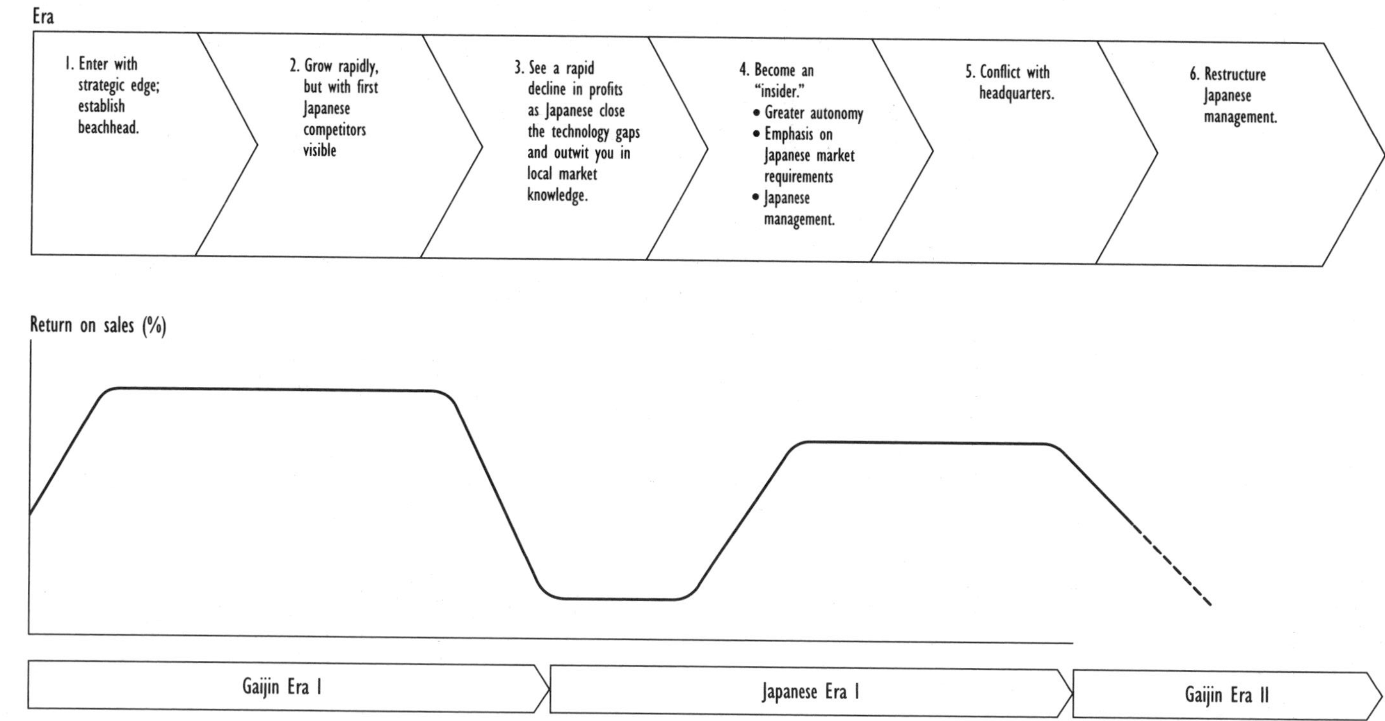
Era
1. Enter with strategic edge; establish beachhead.
2. Grow rapidly, but with first Japanese competitors visible
3. See a rapid decline in profits as Japanese close the technology gaps and outwit you in local market knowledge.
4. Become an "insider."
• Greater autonomy
• Emphasis on Japanese market requirements
• Japanese management.
5. Conflict with headquarters.
6. Restructure Japanese management.
Return on sales (%)
Gaijin Era I
Japanese Era I
Gaijin Era II

Table 1 The Top 100 Foreign Entities by Entry Advantage

TYPE OF ENTRY ADVANTAGE	COMPANIES Total = 100	EMPLOYEES Total = 140,000*	SALES Total = $60 billion*
Other	7%	4%	5%
Legal	5%	4%	5%
Network	5%	11%	9%
Concept/System	25%	17%	11%
Technology	58%	64%	70%

SOURCE: *Toyo Keizai*, "Gaishikei Kigyo Soran."

*Equity-weighted

economy is almost 20 percent. Even excluding the companies' home country employees, Japan averages only some 2 percent of the balance — still well below Japan's share of global GNP.

The progress of some of the leading companies from the West indicates how tough success can be. Foreign companies employ around 650,000 people in Japan. This represents just over 1 percent of the work force of some 63 million in Japan. By comparison, in Hong Kong, with a work force of only some 3 million, the multinationals employ some 450,000 people, almost the same figure.

Yet there are success stories. Foreign companies hold significant shares of the chemicals, pharmaceuticals, and office equipment and medical equipment industries. They are also significant players in parts of the consumer goods and financial services industries. An analysis of these leading foreign companies indicates that they have built their positions predominantly on leadership in know-how, usually technological, or on concepts that did not previously exist in Japan (see Table 1). These two bases of advantage accounted for some three-quarters of the entries. For the balance, advantages range from having an extensive network outside Japan, to rare legal barriers favoring foreign companies, to control of resources, such as the near-monopoly De Beers enjoys in diamonds.

Sustaining a position has often proved harder than entry into the market. Many foreign companies have faced the same problem: As their initial advantage has disappeared, Japanese companies have surpassed them in local market responsiveness and execution, creating a sometimes catastrophic decline in results. This precipitates a midlife crisis in the company, at which point it must undertake a radical review of what will be required to succeed in Japan.

This has occurred in a wide range of industries, from manufacturers of copiers to jeans, from robots to diapers. Indeed, the most dramatic example is probably the plunge in market share that shook Procter & Gamble in the early 1980s. The companies that have survived, or occasionally by-passed, the midlife crisis have typically undergone a significant process of transformation. This has meant not just the creation of products tailored to meet the needs of the Japanese market, but also a significant change in the way the company competes in Japan — the way it deals with distributors and customers and the rate at which it replaces products, for example. This, in turn, has meant the development of a strong local organization, the transformation of the initial advantage into one based on local capability and competence, and the ability to contribute to the global company.

Small and medium-sized companies face these same challenges of getting in and staying in, but usually without the commensurate ability to finance their investment that large companies have. In the ten years between 1982 and 1992, for example, two leading U.S. companies, each with a turnover of around $1 billion in Japan, each injected some $1 billion into their Japanese subsidiaries to cover losses and capital investment. Smaller companies could not consider comparable investment programs. Thus, small and medium-sized companies have sought to meet the challenges in different ways.

GETTING IN

The advantages enjoyed by large corporations have formed the foundation for the entries of smaller companies as well. Among the "concept" companies are marketers of fashion and image-related products. Dunhill, for example, has created a premium brand image in men's apparel in Japan, as have Gucci and Ferragamo in women's clothing. Wedgwood and Royal Doulton have also built significant businesses in Japan. The success of these products has been attributable to both their image and to their unique origins.

Without the resources of a major corporation, many of the concept-based companies came to Japan by first testing the waters, and some through an almost serendipitous process. As the marketing director of one consumer goods company put it, "It was difficult to know where to start. I couldn't read anything or speak to the people. We thought about putting someone on the ground, but we couldn't afford the expense. In the end, the embassy was very useful in introducing us to a number of distributors, and we gave one of them the rights to the product." The international head of an American company had a similar experience. "We intended to do something about Japan, but couldn't see an easy way of doing so. As a result it kept slipping down our list of priorities. Then one of the Japanese distributors approached us about carrying our product in Japan. We accepted."

The challenge of getting in for high technology companies has been different. The competitive nature of the market often necessitates many changes, even just to get started. A U.S. company with a unique computer terminal found itself facing the need for multiple product modifications if it wished to sell more than a few dozen units. The product needed to "speak Japanese," requiring changes not only to its software and operating system, but also to the hardware architecture. Even the case was redesigned — the rugged look that attracted American buyers proved too "heavy" for Japanese tastes. Similarly, a specialist engineering company had to redesign its products to meet the demands of its customers in the integrated circuit business. "We couldn't see why they wanted the changes, and certainly the guys back in the U.S. couldn't. In the end, however, we realized that if the customer wanted it pink with blue spots, that's what we had to supply." As with larger companies, however, the problems of staying in are often greater than those of creating the initial beachhead.

STAYING IN

Even fashion and concept-based companies see significant needs to adjust their products to local tastes if they hope to survive competition and market vicissitudes. Dunhill, for example, was advised by its Japanese partner to expand its clothing business (rather than restricting itself to lighters and other accessories) in order to capitalize on Japan's view of England as the country of the gentleman and of gentlemen's clothing. Indeed, the Japanese word for suit, *sebiro*, traces its origins to the Japanese pronunciation of Saville Row, London's famous street of top-class tailors. By the mid-1980s, Dunhill had become a leading menswear company, and the Japanese, both inside and outside Japan, their leading customers. Similarly, a company making pottery cottages had seen some success with its traditional lines in Japan. Market research showed that it should produce models of places like the St. Andrew's clubhouse — a major British landmark for the Japanese, though probably of little interest elsewhere in the world.

A downturn in fortunes produces the same midlife crisis problems as in larger companies. A medium-sized engineering company saw its share of the market decline from 60 percent to 5 percent and was catapulted into the classic symptoms of the midlife crisis — loss of strategic direction and management upheaval — as it made moves to Japanize the company as fast as possible.

Many smaller companies whose business is based on a single concept have experienced serious problems when their product goes through a boom and bust cycle. Food items have been notorious for this. *Shochu*, for example, a Japanese hard liquor resembling vodka, boomed in 1983 and 1984, with sales surpassing whisky but, by 1986, was back to where it had begun. Oven-ready French fries experienced a similar curve. The boom and bust pattern can occur across product lines as well. In the late 1980s, for example, there was an Italian boom. While it lasted, the boom was good for sales of all Italian goods, from Gucci to grappa; when it ended in 1991–92, Italian consumer goods slumped across the board.

Increased competition is, however, the biggest hurdle to staying in the Japanese market, and the challenges facing high technology companies are often more severe than they are for concept companies. It is not that the market will collapse as fashion changes, nor that there are many substitutes from around the world. Rather, the issue is that Japanese competitors are likely to imitate the product or technology and move rapidly to surpass the foreign company in meeting local market needs. Although patents can provide some protection against this, many companies have found them to be inadequate. A specialist pump manufacturer that created the market for its type of product in Japan found its share steadily dwindling as its Japanese competitors out-executed it. "Our competitors introduced a range of products with a form of automatic control built in. We had already evaluated this avenue at our laboratories in Europe and had decided not to pursue it. Unfortunately, some of the Japanese customers liked it, and away went another five points of market share," reported the regional head.

It has often proved difficult for Japanese companies to compete with fashion and concept-type products. Part of the foreign companies' advantage lies in what is called *honmono*, "the real thing," a highly valued attribute in Japan. The real thing may be Italian designer fashions, English tableware, or French perfume. Even in this context, however, competition cannot be ruled out. A Japanese trading company, observing the success of one line of Italian or French fashion, for example, may work to build a portfolio of such products, establishing relationships with two, or even ten, other producers of similar goods.

The midlife crisis is not preordained. It happens because companies have not prepared in the "fat years" for the "lean years." These preparations consist of building, or having access to, the competences and capabilities required to reshape the business in a Japanese way, and also building the links in the market and elsewhere that will allow the effective leveraging of the parent company's advantages. At the minimum, this usually means the capability to tailor and develop the product line to fit Japanese needs. The choice of a route into Japan is part of this preparation. The company needs to consider both the likely success of the initial entry and the appropriate steps to survive or, preferably, avoid the midlife crisis.

THE ROADS TO FREEDOM

Companies considering an entry into Japan usually think first of establishing their own office. This can be an appropriate first step for those who can see the prospect of immediate revenues, or who have no reasonable way to conduct business except through their own resources. But for many companies unfamiliar with the Japanese market, and facing the prospects of high expenses with low initial revenues, the preferred route is a more gradual one.

GOING IT ALONE

Establishing a representative office or company is a route most frequently followed by professional service companies. (This would exclude other categories of service companies, such as food chains, where this route is difficult.) For some such companies — financial institutions, law firms, trading companies, consultancies, advertising agencies — the opportunities and challenges of being in Japan are as evident as they are for manufacturers of products. The difficulty is that the company's leadership position is not encapsulated in a product, and so cannot be easily transferred. In fact, it has to be created on the spot.

This means sending one or two people to Japan — into the unknown. The first challenge is usually to find a secretary and some office space; these are not formidable tasks, but they add to the cost base. The more serious challenge is to build revenues. Typically, the service companies that follow this route try to piggyback off their multinational clients. They speak in terms of finding a "launch client." Others have leveraged existing relationships with Japanese clients to build a business in Japan. Some law firms have followed this route, though for legal reasons they often establish informal links with a Japanese law firm.

One company that built a business in Japan by way of an existing relationship with a Japanese client is Market Makers, which acts as a representative agent and marketing consultancy for foreign newcomers to the Japanese market. It was founded as a "go-it-alone," without a foreign parent. The two founders each had some four years' experience in Japan and leveraged their contacts to get the business off the ground. Six years later, the business has twelve professional staff and a portfolio of around twelve core clients.

Some larger manufacturers have also chosen to take the plunge directly. Compaq, for example, recently chose to build its own company in Japan because management determined that if the company was to challenge the Japanese manufacturers, as well as Apple and IBM, it needed to hit the ground running. This will allow Compaq to control distribution channel strategy and pricing directly, and to build the feedback loop necessary to learn from the Japanese market and competitors. On the other hand, it has meant major industrial start-up costs. For most small to medium-sized companies, going it alone is possible only after building experience in the market — usually through an agency or an alliance.

ALLIANCES

Small and medium-sized companies, under pressure to achieve a position rapidly, and lacking the resources to finance a direct entry, typically look for alliances. This is defined as a relationship between companies to provide reciprocal access to resources and skills not otherwise available in the open market. These may range from special relationships with one or two distributors or product licensing, to a more formal set of arrangements or a joint venture. As with large companies, however, creating advantageous alliances has proven difficult.

PREFERRED ARRANGEMENTS

Many companies, even when they consider themselves to be "going it alone," are actually in a form of alliance. The partner in this case would probably be a major distributor or a small trading house. This special relationship allows the foreign company to sell goods and learn about business in Japan, without the start-up costs associated with an independent entry.

A small European supplier of mechanical equipment found such a relationship satisfactory for an extended period of time. "We had no time to spare for Japan. We were introduced to a distributor through some friends. The distributor handled our business satisfactorily for many years." For a company that genuinely does not have management time to concentrate on Japan operations, this form of relationship can bring attractive incremental revenues.

A biotechnology company decided that it was unlikely to want to build a presence in Japan in the foreseeable future. As a result, it decided its main interest in Japan was to generate financial returns and to build relationships that would enable the company to have ready access to the main players in the market. It hired as a senior executive someone who had worked for almost a decade with two foreign pharmaceutical companies in Japan. The company has licensed out its products to Japanese and foreign companies in Japan and is satisfied that, given the other pressures it faces, it made the right decision in not trying to build its own business.

The most common problem with this type of relationship is that the Japanese partner, distributor, or licensee, uncertain of the reliability of the foreign company, will pursue a strategy contrary to the foreign partner's best interests. A distributor, for example, will frequently premium-price the product. If, as occurs in many cases, the distributor is inexperienced with a particular product, the sales strategy and promotion are often misconceived. Still, the lessons learned from this type of relationship can be the foundation for a larger commitment to the market.

This can be illustrated by the example of a small consumer goods company that was contacted by one of Japan's leading department stores. The company responded by organizing a visit to Japan and, through embassy contacts, met most of the major department stores. Arrangements were made to supply products to a number of them, achieving turnover of around $1 million. The company became frustrated, however. "The strategy was totally at odds with what we wanted to see. Our prices in Japan were two-and-a-half times what they were in the United States. We were so prestigious — and expensive — that even the Sultan of Brunei was too downmarket for us. Similarly, the displays and positioning in the outlets were out of tune with what we wanted." The experience was enough to whet the company's appetite, however. After researching the market, the company head-hunted a senior Japanese sales and marketing executive away from one of the foreign consumer goods companies. He then hired a small sales force and built the company's sales through expansion in premium outlets.

Many companies also find they soon need to move beyond such relationships. A typical example would be that of a U.S. high technology terminal company. "When we first entered the Japanese market, we gave the rights to the product for a period of three years to a specialized trading house. They found us rather than us finding them. For a couple of years we did about $1 million of sales a year — just about enough profit to cover the costs of an annual visit. The trading company soon told us we had to Japanize the product if we wanted more. To be honest, the sales in Japan were too small for us to spend any time even thinking about that. Then, in 1989, one of our Japanese competitors stole one of our major accounts in the U.S. That opened our eyes. We decided to respond by putting one of our best young technicians into our partner's organization for a year. He persuaded us that we did have to Japanize the product, and found ways to do it. Through him, and some market research, we also found out that the market was developing very differently from the U.S. We decided that, if we were not to miss the boat, we needed to get on with it ourselves. We hired a senior Japanese, in his mid-fifties, who had worked with a foreign-owned electronics company for fifteen years or so. He has built a small sales and service force for us. We still have a long way to go, particularly on customizing the product — but we'll get there."

JOINT VENTURES

A more formal alliance, either a joint venture or a set of agreements to form a dedicated business unit, is another option considered by many small to medium-sized companies. Indeed, excluding financial institutions which have almost all preferred independent entries, most of the foreign presence of smaller companies in Japan is established in this form.

The outcomes of such arrangements can be summed up by the comment: "It is drivers, not cars, that cause accidents." Alliances are neither good nor bad; they are what the partners make them. Alliances have been found by some to be very effective vehicles; others have found them to be painful and costly.

Experience has shown a set of recurrent problems that arise, and on the basis that forewarned is forearmed, entrants to the Japanese market should consider them in making the decision to ally or not, and if so, with whom. A review of over two hundred cases indicates that four classic problems emerge: (1) the two parties have different dreams; (2) the contributions and dependences, upon which the alliance was based, shift; (3) frictional losses consume all the energy of the effort; and (4) corporate amnesia occurs — the foreign partner repeatedly forgets all it has learned about business in Japan. These problems can become particularly severe for small companies where there is little senior time to devote to the alliance.

DIFFERENT DREAMS

"One bed, two dreams" goes the ancient Chinese saying. The dream of the Japanese company is frequently to become a leader in those businesses in which it participates, or to build a basis for the future by entering new sectors. An alliance is a way of achieving these goals. The larger trading companies, for example, have used alliances to diversify into high technology and into fashion and leisure-related businesses. For them, the small foreign company may well be only one of a myriad of relationships. The trading company would like to see the products succeed, but is probably not committed to making any one of them a major winner.

Japanese industrial companies have typically allied with their peers from overseas. The goal is frequently skill-building in terms of acquiring essential business know-how, but there may be little commitment to building the business of the joint venture. Foreign businesses are often more interested in financial returns. As one Japanese manager pointed out, "Our foreign partner came in looking for a financial return. They got it. Now they complain that they didn't build a business. But that isn't what they set out to create."

SHIFTING CONTRIBUTIONS AND DEPENDENCES

As Lord Palmerston once said of Britain's foreign relations, "We have no eternal allies and no perpetual enemies. Our interests are eternal and perpetual, and these interests it is our duty to follow." Business alliances, too, disappear when the partners' interests are no longer being met. At the outset, each party contributes to and is dependent on the other. Frequently, the foreign company has contributed the concept and technology, while the Japanese company contributes the distribution. As time goes by, however, the balance of contribution and dependence is usually lost. Once this happens, it is only a matter of time before the alliance disappears.

The potential problems of an imbalance introduce a difficult choice between long- and short-term needs. The best partner in the short term is likely to be a substantial company, already established in the business. Such a company is, however, likely to lose its dependence soon, either through mastering the skills it set out to acquire, or by finding other suppliers of similar products. A smaller, less competent player may offer less in the short term, but more over the long term.

FRICTIONAL LOSSES

Differences in management philosophy, expectations, and approaches can waste management energy by producing "heat" between the partners rather than business success. "Our [Japanese] partner has never produced a proper sales and marketing plan," complained one Western executive. "Our [Western] partner takes so long to consider obvious points that we are always too slow to act," complained his opposite number. These difficulties arise not because the companies lack the good will to succeed, but because they lack the understanding of one another to make working together feasible. When the alliance has to draw on the resources of the parent companies, such problems become more intense. The mounting frustration can stymie activity and may lead to disillusion and a spiral of decline.

CORPORATE AMNESIA

To compound their problems, Western companies often forget all they have learned over the history of an alliance. A senior Western executive visited his Japanese counterpart to propose an expansion of the relationship. "You know," said the Japanese manager, "I think we should give this the same earnest consideration we did the last time you presented the idea ten years ago. On that occasion, I believe, we were willing to go ahead but you became less enthusiastic for some reason. I hope the affair progresses better this time." The foreign manager, red-faced, muttered his excuses and withdrew to ransack the files and seek out someone who might remember what had happened.

Making an alliance succeed is difficult. Those who have made an alliance work are those who have developed and employed the skills to manage it. As the head of the Japan office of a large European company with many alliances in Japan once joked, "Never do your first alliance; you're bound to get it wrong. Start with your second." For many companies, both large and small, the key to success has been to commit staff to work with the alliance in order to avoid corporate amnesia. For larger companies, this may mean many people; for smaller companies, it is often just one person. This makes the choice of staff even more important, and the need to ensure continuity crucial. A high technology company, for example, sent one of its best software engineers to work with its Japanese partner. The same person has stayed closely involved with the alliance for eight years (to date). A consumer goods company, unable to finance a person dedicated to, and resident in, Japan, has kept the head office responsibility with the same person for the last six years. Even though he does not have the hands-on feel that a resident would have, he has managed to build relationships and has accumulated broad experience in the market.

ACQUISITIONS

Typically a major route for international expansion, acquisitions are of minor significance for foreign companies entering Japan. Total acquisitions in Japan, including those by domestic and foreign purchasers, are around 250 a year — slow by international standards, but growing. The problem for most is that it is difficult to acquire a company in Japan, and doubly difficult to make something of it. In a review of 170 acquisitions that occurred between 1985 and 1990, 40 percent of the target companies fit the classic "distress" image — they were in either financial or strategic trouble. Just under 10 percent, however, were on the receiving end of aggressive or hostile moves. (This may be an underestimate since some aggressive acquisitions are dressed up to appear friendly in public.)

The bulk of the aggressive moves have come from so-called *kaishime*, or greenmailing. Trafalgar-Glenn, a small U.K./U.S.

partnership, established one route for doing this in 1984 when it bought up Minebea's convertible bearer bonds in Switzerland, and then showed up in Tokyo with the equivalent of 25 percent of Minebea's equity. The attack failed — Minebea issued shares to a friendly company, which diluted Trafalgar-Glenn's holding and gave Minebea a safe shareholder base. But the method was clear. Others, including Minebea, have followed the same route, and have been successful. Aggressive takeovers have, therefore, become feasible.

This may seem to bode well for acquisitions by foreign companies. To date, however, all acquisitions by foreign companies fall into the "friendly" category. When Merck took control of Banyu in 1983, the Japanese company had realized that it no longer had enough new products in its production pipeline to remain independent, and turned voluntarily to its joint venture partner of thirty years. Similarly, when BOC became the leading shareholder in Osaka Sanso, it did so through negotiations with the retiring chief shareholder, who thought the company needed a strong international partner to provide technology.[2]

The reason for staying on the friendly path was made clear by the Boone Pickens/Koito struggle, in which — despite much sound and fury — Pickens' leading shareholding of 26 percent did not gain him any control of the company. In private discussions, the chairmen of ten of the largest foreign companies in Japan were unanimous in saying that they did not have the management resources to control a Japanese company acquired through an aggressive move, though they might be able to play the role of white knight.

This presents the foreign company with a dilemma. If it acquires a company that is already under pressure (as several pharmaceutical companies have acquired small generic drug manufacturers), it may gain in scale, but will obtain few managerial skills, little technology, and often an old-style Japanese company that will be hard for foreign managers to handle. If it dreams of acquiring a larger company, it probably has to begin with an alliance, but with no guarantees that a later full-scale acquisition will ever be possible.

Table 2 Routes into Japan: Consumer Goods Company

<table>
<tr><th></th><th>APPROXIMATE SALES</th><th colspan="2">PERSONNEL</th></tr>
<tr><th></th><th></th><th>Multinational Corporation</th><th>Partner</th></tr>
<tr><td>Step 1: Exporter</td><td>$1 million</td><td><1</td><td>?</td></tr>
<tr><td>Step 2: Informal Alliance</td><td>$5 million</td><td>1</td><td>5</td></tr>
<tr><td>Step 3: Joint Venture</td><td>$15 million</td><td colspan="2">15</td></tr>
<tr><td>Step 4: Own Company</td><td>$50 million</td><td colspan="2">30</td></tr>
</table>

STEPS ON A STAIRCASE

Whatever the chosen entry method into Japan, it is, or should be, a first step on a staircase. The small company, faced with the need for an alliance in order to participate in the market, often sees the main objective as getting started. Yet the problem is undoubtedly: "Marry in haste; repent at leisure."

The options outlined above should be seen as ways of structuring the steps in order to achieve business goals. Thus, a company might go through several metamorphoses. One European consumer goods company, with worldwide sales today of some $200 million, exemplifies this (see Table 2). For almost a decade, the company exported to Japan through a trading company. Relationships were cordial, but the business amounted to little. About fifteen years ago, the company changed the relationship and persuaded its Japanese partner to establish a department dedicated to its products, with one full-time representative of the multinational. About eight years ago, the department was split out of the Japanese parent as a separate joint venture company, with both partners holding 50 percent of the shares, together with rights to increase the shareholding. The foreign company did this about two years ago, and now has its own successful entity in Japan.

For many small to medium-sized companies, the choice of goals and steps is difficult. This means avoiding making commitments until management has enough experience. For those that have to move quickly — high technology companies, for example — the costs of building such experience can be high in terms of both senior management time and advisors' fees. Companies that are not under such market pressures should take more time. They should not, however, neglect the experience-building, which requires taking an active role in the business in order to move up the learning curve. The luxury of time often breeds the temptation to avoid attempting to come to grips with the requirements of the market.

Once the need for a larger commitment is recognized, the company should begin to think what steps are appropriate. The questions should focus on where the business is seeking to go, and whether an alliance would meet those goals:

- What do we aspire to be in five or ten years?
- What business capabilities and competences do we need to achieve this?
- What roles might an alliance play in attaining these capabilities and competences?
- With whom should we work?
- How might we structure the alliance?
- What do we need to do to move beyond the alliance?

The answers to these questions must be tested: Is the structure competitive? How is it likely to evolve given the concerns above? What investments — financial and in personnel — is management prepared to make? What risks are management prepared to accept?

A specialist engineering company had relationships with two distributors in Japan for some ten years. These relationships received little attention for many years, until it became evident that one of its Japanese competitors was becoming a serious global threat. In order to combat this challenge, the company decided that it had to aspire to become a number two or three in Japan within the next five years. This meant building a sales and service force of around thirty staff. At the same time, it expected some 20 percent of its product line to be designed and manufactured mainly for Japan, though on common components. To achieve this it had to design products, and tailor its infrastructure, to fit Japan's needs. The company would have preferred to go it alone, but it would not have been competitive. Design skills sensitive to Japan's needs were crucial in making a successful challenge to a strong, entrenched competitor. Thus, it decided that an alliance could provide value in getting the company up to speed quickly.

Many small and medium-sized companies have an interest in participating in the Japan market. For some, the opportunity to build revenues, and cash flow, is given a much higher priority than building a business presence in Japan. They would prefer not to foreclose on the option of building an independent presence at some stage, however, and do not want to lose all control of their strategy. Others aspire to establish a business presence much more rapidly.

The chances of making a mistake in building a business in Japan, even for experienced foreign companies, are high. As are the costs. This often leads to a step-by-step route into the market, aimed at building both business and experience. First, an initial exploratory step of a few sales may shift into a loose alliance. This then becomes either a more formal and substantial alliance, or a small independent presence. Whichever route is followed, the small or medium-sized company needs to put a premium on gaining and maintaining experience, and on viewing each move as another step on a staircase.

NOTES

1. *Kevin Jones and Tatsuo Ohbora, "Managing the Heretical Company,"* McKinsey Quarterly *(No. 3, 1990).*
2. *This is usually given as an example of an acquisition. In fact, BOC currently owns only 25 percent of Osaka Sanso's equity, up from 21 percent when it bought it in 1983, and has convertible bonds and options to carry it to just below 50 percent. BOC is, however, the* de facto *parent — a position achieved through the cooperation of the other (Japanese) shareholders.*

CHAPTER SEVEN

Public Relations in Japan

KIRK R. PATTERSON

第七章

Public relations, often referred to as the "Image Business," is an essential element of any market-entry strategy. Without the right image, a company is doomed to failure, and this is nowhere more important than in Japan, undoubtedly the most image-conscious country in the world. In this chapter, Dr. Kirk Patterson, president of Gavin Anderson & Company (Japan), discusses the importance of communication in the Japanese market and offers advice on how to develop an effective public relations strategy for your company.

For the foreign company, the primacy of image in Japan poses a nontariff trade barrier — no matter now famous a company may be at home, it is probably unknown in Japan. It is as if a foreign businessman, on his first trip to Japan, looked in the mirror and saw no reflection. The foreign businessman and his firm are nonentities in the Japanese marketplace. Helping foreign companies and their products to be recognized in Japan is the role of public relations.

Public relations is often viewed as something that only large corporations can afford to do. This is not true. Any company can undertake a PR program. Successful image-building is less a function of the size of a PR program than of its strategic, ongoing nature. In the final analysis, a foreign company that has its sights set on Japan cannot afford *not* to do public relations.

WHAT IS PUBLIC RELATIONS?

Stated simply, public relations is the process of conveying information so as to build and maintain an effective image of a company and its products in the minds of its various "publics." These publics can include present and potential customers, business partners, journalists, and others.

A key word in the above definition is "process." Public relations is part of the ongoing effort required to establish a strong business foundation. Continuing the image analogy, public relations is akin to assembling a jigsaw puzzle piece by piece until the whole scene is revealed. Patience and perseverance are essential to a successful PR program.

Another key word is "effective," by which is meant the ability to help a company achieve specific objectives. If a company's image is not effective, if it does not help the company attain certain goals, then it is useless. For example, a certain international cosmetics company has for many years spent virtually all of its PR budget for Japan, not to mention a great deal of time and energy, on philanthropic activities, including giving awards to successful women, making donations to community groups, and providing scholarships. These are all very worthwhile activities, and the company is viewed very positively by those few people who are aware of them. Unfortunately, they do little to enhance the image of the company and its products among the mass of women who are its target customers. As a result, the activities do not help achieve the company's ultimate goal, which is to boost sales and profits.

Contributing directly to the bottom line is, of course, the most obvious reason to have a good image. Other reasons might include the following:

- Acquiring new distributors for one's products
- Attracting talented employees
- Developing credibility with local banks, insurance companies, and other key business partners
- Generating third-party endorsements and referrals from journalists, law firms, and other intermediaries

To be effective, a company's image should be strong (the company should be well known), it should be accurate, and it should be positive. More important, because competition is the name of the game, a company's image should be stronger, more accurate, and more positive than its competitors' images. It should also be more distinct than its competitors' images. When a consumer is choosing between similar products, the company with the better, clearer image will get the sale, often at a premium price.

THE JAPANESE CONTEXT

As noted earlier, Japan is the most image-conscious country in the world, and as a result, brand orientation is stronger in Japan than elsewhere. One has only to look at the crowds of secretaries on train station platforms carrying Louis Vuitton or Gucci bags to appreciate this fact.

A particularly intriguing manifestation of Japanese image consciousness took place a few years ago. It had become fashionable for young women to play tennis and, more generally, to be "sporty." Unfortunately, Japan has few tennis courts and the cost of joining a tennis club is beyond the means of most young women. As a result, it became trendy for young women to just walk around Tokyo carrying tennis rackets in their sports bags. They were not on their way to or from tennis games, but at least they projected the appropriate sporty image. Given the heaviness and rather awkward shape of tennis rackets, it was only a matter of time before an enterprising bag manufacturer launched a line of sports bags with fake tennis-racket handles sticking out of them. Reality had caught up with image.

Ironically, the "image business" of PR is not well established in image-conscious Japan. Of the many reasons for this, two are key. First, Japanese patterns of interpersonal communication, which stress modesty and indirect expression, are incompatible with the self-promoting "Look at Me" approach of Western-style public relations. Second, the powerful Japanese advertising industry has made PR activities subordinate to an advertising program, rather than a discrete function linked with corporate strategy.

Although the lack of a well-developed public relations industry in Japan poses certain problems for the foreign company entering the local marketplace, including making it difficult to find a reliable PR agency, it does allow for greater freedom of action. With no clear Japanese PR model, a foreign company can consider almost any PR technique (following the guidelines of common sense and cultural sensitivity) and be fairly certain that it will have an impact. The Japanese public and media are not as jaded as in the West, and so image-building activities can be more effective.

Public relations activities are especially fruitful in Japan because of the tremendous desire for information among Japanese people. The Japanese, both individuals and their organizations, are "information sponges," eager to soak up as much information as possible and with little regard to the immediate utility of that information. There is a widespread belief that information is power, information provides security, information leads to competitiveness. Japanese absorb information whenever and wherever they can, and then they squeeze it out, drop by drop, at strategic moments. In such an environment, public relations can be especially worthwhile because the information a company wants to convey is readily absorbed by its target audiences.

Establishing a Japanese PR program is especially important for a small or medium-sized company because the main alternative to public relations, advertising, is prohibitively expensive in Japan. For example, a full-page advertisement in the *Nihon Keizai Shimbun*, Japan's leading business newspaper, costs ¥18.4 million (approximately $160,000), about 40 percent more than the price of a full-page *Wall Street Journal* advertisement. In addition, compared with advertising, which is useful for reaching mass audiences, public relations is a more strategic, targeted means of conveying information and images to key individuals and publics.

One final point, before moving on to a discussion of specific PR activities, is the linguistic challenge involved in Japanese public relations. To state the obvious, public relations in Japan must be conducted in Japanese. Do not be fooled by the many English-language signs and publications, or by the speakers of English with whom you may come in contact. Be prepared to communicate in Japanese, or do not bother to do business in Japan. And beware, also, of the tyranny of translation — information materials for the

Japanese market should be written from scratch in Japanese, not translated directly from English. (Just think back to the last time you tried to decipher a manual for a Japanese electronics product and I'm sure you will understand why translation does not equal communication.)

A JAPANESE PR PROGRAM: YES OR NO?

Whether or not a company should undertake a Japanese PR program depends on its particular circumstances and goals. Public relations costs money and places an additional burden on the limited time and resources of key personnel. Furthermore, the benefits of public relations are often difficult to quantify and, in any case, may take years to be realized. A decision to conduct a public relations program, therefore, should not be taken lightly, and once that decision is taken it should be implemented fully and consistently.

There is no single hard-and-fast rule to determine if or when a company should initiate a public relations effort in Japan, but the following are a few guidelines:

- If a company is sufficiently committed to the Japanese market to maintain a full-time office in Japan or to have a full-time "Japan desk" in its head office, then public relations is usually justified.
- If the Japanese market represents, or has the medium-term potential to represent, a significant portion of a company's total sales (usually more than 10 percent), then public relations is typically a sound investment.
- Public relations may *not* be appropriate if:
  - a company is not firmly convinced of the value of developing the Japanese market for its products or services.
  - the market for a company's products or services is so small that personal contact can be made with every potential customer.
  - demand for a company's products is principally a function of price, as is the case for many types of natural resources.

By following these guidelines and talking with other people familiar with the Japanese market for your products or services, you can decide if a Japanese PR program is appropriate for your company. If the answer is "yes," then the program must be strategically planned and vigorously executed, as is true of every other aspect of your Japanese operation.

HIRING AND MANAGING A PR AGENCY

Because of the costs involved, a small or medium-sized foreign company in Japan rarely finds it appropriate to have a full-time PR manager on staff. Typically, therefore, such a company hires a PR agency to handle its Japanese public relations under the supervision of the person in charge of the Japanese market. An outside agency can help the company in three broad areas:

- Strategic planning and PR program development
- Launching the company's entry into the Japanese market
- Ongoing implementation and management of the PR program

Responsibility for the third of these areas can often be gradually assumed by the company as its Japanese operation is expanded and consolidated, leaving the agency to provide assistance on a project-by-project basis, and to help generate and evaluate new ideas.

There are many PR agencies in Tokyo, but only a handful that have bilingual account executives and that are capable of providing foreign clients with both solid strategic counsel and competent hands-on program implementation. To obtain the names of appropriate PR agencies, contact one of the many foreign chambers of commerce in Japan or the commercial attaché at your country's Tokyo embassy.

To select an agency, contact each of the agencies and ask them if they are interested in handling your account. If they express interest, send them a set of materials on your company (annual report, corporate brochure, product catalogue, etc.) and an outline of your Japanese business operations and objectives. Ask each of them to prepare a "capabilities presentation," which would give you an indication of their particular areas of expertise, staff size, and experience, and their work for clients in the same or similar industries, noting possible client conflicts. At these presentations, ask the following questions:

- *Who will be the account executive(s) actually handling the work?* Agencies often send experienced senior executives to make capabilities presentations, but after winning the contract they disappear from the scene, leaving the work to junior staff. An agency is only as good as its account executives, so make sure you know who is going to be handling your business.
- *Do they provide PR services to your competitors?* You need to decide whether or not you want an exclusive relationship with an agency (that is, the agency will not work for any of your competitors). The advantage of an exclusive relationship, of course, is that you can be assured of receiving priority attention and you can trust that your information will not fall into "enemy" hands. Exclusivity, however, must be bought in the form of a minimum monthly retainer (discussed later), and so it is therefore likely to be more expensive than nonexclusivity. In addition to lower fees, another advantage of nonexclusivity is that, if an agency has more than one client in an industry, then it will likely have better contacts with key journalists in the field and will have a better understanding of industry trends and issues. There are many arguments for and against exclusivity, but, as a general rule of thumb, if the agency is to be actively making contacts on the company's behalf and otherwise representing the company (which is usually the case), then exclusivity is appropriate; if the agency is providing purely behind-the-scenes support services, then the extra cost of exclusivity cannot be justified.
- *How much turnover has there been in the agency's staff and clients?* Some turnover in personnel, as individuals move to other agencies or assume corporate in-house PR positions, is inevitable in any agency. Similarly, agencies will occasionally lose clients for a variety of reasons that may or may not reflect badly on the agency. You should be on the lookout, however, for excessive staff or client turnover, which could be an indication of serious management or financial problems within the agency.

- *How do they charge for their services?* In the good old days (for the agency), companies paid a fixed monthly retainer, which gave them nothing but the right to use the agency's services, for which they were charged extra. Today, such retainers are dinosaurs. Instead, agencies will charge on a monthly basis for staff-time costs incurred, with such costs calculated by multiplying an individual's hourly billing rate (which reflects that person's experience and seniority) by the number of hours the person spent serving the client. If a company wants an exclusive relationship with an agency and/or if it wants to have priority access to the agency's senior consultants, then it will be required to pay a minimum monthly retainer (usually ¥500,000 to ¥1,000,000 per month), with staff-time costs exceeding that covered by the retainer to be billed separately. Out-of-pocket expenses, plus a 15 to 20 percent administration fee, are charged separately, as is the Japanese consumption tax. As in any business, you get what you pay for, so be suspicious of any agency that charges significantly less than its competitors.

HOW TO DEVELOP A PR PROGRAM FOR JAPAN

Based on the capabilities presentations, you will select the agency that seems best able to meet your needs. Having done this, bring them fully into your confidence. Spend the time to explain your business and what you are hoping to achieve in Japan. Share with them your concerns and your aspirations; help them understand the policies and politics of head office. Above all, treat them as a key member of your staff. Give them access to all the information that would be available to an in-house PR manager. Armed with this information, they will be an invaluable ally in your fight to increase sales and profits in Japan.

The next step is to work closely with your agency to develop a Japanese PR program. The best way to develop this program is to give your agency certain strategic guidelines and budget parameters and then ask for a detailed proposal outlining the overall PR strategy: the particular publics to be targeted; the short-term (less than one year) and long-term (three to five years) objectives; the nature, purpose, and timing of specific PR activities; and the costs involved. Discuss the proposal with the agency and have them make changes if necessary, and then use it as a baseline to provide a structure and focus to your PR program. At the end of every fiscal year, have the agency submit a review of that year's activities and a plan for the next year's program.

This section has stressed the importance of finding a reliable PR agency and using it to develop a well-considered PR program. Certainly, an agency can play a very important role in helping to establish a strong, competitive image for your company and its products. But remember, the agency works for you, and so you must manage and control it as you would an employee. While respecting the agency's capabilities and strengths, you must provide the leadership and set the direction for your PR program. And the above-noted guidelines to selecting and working with an agency are applicable to any consultants — in marketing, advertising, or market research — that you may hire in Japan.

DEVELOPING A DATABASE

Before you undertake an image survey, a media relations program, special events, or any of the other activities discussed later, it is essential to have a computerized database of all key individuals you should be contacting, not only as part of the PR program but also as part of your broader marketing activities. Whether developed by your own office or by your PR agency, a database is essential to a strategic approach to the Japanese market.

The database should include the names, positions, companies, addresses, telephone/fax numbers, and other appropriate information for a variety of individuals, including:

- Journalists at relevant newspapers, business magazines, and television stations
- Journalists at key trade publications, not just those that cover your industry but also those related to your customers' industries (For example, if you sell computer networks to hotels, your database should include journalists from trade publications for both the computer and hotel industries.)

- Japanese journalists based in your home country, including representatives of the major newspapers, broadcasting organizations, and wire services
- *Hyoronka*, or commentators/experts, in your field; often freelance journalists, *hyoronka* play an important role in influencing trends and attitudes in their chosen areas
- Politicians and, especially, government bureaucrats who are interested in or have responsibility for your industry
- Present contacts and potential clients

This database, which needs to be constantly maintained and regularly updated, is the basis for your whole public relations program. It provides you with access to the various publics you must reach if you are to penetrate the Japanese market.

CONDUCTING AN IMAGE SURVEY

A large company typically kicks off a new PR program by undertaking a comprehensive survey of its image in the marketplace, especially as compared with the images of its competitors. Such surveys, conducted through mail-out questionnaires, interviews, and analysis of media coverage, provide insights into how the company is viewed, positively and negatively, and the aspects of the company's image that need to be strengthened. As such, it helps the company devise and refine its PR strategy and provides a useful benchmark against which to measure the impact of that strategy.

Such comprehensive image surveys are not cheap, so small and medium-sized companies often push ahead with a PR effort without undertaking a survey. This is a mistake. To know where you want to go it is crucial to first understand where you are now.

For a small or medium-sized company, a survey can be undertaken that provides useful information without breaking the bank. A relatively low-cost survey can be undertaken by:

- Limiting the number of competitors included in the survey to only two or three companies;
- Relying heavily on online media databases, such as Nikkei Telecom;

- Keeping the number of questionnaires to the bare minimum (for example, by limiting the number to twenty key individuals); and
- Conducting telephone interviews rather than in-person interviews.

Such a survey can, and ideally should, be undertaken as part of the market research conducted to help you define and target market opportunities and obstacles.

MEDIA RELATIONS

The best, most efficient way to communicate to your target audiences is through the Japanese media, notably the print media. More than in virtually any other country, the media in Japan are powerful shapers of the images of foreign countries, companies, and individuals. The Japanese read more newspapers, magazines, and books than any other nationality, and the publications they read have a far higher proportion of foreign content than in almost any other country.

Part of the power of the Japanese media comes from the sheer size of their audiences. The country's five principal newspapers, for instance, are all distributed nationally, with the *Yomiuri Shimbun* having a circulation of 9.8 million and the highly respected *Asahi Shimbun* having a circulation of 8.3 million. By contrast, the *New York Times* has a weekday circulation of 1.2 million, with 400,000 for *The Times* of London.

Japan's leading business newspaper, the *Nihon Keizai Shimbun* (often referred to as *Nikkei*), has a morning circulation of almost 3 million (and about 2 million for the evening edition), which is 1.5 times that of the *Wall Street Journal* even though Japan has only about one-half the population of the United States. Moreover, *Nikkei* carries about 2.5 times more foreign news and on a wider variety of countries and topics than does the *Wall Street Journal*.

Japan also has a more extensive range of trade publications than most other countries. Regardless of your industry, you will find numerous specialized publications aimed at your industry and the industries of your present and potential customers.

Journalist Contacts

It is true everywhere, but especially true in Japan: An important aspect of business success is the network of contacts one develops and maintains. This applies to everything you do in Japan, including the cultivation of journalists.

Take the time to get to know key journalists in your field. Target the five to ten individuals who write extensively about your industry, especially in trade publications, and make it a point to establish a relationship with each of them. Invite them out for lunch or for drinks (but not for breakfast — Japanese reporters are not morning people), not necessarily to talk about particular topics but rather just to get to know them and let them get to know you. Over time, this will give you access to their publications when you have particular stories to "sell in." Of course, there is a *quid pro quo* in this, for these journalists may come to you for favors from time to time, and you should do whatever you can to help them, be it getting data on your industry or spending time to explain some new technological development.

Your cultivation of Japanese journalists should extend to getting to know those individuals who are posted in your home country, especially because most of the foreign stories appearing in the major Japanese daily newspapers are written by their overseas correspondents. When you are visiting head office, make it a point to meet with these journalists. This will not only help you get more or better coverage for your company but will also give you other important contacts when those journalists are transferred back to Tokyo.

Press Kit

Compile a press kit of relevant information on your company, including some or all of the following materials:

- Annual report, including a Japanese-language summary of the report's highlights
- Japanese-language corporate brochure and/or a fact sheet on the company
- Profiles in Japanese, with black-and-white photographs, of the senior executives of the company, including the person representing the company in Japan

- Relevant Japanese-language product information, including black-and-white photographs
- Important and/or recent press releases
- Reprints of favorable magazine and newspaper articles (in English and Japanese) on the company

The press kit should be distributed widely, including being provided to journalists in advance of press interviews, handed out at press conferences, and given to key media contacts. It is important to keep the press kit updated and to always have a supply of preassembled kits on hand.

Press Releases

A critical component of your Japanese PR strategy should be the regular dissemination of Japanese-language press releases. The purpose of the press release is not primarily to have those releases picked up by the Japanese media, but rather to create the image of a company that is dynamic, that is involved in many exciting activities. This will lead to greater interest in your company among journalists and others who receive the releases. The following are some general guidelines for a Japanese press release program:

- The goal should be to send out a press release at least once a month, and more often if possible.
- Make sure that head office sends you all their press releases, preferably in advance so that you have time to prepare Japanese versions that can be issued simultaneously with the head office's releases.
- Only some of the head-office releases are likely to be of interest to a Japanese audience, so ask your PR agency to advise which releases should be distributed in Japan.
- When preparing the Japanese versions, bear in mind the interests and background knowledge of Japanese journalists. In some cases, head-office releases will be too detailed for a Japanese audience and so should be shortened, while in other cases supplementary information will be required for the significance of the release to be appreciated by Japanese readers.
- Often, any one head-office release may not appeal to a Japanese audience, but several releases combined into one may make a

very interesting story. For instance, a British bank that had issued separate releases to announce the opening of four new overseas offices integrated them into one Japanese release that focused on the bank's commitment to serving clients worldwide.

- Always be on the lookout for topics that could be the subject of releases originating out of Japan, rather than out of head office. For example, a U.S. aerospace company made the new Japanese licensing agreement of one of its products the subject of a Japanese press release, even though it was not big enough news to justify a head-office release.
- Send the releases not only to journalists but also to all or most of the other people on your database. This helps keep those individuals aware of your company and its presence in Japan.
- Fax the releases to those Japanese journalists and other contacts who are based overseas.

Press Interviews and Press Conferences

When your company's CEO or other "newsworthy" person is visiting Japan, make sure that you set aside a half day for press interviews. Arrange interviews with two or three key publications, selected on the basis of their ability to reach the audiences that are especially important for your business.

Relative to their Western counterparts, Japanese business publications place less emphasis on company-specific topics when presenting foreign stories, preferring instead to focus on broader issues and trends. In arranging interviews, therefore, it is important to "hook" the message you want to convey with a broader story that will appeal to the journalist. For example, a U.S. law firm arranged an interview with a prestigious business magazine for its senior partner by stressing the increasingly global nature of legal issues, such as the extraterritorial application of U.S. antitrust regulations and the legal enforcement of environmental performance standards.

Japanese business journalists are, by Western standards, very cooperative and non-aggressive. Investigative reporting, with its emphasis on uncovering corporate misbehavior, is almost entirely absent in Japan (except among some of the weekly magazines). Journalists display a genuine desire to communicate information of interest and value to readers. As a result, they often come to interviews with little preparation, and with only a few general issues in mind. This allows the interviewee to take the lead in discussing certain topics, but it also puts the onus on that person to determine in advance what points he or she wants to get across.

It is usually best for your PR agency to arrange the interviews as they can determine the best way to "sell in" a story to a particular journalist or publication. If the journalist is unfamiliar with the company, he or she should be provided with the press kit and other relevant materials; in some cases, it is also useful for the agency to brief the journalist in advance. Japanese journalists rarely speak English, so the agency's account executive will usually interpret at the interview. The agency will also follow up with the journalist afterward, providing additional information as required and answering any questions he or she might have.

Press conferences should be reserved for announcing major news, with "major" being defined as that which is significant to the Japanese public, not that which is significant for your company. Using the names of journalists in your database, the PR agency will invite fifteen to twenty individuals, usually by phone with follow-up by fax, and they will confirm attendance the day before the press conference. The press conference, typically held at a hotel or other public meeting facility, should be conducted in Japanese, using interpreters as appropriate. Your presentation should be kept relatively brief, with at least thirty minutes for questions after your presentation. Most important, full press kits, including the text of the presentation (and hard copies of any slides used) and detailed background materials related to the announcement, should be given to all attendees, as well as mailed to key journalists who could not attend.

Press Clubs

The Japanese press club system has been the topic of considerable discussion in recent years. Press clubs, of which there are about seventy-five in Tokyo, are groups of reporters from the major newspapers and broadcasting organizations (but not magazines) who are stationed at the government ministries and at the nation's various political, economic, and industrial organizations. These clubs have been criticized for contributing to homogeneity in Japanese news reporting. Foreign journalists in Japan have also criticized press clubs because they are generally closed to non-Japanese media and therefore constitute a serious impediment to their own news-gathering activities.

Much of this criticism of press clubs is valid. It is, however, irrelevant for most small and medium-sized companies. The key to getting good press coverage is to cultivate key journalists whether or not they are members of press clubs. If there is a press club closely related to your field, it does not hurt to distribute your press release to it, but that would be as a supplement to, not an alternative to, your major press-release distribution activities. Unless your company is well known and unless the topic of the release is of major domestic significance, the press club journalist is unlikely to read the release, *unless* you have been cultivating the journalist all along.

A few miscellaneous comments on distributing releases to press clubs:

- There is no fixed "rule" for distributing releases to press clubs; each press club (or manager — the position of manager rotates among club members, generally changing every month) has its own regulations or guidelines.
- Typically, enough copies of the press release need to be provided for each club member, plus one extra for the club files.
- One usually needs to make an appointment with the press club for distributing a release.
- Depending on the press club and/or the manager at the time, a PR agency may or may not be allowed to distribute a press release on behalf of a client.
- There may be two or more press clubs to which you should distribute your press release. For example, if your company is issuing a release to announce the development of a new type of pollution-control equipment, the heavy-industry press club and the Environment Agency press club would both be appropriate recipients of the release.

Trade and Specialized Magazines

Japan has a tremendous array of trade and specialized magazines, covering virtually every industrial sector and sub-sector, every consumer segment and sub-segment, and every age group. Regardless of your company's line of business or that of your clients, there is almost certain to be a magazine that reaches precisely the audience you have in mind.

The above general comments on developing relationships with journalists apply especially to those at trade and specialized magazines. In fact, because journalists at these publications are better informed about the industry or market than journalists at the general newspapers and business magazines, they are often easier to approach and are more receptive to what you have to say. Moreover, they can provide you with invaluable insights into trends and developments in your industry, including the activities of competitors.

One reality of dealing with Japanese trade publications is the apparent correlation between a company's advertising and the amount and nature of editorial coverage it receives. For instance, one U.S. company that was having trouble with some of its Japanese employees discovered that those troubles were the subject of a cover story in a popular weekly magazine. That particular issue of the magazine was promoted in subway advertisements reading: "XYZ Company Screws Its Japanese Employees!" in bold, black characters. When an editor of the magazine was asked why the company had been raked over the coals for what was, in fact, a relatively minor problem, the reply was: "If they had been advertising with us over the years, maybe . . ." Certainly, I do not advocate succumbing to editorial blackmail, but it may nevertheless be prudent business, and good media relations, to set aside some funds for advertising in key trade publications.

Media Monitoring

In addition to communicating to the Japanese media, you need to follow what they are saying about you, your industry, and others. Be an "information sponge" and soak up information just as your Japanese competitors do, and then use that information to outcompete them in their home market. The best way to get important competitive information is to monitor media coverage on selected topics, and so one of the key aspects of your PR program should be media monitoring. This can be undertaken by your agency and/or your staff.

The following are a few comments on media monitoring:

- You must decide what subjects you want to have monitored. At the very least, you need to know what the media are saying about your company, both its operations in Japan and elsewhere. Depending on your needs and budget, you may also want monitoring of:
  - trends and issues in your industry and the industries of your present and potential clients
  - your principal competitors, both Japanese and foreign
  - your Japanese business partners
  - your key present and potential clients
- With regard to publications to be monitored, as a basic minimum the morning and evening Tokyo editions of the national daily newspapers should be covered, these being the *Yomiuri, Asahi, Mainichi, Sankei,* and *Nikkei*. In addition, depending on your industry and objectives, you might want to consider monitoring:
  - the principal industrial newspapers, notably the *Nikkei Sangyo Shimbun* and the *Nikkan Kogyo Shimbun*
  - the *Nikkei Ryutsu Shimbun*, covering the retail industry, and the *Nikkei Kinyu Shimbun*, covering the financial services industry
  - regional editions of the national daily newspapers
  - the principal business magazines, notably *Nikkei Business, Toyo Keizai,* and *Diamond*
  - the main magazines for your industry and for your target customers
  - Japan's English-language newspapers and magazines, but only if you need to know what's happening in the foreign community
- The agency should provide you with clipping books on a biweekly or monthly basis (weekly is possible, but it would cost somewhat more), including summary translations for each of

the articles (you can ask for full translations of articles that seem especially interesting, although this can get quite expensive).

- The agency should fax you especially important articles from the daily newspapers within twenty-four hours of when they appear.
- The cost of this service will vary considerably, depending on the number of subjects and publications monitored and the number of articles that are clipped. The agency will charge a basic monitoring fee, plus a per-article charge; translations are extra. There is also a surcharge for an "express" clipping service.
- You should personally subscribe to one of the many fax translation services in Japan, which provide English-language summaries of the main stories in the morning's newspapers by 9:00 a.m. every business day. There are several such services for general business news and specialized services covering particular industries. You should also read the *Nikkei Weekly*, the English-language newspaper published by *Nikkei* that comes out every Sunday, and the *Japan Times* or one of the other English-language newspapers.

PUBLICATIONS

As discussed in the section on press kits, you will need to prepare Japanese-language materials to distribute to journalists and others interested in your company and its products. These do not need to be expensive, glossy publications, but they do need to provide useful information and to project the image of a company that is solid, professional, and well established. For this reason, word-processed, photocopied materials are generally not acceptable. Your agency can advise you on the appropriate type and content of publications that should be produced, as well as coordinate the production. Once you have produced these materials, make sure you distribute them widely. Mail them to those on your database, hand them out at meetings, distribute them at trade fairs.

EVENTS

By organizing special events or by participating in events organized by others, you can significantly raise the public profile of your company. There are three reasons to organize or participate in events. If an event fulfills none of these functions, then it should not be undertaken. They are:

- *News value* The event should attract the attention of the Japanese media and lead to coverage by print and/or broadcast journalists.
- *Educational value* The event should educate journalists and/or present and potential customers and business partners about the company and its products.
- *Image value* The event should enhance the company's image as a respected, established member of the business community.

The types of events you might want to consider include the following:

- *Seminars* Organizing a seminar can be an excellent way to educate key publics about your products or services, especially if they are new or difficult to understand. For example, an international energy futures exchange holds regular seminars in Tokyo to teach sophisticated futures trading techniques to individuals from trading companies and oil companies. Similarly, a leading foreign chemicals manufacturer held a seminar to introduce its new CFC-substitute product, with attendees being primarily engineers from the home-appliance and automotive industries.
- *Receptions* The most common way to announce the opening of a new office or to introduce a visiting chairman is to organize a reception. Typically a late afternoon or evening affair held in a hotel, the reception is a rather expensive and over-used PR vehicle. On the positive side, they are relatively easy to organize and are a quick way to reach all the people in your target publics.
- *Trade Fairs* Regardless of your industry, there is almost certainly an appropriate annual or biannual trade fair in Japan, and perhaps several. Trade fairs are an excellent opportunity to display your wares, make new contacts, assess the competition, and get feedback on the likely market success of your offerings. They are not cheap, however, especially when one considers the cost of setting up a suitably impressive booth (and to have a less-

than-impressive booth would risk creating the impression that your company is either not in the same league as its competitors or is not as committed to the Japanese market).

- *Special Events* To avoid the cookie-cutter feel of receptions, many companies organize or sponsor special events to reach their customers, business partners, and journalists. For example:
  - Several Canadian companies in Tokyo sponsored a performance by a touring Canadian classical-music ensemble at the Canadian Embassy.
  - A credit-card company invited the well-known historian Paul Kennedy to be the keynote speaker at a luncheon for bank representatives.
  - A British multinational sponsored a major art exhibition at one of Tokyo's most prestigious museums.
  - An English-language magazine holds a monthly talk by a prominent Japanese businessman or politician.

These types of events are perhaps beyond the means of small and medium-sized companies, but they nevertheless give an idea of creative alternatives to receptions. For example, instead of a major art exhibition, a company could sponsor a showing of an amateur artist from its country. Another way to reduce costs is for several companies to co-sponsor an event.

- *Product Launches* A promotional event to launch a new product is a common way to generate media interest and, more generally, to raise a company's profile in the marketplace. However, these are usually only worthwhile if either the company is very well-known in Japan or if the product is so revolutionary as to attract media attention on its own merits. For small and medium-sized companies, press releases and, perhaps, press conferences, combined with direct mail, are usually a much more effective and efficient way to announce a new product.

Your agency can take most of the overall responsibility for organizing events. Some of the basic administrative tasks — mailing invitations, processing RSVPs, and handling basic logistical arrangements — can be handled more cheaply by your own staff (if you have a Tokyo office), leaving the agency to provide creative input, liaise with the press, and prepare hand-out materials. However, if you divide responsibility for the project between the agency and your staff, be sure that it is very clear who is handling what function, down to such details as preparing name badges, arranging for the slide projector, and making sure the guest speaker has a glass of water.

Here are some miscellaneous comments on event planning:

Be Creative

There are so many events held in Tokyo that it is important to differentiate your event from the others. So often, memory of an event fades into oblivion in only a few days because one event is much like another. Be daring, and do not worry about "breaking the rules" — Japanese appreciate the new and the different, even if they themselves are bound by the rules (as reflected in the oft-quoted Japanese adage, "the nail that sticks up gets pounded down"). A foreign company can get away with activities that, for a Japanese company, would be considered "strange," as long as it stays within the bounds of good taste.

Look for the Hook

Try to find some unusual way to "hook" your message to something that will attract attention and therefore stick in the minds of attendees. For example, a Tokyo reception for the premier of Ontario, Canada, was transformed from just another cocktail party into a widely covered media event by engineering an exchange of baseball caps between the premier (whose home-town Toronto Blue Jays had just won the World Series) and the manager of the Seibu Lions, the Japanese champions.

Focus on Details

Every little detail must be anticipated and planned for. Start preparations well in advance. Leave nothing to chance. Plan. Plan. Plan. And then execute the plan to perfection. This will require a lot of your time and the time of your staff and/or your agency, but it is time (and money) well spent. Sloppiness in arranging an event will be construed as reflecting sloppiness in how you make your products and how you serve your clients. An image once damaged is difficult to repair.

THE LOCAL MANAGER AS EXPERT

For the small or medium-sized company trying to establish a strong corporate image in Japan, the most effective, and often most underutilized "tool" is the company's Japan manager. By positioning the local manager as an expert in the field, both the manager and the company will become better known and more respected. The real beauty of this approach, of course, is that it is virtually free.

Because high corporate visibility is generally associated with large corporate size, a small or medium-sized company can be perceived as larger than it really is through the PR efforts of its Japan manager. There are, in fact, several distinctly second-tier foreign companies in Tokyo that are viewed as industry leaders by the Japanese because of the high profiles of their local representatives.

The following are some of the ways that the Japan manager can help position your company as an industry leader:

- Cultivating contacts with journalists, especially those covering your industry. Fax them interesting tidbits of information that you come across. Go out for drinks. Provide them with whatever information you can on industry trends and developments. After a while, they will be calling you for quotes for their articles, with you cited as an expert in the field.
- Writing articles on topics related to your business for publication in magazines and newspapers read by your customers and business partners (for Japanese publications, these must be translated).
- Giving speeches to trade organizations, chambers of commerce, industry seminars, and other appropriate gatherings. If necessary, your PR agency can recommend and try to arrange suitable themes and organizations for these speeches, as well as write your speech.

Most important, never turn down any reasonable request for assistance or information. Business in Japan, more than in any other country, is a function of relationships and interdependent obligations. You can never have too many friends. If you help others, they will help you, and so over time your reputation and therefore your business will expand accordingly.

OTHER PR ACTIVITIES

I have described the basics of doing public relations in Japan, but there are several other aspects of corporate communications that might be relevant to your operation.

Investor Relations

The process of communicating to and attracting portfolio investors, usually financial institutions, is referred to as investor relations (IR). A typical IR program for a large foreign company would involve one visit per year to Tokyo by the company's president and/or chief financial officer, with this visit to include one-on-one meetings with key investors, presentations to ten to fifteen representatives of trust banks, insurance companies, investment management firms, and other organizations, meetings with foreign brokers promoting your shares, and interviews with financial journalists. Communication to Japanese investors based in the company's home market is also important.

The Japanese generally invest in large, well-known, blue-chip companies, and so it is usually inappropriate for a small or medium-sized company to undertake a Japanese IR program. However, there are exceptions to this rule. If your company is a medium-sized but growing company with a particularly exciting story to tell, Japan might be an attractive market in which to raise funds. To determine whether or not your company should undertake IR in Japan, talk with your investment banker and with a Tokyo-based IR agency.

Government Relations

It is practically impossible to develop contacts in, and provide input into, the policy-making arena in Japan. Politics in Japan does not lend itself to U.S.-style lobbying. While there are a few individuals who claim to be well connected and to be able to influence government policy, their claims are tenuous and their credibility poor. For large corporations willing to spend vast sums to buy political influence, there might be some value in government relations in Japan; whether it is legal or moral, however, is a different question.

Even the tracking of legislative and regulatory initiatives, relatively straightforward in most countries, is difficult in Japan. To find out what is happening with laws and regulations affecting your business, you need to retain the services of someone who has in-depth knowledge of that business and of who the key players are (a very hard task given that the players change positions so frequently). Such individuals do exist, but they are difficult to find and expensive to hire, generally pricing themselves out of the realm of small and medium-sized companies.

Public relations can, however, be planned with a view to influencing government decisions that affect your business. For instance, a foreign securities firm used an aggressive program of events and media relations to accelerate the time required to receive permission from the Ministry of Finance to provide investment advisory services. In another example, an international manufacturer of medical implant devices held a high-profile, widely covered press conference that played a critical role in its receiving approval from the Ministry of Health and Welfare for use of the devices in Japan.

Employee Relations

We usually think of employee relations as something that only major companies need or can afford to do. That is a fallacy. Even if you have only one or two employees, it is essential that you communicate with them properly.

Your employees are full-time spokespersons for your company. Every time they meet a friend or go to a party, they are representing your company, so it is important that they have a good understanding of your business and are enthusiastic supporters of the company. You therefore need to share information with them, beyond what they need to do their day-to-day jobs, and you need to communicate to them your vision of the company's future, in Japan and worldwide.

Simply taking the time to talk with your staff, over coffee or lunch or whenever the opportunity arises, is usually sufficient in a small office. For a larger office, however, you might need to produce a simple monthly newsletter, updating everybody on important developments in the company. Occasional company social gatherings, such as a staff Christmas party or a cherry-blossom viewing party, are also effective vehicles for staff communication.

Penetrating the Japanese market is difficult for all new entrants, domestic and foreign. The task is especially daunting for small and medium-sized companies, which typically have neither the resources nor the in-house expertise necessary to overcome all the barriers they are likely to encounter.

Public relations is one weapon that can be used by any company, regardless of its size, to help enhance sales and profits in Japan. It is a cost-effective alternative to advertising and, done properly, it can help a company establish a stronger, clearer image than its competitors. To be effective, public relations must be:

- Ongoing. Public relations must be conducted over the long term, in good times and in bad.
- Consistent. The messages communicated through a PR program over time must be the same and must be mutually reinforcing.
- Creative. Public relations must set your company apart from the competition.
- Strategic. The planning and execution of a PR program must be based on clearly defined short-term and long-term goals.

If you follow these key guidelines when undertaking public relations in Japan, you can be confident that not only will you be recognized by Japanese mirrors, but that your reflection will be noticed by those with whom you want to do business.

CHAPTER EIGHT

Advertising, Sales Promotion, and Direct Marketing in Japan

TODD NEWFIELD

第八章

Public relations is one important tool in building your corporate image and sales in Japan. Others include advertising, sales promotion, and direct marketing. In this chapter, Todd Newfield, president of Fact Communication Inc., provides an overview of recent developments in advertising, sales promotion, and direct marketing in Japan from which you can determine the strategy best suited to your needs.

Newcomers to Japan, faced with the seemingly vast differences between the Japanese culture and their own, may be tempted to throw out all the marketing knowledge and experience they have gained in domestic markets. In fact, however, the strategies that your company has developed in the West can be applied to the Japanese market, albeit with some adaptation. Of course, it is difficult to draw up a set of general principles that would apply to all newcomers to the Japanese market; much will depend upon the size of your company, the type of product you are selling, and your budget. But in all cases, it is your in-depth knowledge of your product and your particular objectives that will determine the success or failure of your marketing strategy. Remember these basic principles: Don't sell yourself short; trust your instincts; and, most importantly, adopt a strategy that you feel completely comfortable with.

To determine your marketing approach to Japan, first consider the three ways a foreign company can develop marketing activities in Japan:

- Appointing an agent to handle distribution and sales in Japan

- Establishing an office in Japan and using consultants to develop a marketing strategy
- Developing an in-house marketing team

The one that you select will in large part depend upon the infrastructure, if any, that your company has in place in Japan, your budget, and the level of commitment you decide to make to the Japanese market.

AGENCY ARRANGEMENTS

In this case, your company contracts with one or several Japanese firms to act as your agent (on either an exclusive or non-exclusive basis), responsible for all facets of your marketing and distribution activities in Japan. This represents the lowest level of physical presence for your company in Japan, as well as the least costly option to you. Potential partners include Japanese trading houses, retailers, and specialized organizations with strong distribution power or direct marketing systems. You simply act as an exporter or supplier of your products, which are subject to substantial markups to compensate the agents for their investment in marketing and distribution services.

Enlist the assistance of your government trade representative or JETRO office in identifying a potential partner. Ask them to provide you with a list of companies that meet a set of parameters you have worked out in advance. These parameters could include industry sector, size of company, regional coverage, and past successes in importing foreign products. Your parameters may be quite narrow or as broad as to say, "Give me a list of all Japanese companies that sell jewelry in Japan." Ask your trade representative what successes they have had in the past in arranging partnerships between Japanese agents and companies like yours, and why they were successful.

It is useful, as well, to augment this list by drawing up your own list of potential candidates. There are numerous company directories listing Japanese corporations by sector and activity.[1] Consult with any of your business contacts who have contacts in the Japanese market; this can include Japanese trading houses and Japanese commercial banks in your domestic market, as well as domestic competitors or suppliers who have experience in the Japanese market. In this way, you can compile a list that draws on a diversity of experiences rather than relying on one source, which may have reasons for promoting only a narrow range of companies that do not necessarily converge with your interests.

Once you have a complete list, review it and select the companies you wish to meet. You will also find that, as you create contacts, there will be a domino effect in the amount of information you gather: One company may not be interested in your product, but may know of another that would be. When your list is finalized, contact the JETRO office or your local government trade representative to arrange meetings for you. Because JETRO is a governmental organization, it has considerable *nakodo* ("go-between") power, that is, it has the ability to arrange meetings on your behalf. In Japan, it is important never to underestimate the value of an introduction.

Try to schedule your meetings to coincide with a trade fair in which you participate; this will be a cost-effective way of using your time in Japan. Take the time to look at the wares your competitors have on offer. In addition, leave a couple of days free in order to visit the stores where your type of product is sold. There is one maxim of which you can be confident in Japan: If a product is on the retailer's shelf, it is there because it sells. In Japan, manufacturers are often obligated to accept returns from retailers when their product fails to sell. Look at the packaging, the point of purchase materials, and the assortment of products in your line. Purchase some goods and take them home with you. Have the labels translated; in this way, you can learn not only about packaging requirements, but also about the products your competitors are selling. All of this information will be invaluable in your determination of whether it is worthwhile for you to market your product in Japan. It will also help you to decide whether your product has the necessary appeal for the Japanese market.

The main advantage to working with a Japanese agent is that it allows you to "stick to your knitting." All you are required to do is fill the orders as they come in and keep the relationship working.

You do not have to establish costly Japanese operations; for a small company in particular, the costs of establishing an office in Japan can be prohibitive. You can use this arrangement to test-market your product before you decide to set up your own manufacturing or sales operations in Japan.

The disadvantages of working with an agent are, first, the high markups that must be paid in order to compensate them for the risks they take in holding stock and for their marketing and distribution services, as noted above. Second, you may have little to no control over the image your product will have in the Japanese market, nor its pricing. If your product is a commodity or generic in nature, it is perhaps just as wise to let your agent add value to it by using their own label. If image is an important component to your product, however, you may wish to maintain more control over the marketing. Third, if your product is a "me too" product that can be sourced elsewhere, you can be certain that it will be, if it achieves any degree of success. Your competition can take advantage of the long lead times entailed in your deliveries in order to develop and market their own brands. Finally, if your agent has complete control, you may find that you do not receive the feedback necessary to fine-tune or enhance your product for the Japanese market, nor can you develop an independent feel for the market which could enable you to establish your own operations in Japan at some future time.

ESTABLISHING AN OFFICE IN JAPAN

If you have decided that you are fully committed to the Japanese market, your first step will most likely be to send a company representative to Japan to establish your operations there. It is important to send someone with good marketing experience, someone who has been with the company for a sufficient length of time to have a full understanding of its objectives and corporate strategy, and who is also sufficiently senior to command the attention of head office and the respect of Japanese counterparts.

The expatriate manager will need to hire, on a contractual basis, either an individual or an agency with strong Japanese marketing knowledge and skills. There are numerous ways of finding this help: become involved with your local chamber of commerce and attend their events; make contacts with other foreign companies that have been successful in Japan and learn about their contacts; consult with local marketing associations to source their membership for possible contacts. By widening your circle of contacts, you will soon find the person or agency that fits best with your company, objectives, and budget.

There are numerous consultants and agencies in Japan, and these are discussed below. There are also a number of what I call "aces." These are bilingual, bicultural Japanese nationals with years of experience in industry who work independently or in small agencies. Often they are working independently because the Japanese employment system is unable to reward them sufficiently otherwise. By contracting with an "ace," you can bring to your company a wealth of experience at less cost than hiring a large agency.

There are a number of advantages to working with consultants. Because they are already experts in your industry, you will achieve quick results without the need for costly training. You will have access to their "brains," a Japanese expression that refers to contacts, which will be invaluable when you begin to establish your own in-house marketing team and need to recruit employees. In addition, if you are dissatisfied with their work on one project, it is relatively easy to terminate the contract (when compared with firing a Japanese employee).

Once your activities reach a certain level, you will probably want to build an in-house marketing team. The first way of achieving this really applies only to large international companies that can afford the costs and time required, and I mention it here only because it has allowed for the development of an approach more appropriate for small to medium-sized businesses, which will be described below. Multinational corporations usually raise an in-house marketing team from scratch, using the brand management system. Each brand has a "thick book" which outlines the history of the brand and programs run on it in other countries. In addition, these companies maintain excellent in-house training programs, including sending employees to the home office. For these companies, the establishment of operations in Japan is essentially no different from any other country in which the company operates. If your company falls within this elite group, there are enormous advantages to this system as it allows you to bring your employees up in your own way. One disadvantage, however, is that your employees become valuable to other companies and may be lured away.

The second approach to building an in-house marketing team is a direct offshoot of the first. The P&Gs of Japan have produced a pool of talented bilingual marketing people, which newcomers to the Japanese market can use to fill their own marketing department vacancies. Traditional concepts of lifetime employment no longer necessarily apply in Japan and these employees can be enticed away, though normally at high compensation packages. The advantage for the small to medium-sized newcomer is that by hiring seasoned marketers, you do not need to spend time building your team from scratch.

In addition to marketing experience, it is essential that your Japanese recruits have English language abilities. This is because communication with the executive expatriate staff in the Japanese office, as well as with the home office marketing department, is critical. Ensure that your Japan marketing team has a direct line of contact with your home office, and that you work to build a strong connection between the two. To reinforce this team approach, you should consider sending your Japanese staff to the home office to learn about your company strategy and products. In order to keep your Japanese employees, it is essential that you develop a company policy that does not create polarization between your expatriate and Japanese staff. I have found that one of the main reasons Japanese staff leave a foreign company is because of the "politics" that arise out of perceived differences in treatment and compensation.

ADVERTISING IN JAPAN

Regardless of how you establish your marketing team, you will eventually have to work with an advertising or marketing agency to implement it. Many firms that decide to go it alone and set up their own operations in Japan are initially amazed by the immaturity of Japanese advertising agencies in terms of customer service. This can be traced to the strategies advertising agencies have used in the past to acquire clients. In Japan, many of the largest agencies did not really exist until two or three decades ago. Although Japanese advertising agencies promote themselves as fully integrated agencies able to handle all facets of marketing, their first priority has been to sell media space. In contrast to their Western counterparts, Japanese agencies have relied on their tight control of the media as leverage in acquiring accounts.

To some extent, this is still the case today. Speaking of Dentsu, Japan's largest advertising agency, Karel van Wolferen states in his book *The Enigma of Japanese Power*: "Dentsu is directly responsible for one-third of all advertising on Japanese TV, and virtually monopolizes the scheduling of sponsors during prime-time hours, not to mention the control it exerts through its many subsidiaries and subcontracting firms . . . advertisers wishing to insert commercials in television programs between 7 and 11 p.m. have almost no choice but to go via Dentsu, because it controls their selection and much of the program material."[2]

As a result of this media domination, no "one agency/one client per industry" rule exists in Japan. To avoid conflicts of interest, however, the agencies have established many intracompany divisions to work on the accounts of competing clients within the same industry. Agency employees are evaluated on how much sales/profit they can make from each client, and the largest clients get the best people.

Since the amount of media space is limited to some extent by the fixed number of commercial seconds during golden time on TV or radio, the next sales priority is event marketing. With the "bubble economy" of the 1980s, Japan saw an explosion of regional expositions, trade shows, and corporate-sponsored events handled by major agencies. Event marketing burst with the bubble economy, and since 1991 the number of such events has dropped off drastically.

The third priority is sales promotion and direct marketing. Sales promotion and direct marketing functions are seen as ancillary services, and are often subcontracted out to smaller agencies.

This results in additional costs to the client as two, three, or four levels of companies will be adding their own commissions to the final price.

A QUICK PEEK AT JAPAN'S ADVERTISING AGENCIES

The *Japan 1994 Marketing and Advertising Yearbook* lists some 165 agencies as members of the Japan Advertising Agencies Association. These range in size from small independent creative houses to the monolithic Dentsu, referred to above. In addition, there are over 70 listings for the Japan Marketing Research Association.

In Japan, Dentsu is synonymous with advertising. It is responsible for about one-quarter of all advertising budgets in Japan, and advertisers tend to follow its instructions rather than the other way around. Dentsu is a conglomerate of hundreds of divisions, with well over one hundred film production companies and four hundred subcontracting graphic arts studios under its control.[3] I have heard of bidding competitions between major agencies where Dentsu came out the winner, merely with a letter from a top executive stating, "Pick us. We will do our best!" For major events or campaigns that demand prime time media coverage, Dentsu is the gatekeeper.

Hakuhodo is the second-largest Japanese agency. Its traditional strengths are in marketing strategy and creative development, though it is now improving its marketing and sales promotion activities. Third on the list is Tokyu Agency, which has a strong reputation in sales promotion. This strength comes from its membership in the powerful Tokyu group and its extensive network of retailers, including department stores, supermarkets, and specialty shops. The next in size is Daiko, based in Osaka, Japan's "second city." The fifth-largest Japanese agency, and moving up, is Asatsu (Asahi Tsushinsha), which is said to be the closest in style to a Western ad agency. It lacks the media buying power of Dentsu or Hakuhodo, but makes up the difference with strong sales promotion and direct marketing abilities.

In addition to the Japanese agencies, many international agencies have established strategic ties with Japanese firms, mostly in order to compensate for their lack of media buying power. This has given birth to an "alphabet soup" of agency names. Most of the major foreign agencies have established offices here, and have been quite successful in helping foreign marketers with their advertising and overall communications strategies in Japan.

HOW TO SELECT AN AGENCY

A small to medium-sized company often has difficulty finding an agency. In the major Japanese agencies, employees are evaluated on how much sales and profit they can make from each client. As a result, only those companies which are seen to have heavy media-buying potential will be assigned the top people. Having said that, no agency will turn you away, but the quality of your account team will be directly proportionate to your media-buying power. For foreign newcomers to the market, access to good advertising and marketing support from the Japanese agencies can be very limited.

To deal with this, small and medium-sized companies should consider separating the media-buy function from the creative function, with a large Japanese or hybrid advertising agency contracted as a broker to purchase media space. The creative development, from planning to actual design, can then be handled either internally or with a small planning agency that specializes in creative production. These companies abound in Japan; many are ventures by former advertising agency employees, both foreigners and Japanese. Not only do these firms work directly with clients to develop strategy and creative development, they are often employed by advertising agencies themselves to handle these functions for their clients, at an additional 17.65 percent commission, which would be charged to you.

To contact these planning and creative companies you could join the marketing committees of the various chambers of commerce in Japan and find out from foreign marketers in Japan who they use for their creative marketing. A number of very good creative agencies are run by foreign nationals who have spent a good deal of time in Japan and understand the idiosyncrasies of the market.

DEVELOPING YOUR MESSAGE

At first glance, Japanese mass-media advertising often mystifies the foreign manager. It may be difficult to understand the message the marketer is aiming to project and in many cases even what product they are selling. Famous young actors and actresses, comedians and sports personalities used in dramatic, emotional, and often bizarre and shocking ways are standard fair. Why? Some agencies and advertisers will tell you that Talent X pushing your product will guarantee sales. Newness of execution rather than consistency in brand message seems to be the priority. The question that naturally arises is to what extent do the ads relate to the marketing strategies of the clients.

What works in advertising and what agencies pat themselves on the back for are often unrelated. One approach to understanding advertising in another country, and the "who's who" amongst the agencies, is to look at advertisements and promotions that have received awards for excellence in conception and technique through unbiased selection by industry associations and consumer representatives. The United States abounds with such award programs. In Japan, however, there are fewer benchmarks to draw on, the major one being the Dentsu Advertising Awards.

Contact any large foreign bookstore in Japan to obtain a copy of the *Japan Marketing and Advertising Yearbook*. Unfortunately, the book does not list the agency which worked on the campaign or any hard data on actual results in terms of sales increase, awareness, or percentage recall, but it does give an interesting overview of the winning advertisements in the various media, and sheds light on trends in the industry.

CORPORATE BRAND VERSUS INDEPENDENT BRAND

Much of the advertising by Japanese marketers is centered around building and reinforcing awareness of the corporate brand name rather than individual brands or products. Kirin, Koa, Lion, Shiseido, Sony, and other leading Japanese companies promote their corporate name, trademark, or logo in every facet of their communications activities — right down to having every employee wear the company logo on his or her lapel. Under this corporate umbrella, marketers quickly launch and scrap products as consumer preferences or market conditions change. A strong corporate brand is seen as an effective way to quickly obtain market share for new products, while saving on market entry costs.

The downside is that these multiple new products have short lives because they lack independent brand loyalty among consumers and suffer when competing products enter their newly established niches. Large multinational marketers, let alone small or medium-sized companies with only limited corporate brand awareness, find it a costly exercise to continuously update the product line and conduct the associated advertising campaigns to build and maintain market share.

However, foreign firms like Philip Morris and Procter & Gamble have been successful in employing independent or free-standing brand systems. Each brand maintains a distinct personality and brand loyalty, which is built up through consistent theme advertising, in some cases lasting over many years. Although heavy initial investment is required to build a strong brand franchise, once established, the long-term brands are very profitable and generate funds which can be channeled into launching new brands targeted at different markets. PM's highly successful Lark cigarettes are a case in point. Lark was launched with the theme "Speak Lark" over ten years ago. At that time "Speak English" was a national goal, so the "Speak Lark" concept tied in well. The same theme has been used for so long that to almost every Japanese consumer the "Speak Lark" theme evokes emotions and recognition of the brand.

SOMETHING NEW

In developing an advertising strategy, or a market entry strategy for that matter, one needs to understand the Japanese love of all things new. New is better. New is exciting. And new products, brands, packaging, and advertising are constantly demanded by consumers. Panasonic, in its well-known advertisements starring George Lucas, stated frankly, "Always Something New" as the theme of their corporate advertising. In 1990, Japan saw the launch of 720 new beverage products, compared to 642 in the United States, a country with twice the population. This is good news for foreign advertisers. Your product is different, and it is new. Use this in your advertising.

SOMETHING COPIED

Japanese marketers are also very good at copying. Not everything can be new, so when a new product or advertising angle takes off, it will be followed quickly by hungry competition. For example, the Fuzzy Logic concept was first incorporated into washing machines and was an instant success. "New Fuzzy" became a buzzword that reaped profits and spawned a new range of products: Fuzzy irons, rice cookers, vacuum cleaners, and ranges all emerged within months of the success of the original Fuzzy washing machines.

If you do launch a successful product, be prepared for instant competition. When the FiberMini drink was launched in 1991, it was regarded as one of the top products for the year. Targeted at health-conscious consumers, the product was billed as a fiber drink with extra vitamin C. During the next year, dozens of similar products were launched by competitors, and FiberMini's sales were squeezed dramatically.

In the tobacco industry, Philip Morris has been successful with Marlboro, Lark, and Virginia Slims. With only a 15 percent share of the tobacco market, PM relies on consistent independent brand advertising and promotion, from which they have built strong loyalty among smokers. Japan Tobacco, with over 80 percent of the tobacco market, decided to pursue the typical Japanese strategy of launching new products to win back (or at least maintain) market share. From 1989 into the early 1990s, the market saw the launch of twenty-six new brands and/or brand extensions.

The strategy of multiple new launches failed to win back market share in the face of the stronger independent brands system enjoyed by the foreign tobacco companies. What is now evident is that JT has changed its strategy to win back market share by copying its competition's successful advertising and promotion programs. Responding to Marlboro's success in motor sports sponsorship, JT's Cabin now has its own racing team. Lark's international espionage and intrigue image features a secret agent, and Cabin now uses a similar motif for its advertising. Virginia Slims' strong direct marketing program is now being imitated by Caster Bevel. Marlboro was extremely successful with custom-logo Zippo lighters used as awards in a closed lottery. Not surprisingly, JT has similar promotions for several of its main brands.

THE SEASONS

Japanese pride themselves on a clear distinction between the seasons; this is reflected in menus, clothing, and, of course, advertising. Foreign advertisers would be wise to take note of the seasonal nature of Japanese advertising, and even more so for promotional offers and trade incentives. Point-of-purchase materials also change with the seasons. Smart marketers must adapt to seasonal themes if they want their displays to be set up. Advertising for TV, print, and outdoor sites tends to change with the seasons and evoke emotions and brand association with traditional seasonal imagery.

THE USE OF "TALENT"

While many Western actors and actresses stay away from commercials to avoid overexposure, in Japan the use of *tarento* ("talent") is standard. Even Western mega-celebrities, who would not be caught dead in commercials in their home countries, frequently sell cars, motorbikes, stereos, instant noodles, and vitamin drinks in Japan. Arnold Schwarzenegger has become a fixture for his in Cup Noodle and "stamina drink" commercials. Woody Allen, George Lucas, Madonna, Michael and Janet Jackson, Paul Newman, Charlie Sheen, Peter Falk, Harrison Ford, and even Sean Connery have all appeared in exclusive, Japan-only commercials.

CHOOSING MEDIA IN JAPAN

Spending on advertising in Japan dropped 4.6 percent to ¥5.5 trillion in 1992, the first decline in twenty-seven years. According to a survey by Dentsu, ad spending may decline by another 1.5 percent in 1993. This is good news for small and medium-sized companies coming to Japan in that agencies are hungrier for your media dollars then ever before. Third-priority sales promotion and direct marketing are growing areas, so agencies are scrambling to improve services in these fields as well. Only time will tell, but a general shift toward a more competitive buyer's market can only help foreign firms' marketing efforts in Japan.

The four major mass media vehicles for advertisers are the same as almost anywhere in the world: newspapers, magazines, television, and radio. As with any industrialized country, your media mix will be based on what you plan to market, your target audience, and how much you are willing to spend. The following section briefly describes the major media vehicles, though more detailed information can be obtained through advertising agencies or the *Yearbook*.

TELEVISION

Expenditures on television advertising have grown dramatically since 1985 but slowed in the latter part of 1991, when the growth rate dipped to 4.7 percent. In 1992, ad spending on TV decreased by 1.6 percent. This may lead to new opportunities for foreign advertisers to purchase prized slots; however, costs are still prohibitive for small and medium-sized firms. Firms wishing to advertise on TV, are well advised to work with one of the larger Japanese advertising agencies who control this media. As anywhere, TV advertising is best suited to building brand awareness and support for the mass selling of consumer products.

NEWSPAPERS

In 1991 newspaper advertising expenditures dropped for the first time in twenty-six years, a decrease of just over 1 percent from 1990. In 1992, spending on newspaper ads plummeted 9.5 percent. Circulation in 1991 was over 52 million, with a penetration of 1.24 copies per household. Newspapers are used for corporate advertising, brand advertising, promotional advertising, and, since October 1990, coupon advertising — though not to the same degree we see in the West.

MAGAZINES

According to the *Yearbook,* there were 4.6 billion magazines printed in 1991. Most magazines are either published weekly or monthly, with weeklies exceeding monthlies in both number of copies and sales volume. With over 2,300 titles and 29.8 copies sold per person per year, magazines have been favorite advertising vehicles for marketers. From 1988 to 1990, advertising expenditures saw double-digit growth, and new launches soared to 165 in 1991. Since the last half of 1991, however, the magazine publishing business has slowed with the rest of the economy.

Small and medium-sized companies that decide to conduct advertising in various magazines should set up a system to compare effectiveness between the different publications used. Response cards, customer service numbers, and promotional advertising can all be used to accomplish this. In September 1991, I put together a promotion for a major foreign advertiser which involved a phone-in sweepstakes using a theme-related voice-processing system. The system enabled the brand to track respondent demographics and response rates of each magazine used in the promotion. From this, we could determine which magazines were cost-effective in reaching the target audience and which were not, and the advertising strategy could then be adjusted accordingly. While this is standard practice in the West, it is relatively new in Japan.

RADIO

As with magazine advertising, radio advertising expenditures increased at a double-digit rate from 1988 to 1990, and then dropped sharply by 3 percent in 1991. Service, leisure, automobile, food, beverage, and tobacco companies have been the major users of radio advertising. It is sometimes difficult to get good rating data on programs to determine listening audience, however. Many marketers believe that radio will play an increasing role in the future and can be a targeted delivery vehicle for both corporate and brand advertising.

OUTDOOR ADVERTISING

Corporate identity and tobacco advertising have been the driving forces for large outdoor advertising. With the fall in land prices over the last two years, many in the industry expected outdoor advertising costs to decrease as well. However, strong demand for highly visible space has enabled media companies experiencing falling revenues from other media to charge increasingly higher rates for outdoor space.

Another growing medium for outdoor advertising is large-screen color TV. The number of these outdoor TVs is growing; Tokyo now has them in most shopping and entertainment districts. An exciting use of these large screens is as a backdrop for special promotional events. Transit advertising, outdoor ads, and large-screen TV can be used together to form a "JACK promotion," a Japanese term derived from the English word "hijack," where the advertiser literally takes over a major entertainment and shopping area for one or several days. This high-density advertising combined with product sampling on location is used to create a strong impression and awareness among consumers. As an interesting twist on JACK promotions, in the early 1990s, Pepsi "train-JACKed" the Yamanote line, which runs around the center of Tokyo, so that the only ads in the cars were for Pepsi.

SALES PROMOTION

Although advertising and PR will undoubtedly be important for small and medium-sized companies coming to Japan, creative sales promotion and direct marketing offer unique ways for these companies to distinguish themselves from other marketers and to build up tangible sales.

Sales promotion in Japan has traditionally been seen as merely a sales support tool. As such, most sales promotion planning has taken place within the sales departments of the marketer and not through agencies. Sales promotion programs would be established and run over several years, with only slight adjustments. The majority of the programs are of the "me too" variety, lacking any real executional creativity except in respect to original premiums. Sales promotion is still for the most part considered a means to generate a quick, yet temporary, sales increase. This is starting to change, however.

Two main factors have fueled this change in sales promotion thinking. Foreign companies coming to Japan have brought with them extensive sales promotion experience gained in their competitive home markets. Japanese companies, which had always relied on their production power to turn out new products as market conditions changed, began to take note of how foreign multinationals used strategic marketing and promotions.

It would be easy to argue that Japan's sales promotion industry lags at least five years behind that of the United States, and hot new ideas will continue to be imported from the West. The structure of the industry itself is a clear sign of its immaturity. There are few real sales promotion agencies. Most firms claiming to be sales promotion agencies generate almost all their revenue, not from sales promotion planning or promotional execution, but from printing or supplying premiums. But with the increased demand for new sales promotion planning, Japan's advertising agencies are now starting to build up their sales promotion divisions.

Another factor which is making many firms look at sales promotion more seriously is the change in the Japanese consumer. Once thought of as a very homogeneous, middle-class society, we now see the identification of specific target groups within it. Examples include: *torantan* — single 30-something working women; *hanako zoku* — young women with lots of money to spend on food and travel; *jukunen* — married couples over forty with no children at home; and *dai ni no jinsei* — senior citizens free of responsibilities for grandchildren and enjoying a "second life." The strength of sales promotion as a means of targeting these groups and to support long-term residual value is starting to be recognized.

Sales promotion campaigns offer the small or medium-sized company some of the most potent tools for obtaining vital information about prospective customers. You will no doubt recognize most of the methods, and many are rather simple. Where the challenge lies is in setting a clear objective and then developing an appropriate offer that stands out among the clutter and encourages your targets to respond.

The first step to a successful sales promotion is to set objectives. Traditionally sales promotion is used to:

- Reach new users and encourage purchasing
- Obtain trial for a product
- Hold on to current users of a product

- Encourage repeat usage of a product
- Neutralize competitive advertising or sales promotion
- Reinforce brand advertising

The additional objectives that small and medium-sized-companies should demand from their promotions are:

- Building a database of prospects and users
- Monitoring the cost-effectiveness of one promotional approach versus another
- Finding out which areas and markets respond to which types of promotions
- Profiling your key target or heavy user
- Monitoring where trade is supporting your consumer promotions and where it is not

This second set of objectives gives companies a vital base of information from which to plan, develop, implement, and monitor strategies to win market share in Japan.

DEVELOPING YOUR PROMOTION

The next step in developing a meaningful sales promotion program is deciding on the offer. Consumers today are quick and smart — they will look at an offer for a few seconds and if the value isn't there, they'll pass it by. This section provides an overview of some of the tools available in Japan.

LOTTERIES

One of the most popular sales promotion tools used to build a database of potential consumers and prospects is the sweepstakes, or *open* and *closed* lotteries. An open lottery is a promotion which awards substantial prizes on the basis of a chance drawing or some form of contest. For legal reasons, entrants are not required to purchase products, so these programs do not necessarily translate directly into sales. Prize values are limited to ¥1 million (approximately $10,000), much less than in most Western countries. Foreign travel has been a very popular offer due to the increased emphasis on leisure in Japan (and in part the strength of the yen), and overseas trips have consistently accounted for nearly 10 percent of all open lottery awards in the last ten years. While in the late 1980s top destinations were the United States, Canada, and Europe, hot destinations are now Hong Kong and Hawaii, and theme-related tours have also become popular — an Australian adventure, dinner with a star in New York, or a gourmet tour of Hong Kong.

In order to build up lists of prospective purchasers and target specific demographic groups, companies offer personal electronics, original items, gourmet-related premiums, and even their own product as awards for these campaigns. Pocari Sweat is a popular sports drink in Japan, and Pocari regularly offers a year's supply of its product as prizes in their promotions. For small and medium-sized companies, this may be a more economical course than a trip. In selecting a prize, you must decide who your target group is and what data you want to gather. A campaign offering foreign travel or other high-value consumer electronics as incentives would undoubtedly garner higher responses than the Pocari offer, but if your objective is to build a list of hard-core users, the latter would be more appropriate.

Open lotteries can also include quizzes or surveys. With a quiz, the entry question is usually designed to build brand awareness. With a survey, the objective is to gather specific data. It is often said that Japanese tend to be honest when answering questions, and the percentage of usable data is generally quite a bit higher than when surveys are done in the West. Open surveys with write-in redemption cards or telephone-entry are used to build sales leads. Open lotteries aim at promoting brand awareness and building excitement around the product. Unlike standard media advertising, however, sponsors can monitor effectiveness through response tracking, as well as obtain important demographic data.

The high-value awards and mass media advertising associated with open lotteries make these programs costly. In addition, consumers are not required to purchase in order to enter. Another form of sweepstakes, the closed lottery, or "must buy" lottery, does require purchases and has become one of the most popular promotion vehicles among major marketers. The process is the same as in an open contest, but the applicant must purchase the product to enter. The current ceilings on prize values have become quite controversial, with marketers generally in agreement that it is much too restrictive. For some consumer items, prize values are limited to the lesser of twenty times the value of the product or ¥10,000.

ORIGINAL PREMIUM OFFERS

One way companies have overcome the limits mentioned above is by offering original items. Original premium offers have become very popular in Japan, and some marketers have reached legendary status because of the almost bizarre items they have offered consumers to motivate purchase of their product. Nisshin Foods is famous for its Banbangi brand promotion, which drew millions of responses with the offer of an original character item — a bird with two clocks for eyes. The unique feature of this clock was that it would call out "Banbangi!" at strategic snack times, to remind consumers to eat their instant noodle product.

VALUE AND REWARD

The keys to successful promotions are value and reward, with current trends toward immediate value and immediate reward. With faxes, overnight delivery services, computer modems, and call processing, consumers are accustomed to getting what they want without having to wait. We are starting to see a trend, led by foreign companies in Japan, wherein rewards are delivered on the spot.

The tobacco industry, in particular, has taken up this challenge. In the mid-1980s, foreign tobacco companies began to use sweepstakes to promote brand awareness in a market dominated by Japan Tobacco. Lotteries were used that received approximately 500,000 responses nationwide. Soon, however, Japan Tobacco began to follow suit, and consumers became bored with the programs, causing redemption rates to fall 20 to 30 percent each year. The challenge for marketers was to develop stronger incentive items and de-emphasize delayed promotion techniques in favor of more immediate delivery and gratification for the consumer.

Marlboro broke new ground with its collector Zippo lighter promotions. Philip Morris's Merit brand offered the chance to win beer tickets with purchase, with the tickets awarded in-pack instantly. Lark's 1992 fall promotion was even more innovative, the first in Japan to offer an instant lottery through interactive call processing. With the telephone tie-in, consumers were immediately informed if they had won or not, and the company received immediate information about the effectiveness of the campaign — who was entering and what media motivated entry.

Rub-off and in-pack games also add immediacy to sweepstakes promotions. Rub-offs themselves are old hat in the West, but we are starting to see more and more marketers packing innovative games with their products in Japan.

COUPONS

Although coupon advertising has been allowed since October 1990, few are included in newspapers. In July of 1991, Coca-Cola Japan made the first major coupon offer. It was delivered through seventy-six newspapers and was redeemable for a free bottle of either Coke or Coke Lite. Japan still lags far behind the United States and Canada regarding manufacturers' coupon advertising due to its fragmented distribution and clearinghouse procedures, and the effectiveness of couponing as a long-term strategy is still under debate.

SOCIAL MARKETING

Another recent promotional import from the West is the cause-related promotion or social marketing promotion, which aims to give something back to society. Cause-related promotions, which show no sign of leveling off in North America, have started to appear more and more in Japan. Retailers and marketers raise funds for various causes to project positive brand and corporate images.

DIRECT MARKETING IN JAPAN

The integration of direct marketing with sales promotion is just starting to get off the ground in Japan, led by U.S. firms such as airlines, credit card companies, and tobacco manufacturers, who top the field in their home markets. More and more companies are now realizing the value of using sales promotion techniques to build databases, which are then used in direct marketing programs to sell their products.

In the mysterious, complicated, and expensive world of advertising and retailing in Japan, direct marketing is *particularly* mysterious, complicated, and expensive. Whether you are selling imported goods by catalogue or promoting your wares by what you thought were tried-and-true direct mail advertising techniques, Japan will undoubtedly frustrate and confound you. And you'll be in good company: Sears has tried and failed for years to crack the market, and Reader's Digest recently pulled out due to declining revenues. Direct marketing in Japan is not for the faint of heart or underfinanced, and particular care must be taken in the following areas:

- Japanese postal regulations for bulk mailings are ambiguous and often loosely interpreted depending on the postmaster and his relationship with the mailer. However, those mailers who are willing to spend a good amount of time and money courting the local postmaster may receive bulk permit approval on even the most questionable DM packages.
- Quality lists are extremely rare; most are shamelessly compiled from telephone directories and company staff lists. Lists of substance, such as magazine subscribers or qualified DM shoppers, if they can be found, tend to be quite expensive and the owners will often require renters to use their own overpriced lettershopping services.
- Size limits are enforced to the millimeter and run counter to standards established in the rest of the world (although the aforementioned local postmaster may find room for exceptions).
- Although the postal service in Japan is probably the finest in the world, discounts for bulk mailing are minimal and you'll probably find bulk rates in Japan more expensive than first-class rates in your home country. What's more, although Japan has officially agreed to honor international postal bulk regulations, advertisers mailing from low-cost ports such as Hong Kong or

Singapore into Japan may often run into inexplicable delays in receiving approvals.

In spite of these difficulties however, DM is one of the few areas of retailing and advertising that has seen steady increases during the last decade, even in the recessionary economy of the early 1990s. The growing number of working women with less time for daily shopping, combined with the simple fact that DM in Japan was dismally underdeveloped even as little as ten years ago, have resulted in annual growth consistently over 10 percent.

More importantly, for some companies interested in entering the Japanese market, direct marketing may be the *only* way to do so successfully. To find out if DM in Japan is right for you, ask yourself the following questions:

- Has DM worked for me in my home country?
- Am I selling a high-value product or service that appeals to a narrow segment of the overall market which may be difficult to reach in mass media advertising?
- Do I have a relatively limited budget that prevents me from setting up full-fledged operations in Japan?

The last question is crucial to many companies interested in the Japanese market. Considering Japan's fierce competition, costly real estate, and intricate, exclusionary distribution system, the idea of using a controlled test mailing to judge consumer response to your product, followed by direct order fulfillment from your home country in lieu of a Japan-based sales office and warehouse, may be the ideal way to test the Japanese market with a minimum of risk.

The three most important areas to consider when planning a DM campaign in Japan (or anywhere in the world for that matter) are lists, tools, and strategies. The following primer on these three subjects should be a good first step for those interested in entering the Japanese market.

MAILING LISTS

Many DM professionals in Japan agree that here, more than in any other market, having the right list is the key to a successful DM campaign. The Japanese list industry is quite young compared to those in Europe or North America, and good lists are extremely hard to come by. A number of factors have caused this unfortunate situation: Few magazines are sold by subscription, so subscriber lists (with one important exception to be covered in a moment) are almost non-existent. Catalogue companies jealously guard their lists and will rarely rent them to other users, whether they are competitors or not. And finally, there has been little pressure on the industry to produce quality lists. During the booming 1980s, fortunes were being made from names compiled from the telephone directory, so why make the effort to put together a real list?

Fortunately, lean times have improved the situation dramatically. Catalogue companies, anxious to generate extra revenues, are releasing their DM-responsive lists for rental to selected companies. Faced with declining rental revenues, the list companies themselves have begun developing high-quality databases of businesspeople and consumers with relatively specific (for Japan) selections.

On the consumer list side, one of the best lists available is from Japan's mass communications monolith, Fujisankei Communications. The Fuji group dominates Japanese broadcast, publishing, and music media. Their specialty Fuji DM Fan list is one of the most expensive in Japan, and you will be required to use Fuji's own exorbitantly priced lettershop as well. What you get for the money, though, is an up-to-date selection of more than 4 million consumers who have completed a detailed lifestyle and demographics questionnaire. One particularly interesting category is shoppers who have responded to Fuji TV's home shopping program — a rare example of a DM-responsive list in Japan. (Trivia buffs will be interested to know that, in 1990, not one but two $250,000 Ferrari F40s were sold through this show.)

Speaking of cars, another unusual list in Japan is the Internet Car Owners' Database. With personal information on 400,000 owners, plus their car's make, model, and year, a smart DM advertiser in the auto industry could target owners of competing manufacturers' models with a particularly aggressive marketing blitz. What's more, Japan's strict (and at around $2,000, astonishingly expensive) registration inspections, which start regularly after the third year of ownership, mean that most owners trade in their cars at about the two year and eleven month mark. What would the average auto marketing executive give for the list of a competing manufacturer's car owners who are planning a trade-in by a specific date? In this case, it would be the measly cost of a list rental.

Two other consumer lists of note in Japan are the Kennedy International Omnibus Database, and the Kozuka Shokai DM Shoppers Database. Kennedy International is a list owner and broker with a number of English-speaking staff, and has recently undertaken the development of a lifestyle and shopping-habit database of Japanese consumers. The 100,000 individuals in this database can be sorted by such categories as catalogue shoppers, overseas travelers, and computer owners — all of potential interest to overseas marketers.

The Kozuka Shokai DM Shoppers Database is compiled from a number of catalogue users lists, including individuals who have purchased $4,000-plus designer watches and jewelry by mail, and those who have purchased imported goods from a U.S. fashion goods catalogue. Kozuka Shokai also owns a number of specialty high-income lists that would be of use to marketers of luxury goods from overseas.

In the field of business-to-business lists, the strongest contender is the Tokyo Shoko Research (TSR) database. TSR actually maintains mailing lists as a sideline to its credit rating service, but this list is one of the best in Japan. With top executives' names, extremely up-to-date listings, and information on over 400,000 companies segmented by 8,000 industry groups, this database could be used in almost any business-to-business context.

Another unique offering in the Japanese list scene is the Nikkei Business Publications list. Nikkei offers the only business magazine subscribers' list in Japan — over 1 million individuals with specialty interests such as business, economics, and computer science. As with other quality lists, Nikkei labels are pricey and the company requires renters to use their own in-house lettershop. This list will cost you in more ways than one, so do your cost-benefit analysis carefully before you mail.

Finally, two specialty lists from the aforementioned Kennedy International should be noted: International Businesspeople and

Professional Women. The International Businesspeople list contains almost 30,000 English-speaking executives in Japan. This list has a reputation for high deliverability and is a favorite of English-language publishers looking to crack the Japanese market. The 50,000-name Professional Women database contains information on women in fields such as medicine, accounting, and law. Catalogue marketers would do well to consider this list of high-income individuals with little free time for traditional shopping.

TOOLS

Because of Japan's high costs for creative development, printing, list rental, and postage, mailers are constantly looking for new ways to cut corners or circumvent postal regulations. Printing in and mailing from low-cost ports such as Hong Kong, Singapore, or Malaysia would seem to be an obvious answer, and some experienced mailers in Japan have used this technique to their advantage. Extremely light-weight self-mailers are frequently used to take advantage of the Surface Air Lift rates which favor such packages, but be forewarned: Although the Japanese postal ministry has in principle agreed to international bulk mail regulations, it doesn't like having its business taken away by overseas operators; nor do Japanese DM agencies, printers, and lettershops appreciate the added competition. Expect a fair amount of bureaucratic foot-dragging before you receive final approval for your mailing.

Savvy local mailers have taken advantage of a loophole in Japanese third-class magazine regulations which allows practically anything to be mailed out at bargain rates as long as it is at least 50 percent editorial and is mailed at semi-regular intervals. The result has been a number of ad magazines which contain "articles" full of exciting and useful information about the advertisers located on the same page. Some of the more brazen DM agencies are even producing catalogues in this format, but the postal ministry has begun to strike back and more than a few third-class permits have been revoked recently.

One third-class magazine which has escaped this fate is *The Earth*, which is mailed as an eight-page, four-color tabloid. One advertiser will buy an entire issue, and all editorial and ad space are then dedicated to that particular client. Mailing costs plummet from ¥120 for bulk mail postage to ¥29 for third-class magazine postage; on a mailing of 100,000 pieces, the savings amounts to nearly $100,000. These cost savings, combined with the impact of having an oversized, full-color magazine arriving at the homes of your target customers, could give you the best bang for your DM buck in Japan.

STRATEGIES

In spite of the difficulties inherent in entering the Japanese market, a number of foreign companies have not only survived but prospered through strategic direct marketing use. The following brief case studies may help you to plan your own successful campaign.

In the mid-1980s, BMW launched what was to become one of the most successful auto-related promotion campaigns ever seen in Japan. By 1990, BMW was Japan's number-one imported auto make, and easily sold every car it could ship into the country at prices at least 50 percent higher than in any of its other markets.

BMW and its agency, Asatsu, began their campaign by developing a specific mailing list for each of its model lines: young, sports-minded individuals for its smaller sports models; business managers and owners for its mid-line models; and owners of yachts, golf club memberships, and resort homes for its top-of-the-line models.

Specific third-class magazines were then created for each model line, each containing editorials on the joy of driving and the sterling history of BMW (exactly 50 percent of each publication was dedicated to this kind of information — the minimum required by the post office to qualify for magazine rates), as well as specific advertising information on the model's features and prices. Readers were asked to return a postage-paid postcard with demographic and lifestyle information, and had an option to have a local dealer contact them to arrange a test drive. BMW then used these responses to develop their own in-house database for future DM mailings.

Over the four years that the campaign ran, over 5 million magazines were mailed and response rates averaged a surprising 11 percent. Responders cited the magazines' oversized format and stunning four-color photography as the main reason they were attracted to these DM packages. And as mentioned before, the impact on BMW sales speaks for itself.

Another Japanese market success story centers on American catalogue marketer L.L. Bean. For years, L.L. Bean found that Japanese consumers were making huge orders from its catalogues even though there were no Japanese-language versions available. And, according to rumor, Japanese tourists were descending on its Maine-based retail store and spending thousands of dollars, only to resell the merchandise on their return to Japan.

Anxious to cash in on this shopping frenzy but leery of the difficulties of setting up shop in Japan, Bean opted to manage its warehousing and shipping operations in the United States and express mail its merchandise to Japan. Japanese translations of its catalogues were prepared, lists were tested and rolled out, and the whole operation was so successful that L.L. Bean has now opened its first retail outlet in Japan. More importantly, it was able to open that outlet *after* it had been able to carefully judge the Japanese market's response to its merchandise through the low-risk method of U.S.-based warehousing and shipping.

Small and medium-sized companies, not in a position to produce their own catalogues, have opportunities to feature their products in other private direct mail catalogues. Companies like Visa, Diner's, JCB, and Million have entered the DM business with their own original catalogues, targeted at their membership. Currently, credit card catalogues are more open to new and unique (foreign) products than the more traditional Japanese DM catalogues.

Remarkable growth and change continues to take place in the Japanese marketplace, and many new opportunities exist for foreign products and companies that gear up for this challenge. Advertising, sales promotion, and direct marketing offer an array of tools that foreign marketers can use to obtain results in Japan if they are designed with a sense of strategic purpose and the emotional support of those who implement them. As with any enterprise, understanding the market, the players, and the tools available, followed by careful planning and imaginative execution, are critical to success. And although there is no fixed or secret formula particular to this market, foreign marketers could learn from a popular motto emblazoned on notebooks in Japan: "See, Plan, Do."

NOTES

1. *There are a number of directories available to assist you. Examples are the* Japan Company Handbook, *published by Toyo Keizai Inc., and* Industrial Groupings in Japan, *published by Dodwell Marketing Consultants. These are both updated regularly.*
2. *Karel van Wolferen,* The Enigma of Japanese Power *(Basingstoke: Papermac), p. 233. Originally published in 1989 by Macmillan.*
3. *Ibid., p. 231.*

The author wishes to acknowledge with thanks the assistance of Fred Love in the preparation of this article, particularly the direct marketing section.

CHAPTER NINE

Marketing Value-Added Products to Japan

MICHAEL LESLIE

第九章

Traditionally, most of Japan's non-oil imports have consisted of resource products; as recently as 1985, these products accounted for nearly two-thirds of the total. The balance of Japan's import mix has changed, however, such that in 1991 resource products accounted for only 50 percent of imports. For many Western countries, Japan's increased demand for value-added products, while representing a tremendous opportunity, also requires a restructuring of traditional trading practices. In this chapter, Michael Leslie, president of Nakodo Consulting Inc., discusses the merits of tapping into that demand and the marketing skills that are required to achieve success.

To add value is to take a product and, by adding services or modifying it, increase its resale value. Examples would be taking raw lumber and transforming it into a chair, turning a side of beef into beef jerky, or taking computer chips and assembling a computer.

Adding value can also mean moving a product further along the processing line to higher and higher steps of development or value-added stages. The processing of sides of beef into boneless cuts is but one step; the slicing of that beef into jerky and then packaging it into retail packages are additional steps, each increasing the resale value and moving the product further along the processing chain.

Commodities, by contrast, are generally goods that require only three factors for sales success: price, quality, and delivery. A commodity is usually sold in large volume to an end user or manufacturer who adds value to it by making something from the raw material. In general, commodities tend to be natural resources or bulk agricultural products and are either renewable, such as timber products and wheat, or nonrenewable, such as natural gas and coal. Exporting these products is relatively easy, and countries like Canada, Australia, and New Zealand have been especially good at selling both forms of commodities.

A recently released report by the Canada-Japan Forum 2000 was quite blunt in its appraisal of Canada's efforts to penetrate the Japanese market. While noting that Canada has a near balance of trade with Japan, the report pointed to the fact that, overwhelmingly, sales to Japan are the result of Japanese initiatives to source products, not Canadians aggressively selling their goods in Japan. The report noted this indicates "a lack of export skills" on the part of Canadians.[1]

Similarly, a recent article describing Australia's exports noted: "Australia has filled the role of supplier of raw primary commodities at low cost for decades — first to England, then to the United States, and now to Asian markets. But in exporting US$9.7 billion of basic agricultural commodities last year, Australia also exported jobs and capital."[2]

In the United States, similar concerns face the traditional commodity industries such as steel and agricultural production, including eroding prices, increased foreign competition, and declining profits.

As the world moves toward global trading, our dependence on the export of commodity goods cannot continue unless we are prepared to accept the resultant lower standards of living. The successful conclusion of the GATT round should mean more open trade and perhaps lower prices for commodities, as other countries move their competitively priced goods into our traditional markets. The supply and demand variances and risks of the commodity markets, boom and bust production cycles, risks of natural disasters such as crop failures, and ever-declining natural resource bases — all these contribute to the need to diversify and enter the value-added production market. We cannot afford *not* to add value. The challenge will be how quickly we can make the changes needed in our production sectors to survive and meet the market challenges of the future.

By moving away from bulk commodity items to more value-added products and production systems, we can increase the revenues to our firms and to our nations' GNP. This higher income will mean more jobs, higher wages, and a more secure future in the global marketplace. We will see the impact of this additional manufacturing upon the entire economy. Adding value will result in more highly skilled and highly paid jobs, a broader manufacturing base, and a more stable economy.

MARKETING VALUE-ADDED PRODUCTS

Adding value will demand the development of new skills. You will find yourself taking part in the design, preparation or construction, and sale of your product. In marketing value-added products, you must adopt an aggressive approach — you must make orders happen, not merely fill orders as they come in, as is often the case with marketing commodities. Because there are more variables involved than just price, quality, and delivery, you need to be market-reactive by developing products, seeking out consumer needs, and locating and utilizing new technologies. In order to modify or create a product to fit the consumers' requirements, you will need to study what the consumer needs, desires, believes, and understands.

Although this will involve considerable time and expense, you have the opportunity (which you do not have with resource products and commodities) to create a brand for your product, one that will build customer loyalty. Many people believe French mustard is the best in the world, and yet almost no one realizes that the seed for that mustard may have been grown in Canada. The best pasta products are often made from North American wheat, and the dry beers of the world come from malt made from barley exported from the Canadian prairies and the American Midwest. By adding value to your product, you differentiate it from your competitors' products. If your brand and quality are successful, you will also have less price competition, as brand products generally sell for a premium over generic or new entrants' products. By creating strong brand images, you can minimize the risk of substitution and link your image to features or concepts that your competitors will have a hard time copying. Be flexible and creative, and always remain a moving target.

The need for service for your products will also increase. Service when selling a commodity consists of meeting three demands: lowering the price, shipping exact quantities, and making speedy deliveries. By adding value, your customers' needs will increase beyond these three items. They may need after-sales service, a wide variety of delivery or payment alternatives, or risk-minimization methods such as inventory protection.

WHY TARGET JAPAN FOR YOUR VALUE-ADDED PRODUCTS?

Initially, because the basics are all there: the consumer market is large and sophisticated, and consumption is growing rapidly every year; it is a market where Western companies often enjoy enormous cost advantages over local producers, especially now that those high-cost local producers are no longer hidden behind fortress-like protectionist walls; and there are 125 million wealthy consumers in Japan who are willing to pay top dollar for products, as long as they can be assured of receiving quality goods. And because the Japanese consumer is extremely quality-conscious and the distribution system elaborate and hard to access, sales success in Japan will practically guarantee that your product and the sales team can succeed anywhere. Experience in product development and marketing gained in Japan will train your staff in the skills needed to compete in the global marketplace.

The opportunity is huge, but so are the challenges. Japanese consumers are a study in contrast: they want to try new products, but at the same time are insecure with products that are really different. As a newcomer to the market, you must tap the pulse of trends and take advantage of this contradictory wish to be an individual and yet still be accepted by the group. Teenagers in Harajuku, a trendy part of Tokyo, rebel against conformity by dressing in exotic clothing and coloring their hair shades of green, but only as part of a group of similarly attired friends. It is fine to be different from everyone else as long as you have company in that rebellion.

The same holds true for new products in the market. When everyone has a Sony Walkman, it is trendy to have the latest version, perhaps one with a TV attachment, or wireless earphones. To buy a similar radio cassette from a Western manufacturer that has no track record in Japan, however, would not be an acceptable risk to most Japanese consumers due to fears of unreliability.

The Japanese market is constantly changing as new trends, opportunities, challenges, and rewards arise. Why is it that businesspeople from other countries find the Japanese market so baffling? Is it simply because of the cultural differences? Japan has a very strong traditional culture, which explains much about its customs, manners, business practices, and consumption patterns. But I would add that it also has a volatile modern popular culture that is altering society faster than even the experts can track.

Not that Japan experts don't try. Go to any bookstore and you'll find a shelf full of titles "explaining" Japan. But you have to be careful about accepting neatly packaged marketing theories about Japan. They may accurately tell you "what has happened," but they are much less useful in deciphering the billion-dollar question: "What happens next?"

Some important current trends to watch and tap into are: the desire to make everything smaller and easier to store due to the lack of space in Japanese homes and apartments; the trend to add buttons and buzzers — sometimes minor improvements or added gadgets to existing products; and the trend to safer, more health-conscious diets as consumers worry about excessive additives, hormones, or residues of chemicals used during or after production. In the Japanese food market specifically, we have noted a number of trends. At the same time as retail prices are dropping, imports are rising and domestic production stagnating or declining. Per capita consumption of expensive so-called "gourmet foods" is growing. Tastes are also changing. While the Japanese once used only thin slices of beef in cooking, approximately 50 grams per portion, they are increasingly moving to larger Western-style portions, such as 200-gram steaks and 120-gram hamburgers. This dovetails with a growing health consciousness and a trend toward leaner cuts of meat.

In Japan, there is also the fashion aspect to consider. That is, once the Japanese catch on to a new product or concept, within weeks everyone's got to have it. One example of how conventional wisdom in the food sector was turned on its head occurred recently.

"The Japanese don't really eat cheese," they used to tell cheese exporters. "Because animal fats were only introduced to the Japanese diet in fairly recent times, they consume only very modest amounts of the blandest processed cheese, and they loathe blue cheese or anything with a cheesy smell." This was true ten years ago, and all sorts of historical and cultural explanations were offered to explain why. Consequently, most cheese producers didn't waste their time on market development in Japan.

But fashion can catch fire in Japan. And, in fact, several things happened concurrently to cause a revolution. Having discovered fine wines, Tokyo sophisticates started to experiment with gourmet cheese to accompany it. Pizza caught on in a big way when Domino's started home delivery. Cheese quickly moved toward being fashionable in the Japanese diet, and the more accustomed they became to eating cheese, the more adventurous they became.

Soon bizarre market surges started to crop up. A fashion-lifestyle magazine called *Hanako*, one of the trend-setting magazines for young women in Tokyo, ran a feature on the Italian dessert tiramisu, which contains mascarpone cheese. The article listed half a dozen eateries around Tokyo that carried this item, describing it in mouth-watering terms. Within a day, there were block-long lineups at all the restaurants mentioned in the article. Within weeks, restaurants all across Japan were carrying it. Within months, there was a worldwide shortage of mascarpone, as Japanese buyers snapped up all the inventory in Italy. Even now, three years later, you can still find tiramisu-flavored ice cream and candies.

The Japanese market is full of opportunities like this. All you need are some basic skills and an understanding of what it takes to make a product a success in the market.

CORPORATE COMMITMENT TO JAPAN

What is needed to begin value-added processing for the Japanese market? First, you must have a core business to sustain your company while the Japanese market is being developed over the long term. You probably should not be undertaking market development in Japan if you don't have a stable, profitable business operation at home.

Second, you need the corporate desire to succeed. The senior management of your company must confirm that they have a real desire to enter the Japanese market. Since the decision to begin means committing for the long term and dedicating staff and time to the effort, it is a decision that cannot be taken lightly. You will be tying up capital, as well as research and development funds, for a number of years prior to receiving any payback. This type of future goal-setting and focus must be made by senior management and have their full, ongoing support. Any retreat from the market after a short time will result not only in the loss of all efforts and investments made to date, but may also damage the reputation of the firm in the marketplace and adversely affect any future initiatives.

It is best to create an export team whose only goal and responsibility is the success of your Japan project. By giving that team the sole job of developing the export market, they will have one focus and the dedication and persistence necessary to complete the challenge. They should not be distracted by other, time-consuming responsibilities, such as domestic purchasing or sales in other markets.

Once the senior management is committed to the project, they must remain easily accessible to the product development and export team, providing them with the support and resources necessary to succeed. Preferably, a member of the senior staff should attend team meetings to provide guidance and support over the long development process. Access to senior managers will help the working-level staff to motivate production lines. Your staff must have the authority to develop samples and be able to rely on the active participation and support of your domestic corporate resources. For example, all their research and sales efforts will go to waste if your local factory refuses to make less than container-lot sizes as samples, pursuant to another management edict to cut down on inefficiencies in production.

You must maintain a long-term outlook because it will take three or four years to develop strong business relationships in Japan, and profits will not begin to arrive until year four or five. It takes a great deal of time and effort to develop the exact product mix, recipes, or designs that will succeed in the Japanese market. Your staff need time to develop relationships, to create product demand, to locate distributors, to confirm retailer demand, and to set up infrastructures such as documentation, custom clearance systems, and storage space. Equip your teams with a budget and a time line that allow the project to progress smoothly over the long term. Don't force them to go, cap in hand, to get funds for every luncheon or sample expenditure.

In Japan, success comes only after you have paid your dues and become an insider in the family-like relationships of Japanese business. The other approach, one many American automakers seem to be taking, is to complain about the perceived unfairness of the Japanese system. The Japanese government may respond by changing relevant laws, but they cannot change the way business-people think. Leave the complaining to others, and concentrate on building the connections and the trust that will win you a position as an insider.

MAKE CONNECTIONS THAT WORK FOR YOU

Connections are essential. It takes time and hard work to become an insider and develop those connections. The Japanese prefer to do business with firms they know and trust, people they can count as friends. The bad news is that Japan does not like doing business with outsiders; the good news is that this means all outsiders, including new Japanese entrants and other competitors and their products.

Consequently, you cannot keep changing your marketing staff for every trip to Japan; it takes time to develop friendships and relationships. You must also take into account the rotation of staff that occurs in most Japanese companies. If you visit only once a year, you could return to find your sole contact in the company, the wine buyer, has been transferred to ladies' underwear or, worse yet, posted to Geneva. His replacement may have been wined and dined by your competitors for five or six months and have no idea of your company's existence. By creating relationships at all levels within the company, you ensure that as changes occur, you always have guides and supporters in the company. And as the people with whom you've developed connections are promoted over the years, one or two of your contacts may rise to positions of authority where they will be pleased to help a long-term friend.

Constant customer contact is key. Customers like to see your face regularly, and they are always pleased when you remember to send presents during Japan's two gift-giving seasons, July and December. If you cannot maintain an office in Tokyo, hop on a plane frequently or phone and fax to keep in touch if your contacts speak English. When you visit, bring samples of new products and small mementos targeted at each buyer's hobbies or family members. All of these things will keep you and your firm current in the mind of your buyer.

In the Japanese way of doing business, relationships count more than contracts. If you work in a big company, you buy from the people you know will deliver — your friends and long-term business connections. Even if someone comes in with products that are cheaper than the usual supplier, the Japanese partners you develop will stick with the supplier they can count on.

When asked why things work this way, one Japanese customer mentioned his experience with Canadian pork suppliers. His company wanted a guaranteed supply of pork and spent several years developing a connection with a Canadian supplier. But one season, when American buyers offered the Canadian exporters prices a little higher than the long-term Japanese contract price, the Canadians sent all of their product to the United States and shorted the Japanese buyers. The Japanese buyers gave up doing business with the Canadian suppliers and redirected their long-term contracts to Danish and Taiwanese suppliers instead.

From the Canadian company's perspective, their actions may be understandable, but in the Japanese context, they were incredibly short-sighted and mercenary. Why give up a long-term relationship just to gain a few dollars over one season? The best strategy for the Canadian exporters to have adopted would have been to phone the Japanese buyers and explain that, while they could have made a profit by diverting their product to the United States, due to the high value placed on the relationship with the Japanese company, they had passed up the opportunity. This would have been the first step toward becoming an "insider." In the Japanese system of obligation and responsibility, the Japanese buyers would now owe the Canadian exporters a debt, and would expect that favor to be called at a later date.

It is this type of mutual respect and obligation that cements relationships and solidifies business dealings in Japan. A distrust of contracts and reluctance to enforce the fine print has given Japan a need for very few lawyers. In fact, bringing a lawyer to the table while discussing a contract signifies a profound lack of trust, and may defeat the deal before negotiations get under way. In order to be able to conduct business without contracts, the two partners must know each other very well, and understand each other's goals, concerns, and profit motives. This type of tied obligation causes both sides of the relationship to seek mutual benefits and not to take advantage of the relationship; both parties understand that if an unfair advantage is given or taken, the opposite side will recall the favor or advantage at a later date.

YOUR MARKETING TEAM

The Japanese market is infamous for the success of insiders and the exclusion of outsiders. If you are to succeed, you need to cultivate business contacts in order to become part of the insider network in your industry or distribution network in Japan. These contacts are vital both for gathering information and for opening doors to export sales. This is particularly crucial in Japan, where you should avoid making cold calls. In a society held together more by personal relationships than contractual obligations, a close working relationship is the essential prerequisite for winning business. That being the case, there is another requirement for success: The human resources needed to develop and maintain close connections.

You need people who know your company and its products, and who understand your corporate goals. They must also have an understanding of the Japanese market and methods of doing business in that culture. First, you will need Japanese employees who know your ways and who can also function well in their own business culture. But you also need Westerners able to function in Japan to act as the link between the Western way of doing business and the Japanese.

One option is to hire market development specialists in Japan as part of your staff. Some firms bring in aggressive market development firms on a contractual basis. These firms are often expensive, but should be able to speed the introduction process for your products. They should be judged on their connections in the industry, not upon their English-speaking ability. They should not only work to introduce your product, they must also introduce you and your staff to the people they know, to ensure that when their contract expires, you are able to follow up on the efforts initiated on your behalf.

If hiring local product development people is not an option, there are a number of alternatives that are cost-effective and will help to ensure that you get local input in your product development. One such measure is involving your local Japanese distributor, your customers, and perhaps local suppliers in the development process. All will have their own contacts and networks who will give you feedback on your new product — topical and precise information on how it is being received and what you should change. By involving your buyers in the product design and creation phases of your program, you will not only ensure that they join with you to produce a product most closely suited to their customers' needs, you will solidify the relationships needed to make the product a success. By consulting them, you get not only the benefit of their different perspectives, you also give them a vested interest in the success of the product: Everyone wants their own project to be a winner.

SELECTING AN AGENT

When selecting an agent to sell your value-added product, avoid an exclusive marketing agreement. The risks of such agreements far outweigh their advantages, and Japan is full of stories of "exclusives" gone bad. For example, you may find that your agent will develop newer, more advanced versions of your product under their own labels; they may decide to sell limited volumes of your product in order to maintain prices, while you wish to sell greater volumes by lowering prices; or they may want your product as one of a dozen or more competing brands, using your product only to enable their firm to present a full catalogue of goods, rather than aggressively marketing it.

Rather than an exclusive arrangement, it is better to use a limited-term agreement for a few, selected products. In addition, some products are better sold through parallel or competitive distribution routes, using competing agents, as long as the target markets are non-competitive. Examples of this can arise where different firms market the same product in different regions, or where one firm sells to the department store gift trade while the other markets to mail order catalogues. By selling to both, you may increase the sales of your products through both routes. You must give the firm you choose enough time to effectively introduce the product. This means you have to be willing to wait at least three years, and you should not change distributors after that period unless you are willing to give new distributors a similar amount of time to develop the market.

Once you select your partner and are comfortable with them, work to motivate them to sell your product. You can do this by traveling to the market and working with them on sales calls as frequently as possible. Another way is to second some of your staff to work with them over a longer time period. By providing staff for training in your distributor's office, you not only gain better-trained, more market-aware staff, you also ensure that your product and its sales results are constantly in the mind of your distributor. And by having a person on the ground in Japan reporting on the results of test marketing or interpreting customer suggestions, you can shorten your product development times; you can receive reports, in your own language, of meetings and product development results as they occur.

If you open sales support and R&D offices in Japan, you can have your own staff conduct sales and obtain customer feedback directly, or work between all of your agents and their sub-agents to serve as a communications conduit for your organization. Once again, the rule is that the more often your product and your company are in the minds of your distributors, the better your product sales results will be.

DECISION-MAKING IN JAPAN

As noted above, in the design and marketing of your value-added products, you must involve your buyer in all stages and have as many people in his company "buy into" your product as possible. In many Japanese corporations, decisions concerning product ideas or development are made during regular meetings. In most cases, however, people with new ideas will have met informally with others to solicit support prior to the meeting. Thus, when the ideas are floated at the formal meeting, the group as a whole opts to proceed with the product or project. By achieving consensus through these one-on-one consultations, the formal meeting becomes simply a public display of commitment for the projects or ideas put forward. This round-table, consensus type of decision-making process can be very time-consuming, but once the group has agreed to something, implementation is smooth and speedy.

It is important for the foreign company to understand how this process can work for or against them. If you and your products are presented only at the formal meeting, you may not receive a proper or positive hearing. But by undertaking the *nemawashi*, or preliminary groundwork prior to the meeting, you can be more assured of a positive reaction, or at least that no surprises come out of the discussions.

You or your representatives can ensure that your needs and concerns are addressed and that the solutions proposed fit within your guidelines by maintaining close contact with your Japanese counterparts during the crucial pre-meeting, information-gathering stages of the decision-making process. To make contacts like this, you must work with the same company for years; once inside that company, get to know people at all levels within it. If your contacts are widespread, your product will be positively represented by several contacts and friends with varying levels of seniority and responsibility during this crucial consensus-seeking stage.

WHEN YES MEANS MAYBE

In order to market value-added products in Japan, you need to study and use as many skills and techniques as you can learn from the market. The key to this learning is listening — not to what is said, but to what is meant. The Japanese desire to retain harmony and to save face means you seldom hear the word "no" in conversation. Words and euphemisms like "that would be difficult" and "I will see what I can do" replace "no." Even the word *hai*, which in the dictionary is translated as "yes," can mean not only "yes," but also, "yes, I heard you" or even "yes, I'm paying attention, but I disagree with you." One has to be sure to hear the meaning, not simply the words.

One of the companies I dealt with during my training suddenly had its order levels drop to near zero after gradually building up volumes over a number of years. When the manufacturer asked for the reason, he was told that his product was too expensive. He sought discounts on ingredients, pushed for lower freight rates, and undertook dozens of other cost-cutting measures to lower prices. The customer was never satisfied, however. In desperation, he took a junior staff member from the Japanese company out for dinner and, after a few drinks late in the evening, he said, "I can't seem to get the product just the way you want it. Please help me; tell me what I need to do."

Unexpectedly, the junior employee explained, "My new boss and the president of your competitor's company have been friends for over fifteen years; we have been buying the product only from them ever since my boss took over last year." By understanding the true problem, he was able to work to solve it. He arranged for the new boss to come to Canada to golf, to meet local government officials, to be greeted at a VIP reception, and to be given a plant tour. He generally made every effort to show how highly he valued the business and to become closer friends with the buyer. Gradually the business came back, and a more secure business relationship developed.

MARKET RESEARCH

In the Japanese market, as in other countries, careful research and study of the consumer is necessary to uncover appropriate niches and market opportunities, and to determine the modifications required to enable your product to fill those niches. In familiar cultures, where the culture has developed from a background similar to your own, it is possible to undertake this study yourself; in Asia, it is better to capitalize on the experience of local product specialists whenever possible.

How do your get your product ready for a market like Japan? Generally, it is safe to assume that your product will probably not be acceptable in its current form. As a result, the approach you should take should be one of market development: You should study the market and the consumers, and identify what they want or need, then build your product to fit that need or, if possible, modify an existing product. With specific reference to the food market, for example, you may find that your products do not suit Japanese tastes, that certain additives and food colorings are not permitted, and that package sizes may need to be adjusted, due to space concerns in the home.

One Western beef supplier looking to enter the Japanese market noted the decline in the numbers of trained meat cutters in the work force and the high cost of Japanese labor. From this he deduced that there was an opportunity to custom-cut individual steak portions and deliver them frozen to Japan. He went one step further than most, however, and identified several other significant factors. These included the need for identically shaped steaks that would match the plastic food samples displayed outside the store; garbage disposal problems for waste fat and trim; excessive tariff charges added to high-value beef products; the need for exact thickness specifications to allow standardized cooking times; the demand for tenderness; and, finally, space and handling capacity of the Japanese buyers.

The beef supplier then set out to address these needs. Using the highest quality product, he trimmed away the waste and shaped the product in a specially designed machine that squeezed the partially frozen product into the ideal steak shape. A mechanized cutter assured that all steaks were the same thickness and weight. Strict quality and sanitation controls were introduced to ensure high levels of safety and security for the product. White boxes were used that would show any abuse or damage during transit, and these were made smaller to suit the smaller freezers of his Japanese buyers and to take into account the concerns of the part-time staff who had to lift them. He selected as a partner a large meat wholesaler who could accept full container loads to keep freight and tariff charges as low as possible. His partner's national distribution system was able to deliver this large volume all over Japan in a cost-effective manner.

The beef supplier captured a niche for himself by determining the needs of the market and modifying his product in a steady, dedicated, and patient fashion to meet those needs.

ADAPT, ADAPT, AND ADAPT AGAIN

Once you have determined your target market, you may note some interesting similarities and differences due to both culture and traditional consumption patterns. Differences in culture can cause all kinds of spin-offs that may affect your product development. As an example, for cultural and religious reasons, the Japanese did not eat meat or dairy products for a long period in their history. This means that the market for these products is still developing, unlike in European-based cultures such as the United States, Canada, or Australia, where meat and dairy products have been primary food sources for centuries. As another example, the Japanese still eat fresh whipped cream with their desserts. An artificial cream filling in your product might sell in Canada or Australia but not in Japan, where the consumer demands the real thing.

To take a product you make now and modify it to meet the needs of the Japanese market, you need to be creative and adaptive. In order to develop their products, many Japanese manufacturers work hand in hand with the retailer as well. They float retail products in either regular stores or in shops specializing in trendy, limited production, new releases. By doing this, you are then able to take this direct consumer feedback to your R&D teams and to the production line and make the suggested changes and retry the product in its new form. Whenever possible, use existing mechanisms and resources to assist your own product development efforts.

When manufacturers of beef jerky initially targeted Japan, they found their product required numerous modifications. The taste had to be milder, using less salt, less spice, and no preservatives. Once these changes had been made, the manufacturer hit additional import barriers: The product had to have a lower water activity to be accepted under Japan's strict import sanitation codes. When this maximum water activity level was met, it was noted that while the jerky kept for months in North America's dryer climates, at the much higher humidity levels of the Japanese summer, it mildewed very quickly. Moisture levels had to be further reduced to ensure the product was shelf-stable over the summer months.

Drying it down to lower moisture levels created other problems: The jerky became almost impossible to chew and exploded into fragments when put in the slicer. Achieving the delicate balance of the exact moisture content to fit these challenges on a consistent basis entailed a five-year development program. Samples were repeatedly sent into what to the manufacturer seemed to be a black hole. After five years, however, quality improved and the size of the orders grew at such a phenomenal rate that additional production capacity was required.

The Japanese market is full of success stories, and many of these are about people who challenged the rules and commonly held beliefs in a persistent and dedicated fashion. Experts told the president of McDonald's Japan, "The Japanese will never eat standing up," and "They won't eat beef," especially using disposable cups and wrappers, which was thought to project a cheap image. But he persisted and today McDonald's Japan is one of the most successful chain restaurants in the world, with over 850 outlets across the country. In fact, many young Japanese believe that McDonald's is a Japanese company! McDonald's has also continually adapted their product offerings to reflect Japanese tastes — witness teriyaki burgers.

The Japanese, like people all over the world, have varying tastes and each is an individual. The key to success lies in determining your market niche, and deciding what that niche requires and how to tailor your product to fit those requirements. It is pointless to try and force your existing product on the consumer if it is not what they want. You must remain flexible and innovative. If there is a market for your product, and the buyer wants you to change the formulation, does your corporate pride prevent you from changing it? Do you reply, "My grandfather developed this recipe (or design) and it has been good enough for the North American market for a hundred years," or do you change it to fit the Japanese consumer's needs and tastes? If the Japanese order your potato chips flavored with seaweed, do you import the seaweed and make the product, or give up the order? Japanese consumers did not like the taste of sugar-free Coke, so Coca-Cola added a little sugar to its Diet Coke recipe and created a new brand for the Japanese market called Coke Lite. There is still no regular "Diet Coke" in Japan. Do you sell what the consumer wants to buy or what you want to sell? This is a critical question. You must be market-responsive, adaptable, and flexible to succeed in Japan.

IN-MARKET TESTING

In Japan, many companies use the concept of "in-market testing." Trial releases, early previews, and prototype marketing provide many benefits. The retail testing of partially completed, value-added products earns your company revenues while allowing you to fine-tune your offer with the benefit of early feedback from the consumer. First, release what you think is a finished, acceptable product to the market, then modify it to meet the needs identified by the consumers. For example, if you are developing a five-colored product line, float only the first color prior to spending money on the others. You can then fine-tune the next colors, based upon feedback from the first launch. The product can then be further improved during the second and third generations, and additional options added. This concept of constant improvement may be one of the greatest reasons for the success of Japanese products around the world. Product enhancements are added, not merely as corrections of errors as occurs in the West, but in response to direct customer feedback.

You cannot accept success as your due; it can be short-lived. Be sure to have new products or enhancements in the wings to follow up with after the glow wears off your existing products. These might be variations on the theme or twists on the concept or even new products targeted to the original consumers. Rest assured, if you have a successful product, you will soon have innumerable competitors' look-alike products flooding the market, challenging your brand and market share. These companies have the luxury of reverse engineering and will not have expended the advertising dollars to create the original demand. Successful value-added product development means always seeking to be ahead of your competitors and taking nothing for granted.

OVERCOMING DISTRIBUTION BARRIERS

Flexibility and creativity are essential in establishing a distribution system for your product as well. When Kodak made an aggressive move to enter the Japanese market for disposable box cameras, they were faced with a distribution problem: Their Japanese competitors pressured vending machine operators and retailers not to deal with Kodak. Kodak didn't cry to the U.S. government about unfair business practices. Instead, they very quietly bought vending machines and gradually established retail relationships over time. You might not have the ability to buy your own vending machines, but there are other ways of overcoming the barriers your competitors place in your path.

When Perrier wanted to enter the Japanese market, it did not seek the French government's assistance to pressure its Japanese competitors to distribute Perrier products, which would have required them to sell in direct competition with their own products. Instead, it set up a trading relationship with a whisky company. Perrier knew that whisky companies in Japan specialize in hauling bottled products to restaurants, bars, retailers, and liquor outlets all over Japan. The fact that over 80 percent of the bottled water sold in Japan is consumed as a mix for whisky made this relationship a natural, strategic tie-up.

We have discussed how two large companies worked to overcome some of the barriers presented by the Japanese distribution system. As a smaller company, you must seek to cultivate strong links with niche suppliers who serve the customers to whom you wish to sell, a painstaking task given the intricacy of the Japanese distribution chains — you may find there are as many as twelve layers of middlemen between you and the customer. Understanding the system can leave you feeling that you are unlocking a puzzle. No one wants to reveal all the links of the chain, but in chatting with contacts, you will gradually find out where all the pieces go and uncover the relationships that hold them together.

In some cases, you can then attempt to shorten the distribution chain by selling to the last link, but the simple facts of the time required for delivery, the distances involved, and the demand for smaller, more frequent deliveries required in Japan, may hinder your attempts to achieve this. In fact, it may not always be the best idea — in doing so, you may make enemies out of people who could be useful in the future. Getting products from your plant to the market can be a major challenge, and you may find that you need the myriad small distributors and middlemen with their little trucks to get your product delivered in a timely manner.

Distribution for value-added products differs from distribution of commodities, primarily in terms of volume. Commodities generally require very simple bulk shipping methods, while designer chocolates or hand-carved rocking chairs require more sophisticated packing and shipping systems. Inside Japan, this may be further complicated by the fact that your customers may wish to receive home delivery after they see the display model in the store. You will need storage for your inventory and a mechanism for home delivery. Selecting a partner for distribution may become more critical than marketing the product.

Working within your existing commodity distribution systems may not be the most practical way to handle the market for your value-added products. If your current Japanese partner is a trading house, the trend to the smaller volumes associated with value-added goods is not going to be to his liking; he is used to making his money on the volumes of the commodity business, or how many containers he ships a week. In addition, your traditional commodity customers and distribution partners may have been selected because of their connections with large users of the raw product. Your new value-added venture, however, may require partners in the distribution industry or a noncompetitive sales industry. Thus, you will have to identify new partners and distribution routes for your products and services, but in the long run the changes and diversification they create are better for your firm and its overall corporate survival.

MARKETING TIPS FOR THE JAPANESE MARKET

MASS MARKETING

If your product or service is new or different, you face the challenge of educating the mass market and making it aware of your product and where to buy it, or of focusing on niches that are smaller, and yet large enough to handle in a cost-effective manner. It becomes a question of resources and the marketability of your new product. If your product needs large consumption numbers and you have the corporate resources and commitment to launch nationally, you can create a media-initiated market for it in the short term. If you are limited in promotional resources or production capability, you might wish to focus a little more closely upon niche market opportunities and settle for slower growth. Since advertising in Japan is very expensive, you must judge the value of mass advertising methods and the speed of returns versus the high cost.

If you opt for the mass marketing route, you must be careful to avoid the boom and bust phenomenon. Don't get caught producing a product designed and priced for the top of the trend's market demand cycle. In Japan, just as quickly as a fad starts, it can die. This has occurred with many products in Japan, from the boom in demand for dancing plastic flowers to the recent huge demand for beef small intestine to make a newly popular stew. Many exporters get into trouble when they design and market to the boom, expand production outrageously to meet the new demand, then fall flat when the boom busts and the market reverts to its original size or price range. The savvy marketer aims at the expanded residual market and the more stable prices that remain after the boom, for this is the opportunity in the long term.

PRICING

When introducing a new product, it sometimes works best to take profits later and invest in the relationship initially. By keeping the costs low at the beginning of the marketing relationship, you allow your partner to focus more of his resources on marketing and selling the product and gathering the valuable feedback you need. As you fine-tune your offer, it will be more readily sold at higher prices. One North American manufacturer made a decision to break even on the selling price to his distributor for one year, and to lose money on the project initially by focusing additional promotional funds on its introduction. They added their own dollars to those of their distributors, and opened their books to them to show their commitment and trust. After the product launch and the modifications needed to sell the product for a premium were made, the margins on the product were gradually increased. Both sides cooperated to ensure the product was a success and was suitable for the consumer, before profit margins were taken.

Often products may have small cosmetic or distribution problems that restrict the price levels that can be achieved. The reasons for a customer's reluctance to pay what you consider a fair price may have little or nothing to do with the product itself. Perhaps it is simply that your master carton weight is considered too large, and the staff in the warehouse cannot handle them without back strain; or maybe the boxes are too weak for ocean shipping and, as one box collapses, it crushes others in the container. This may result in ruptured packages and soiling of labels; in Japan, a soiled or slightly worn or torn label means the product must often be discounted over 50 percent and sold in a "damaged goods bin." By offering the product at a very low initial price you will make those first sales that are essential to getting the feedback required, which will then allow you to make the changes needed to get a premium price for your product.

FOREIGN EXCHANGE MANAGEMENT

Since the yen bounces around a fair bit against most Western currencies, you have to be adept at hedging your cash position. When designing products for the value-added market, you need to ensure your returns will be adequate should the exchange rates turn against you, both in accessing raw material for your product and in selling those products for a stable return to the Japanese market.

PACKAGING

Value-added products require sophisticated packaging that is appropriate to the market. Not only the size of the box but its color, shape, quality, and many other factors may reflect positively or negatively upon your product even before it has had a chance to speak for itself. Cultures view different colors differently: While red is lucky in China, in Japan the same color may be viewed as gaudy. Or you may find that you need dividers in your boxes to keep the product from rubbing and damaging labels during the long ocean voyage.

SHIPPING

Another barrier to new product development is the "chicken and egg" problem of shipping less than economical lot sizes. When new product launches are undertaken, most Japanese buyers are very conservative and want to order the minimum lot to minimize their risk of not selling all the product. You must be willing to make less than full batch lots for samples and initial orders, and then to work with your Japanese partners to increase their orders to economical unit sizes. If you insist on a full container load, you may kill the order before it is made. Similarly, you should always quote your initial prices based upon ocean freight rates even though initial orders may go by air. This initial price offer will be used as the basis to determine if your product is competitive with existing products in the market which are probably coming in by ocean. Thus, if you quote based upon air freight rates, your product will look expensive compared to your competitors' products. You may even go so far as to subsidize the first few air freighted loads until your Japanese partner can make up an ocean container load. Let them know you are subsidizing the initial orders to help them get to full container orders. Remind them of this goal, and work with them to get to this larger order as soon as possible. They may also be able to suggest innovative means of lowering costs: They may refer you to other companies in your market with whom they do business in order to consolidate shipments, to source lower-cost raw materials, or to provide cheaper freight rates.

QUALITY CONTROL

The need for service increases because of the complex Japanese distribution system. If there is a flaw in your product, the repercussions will reverberate all along the chain. You need to guarantee, deliver, and supply the just-in-time delivery service to which the Japanese buyer has become accustomed. This system suits Japan for many reasons, but mainly because it cuts down on the costs of inventory and storage space requirements. This makes delivery times, exact order quantities, and deadlines even more demanding. Should an error occur in delivery, such as a mix-up in documentation that delays a cargo, or a box of parts omitted or shipped in error, an entire plant may have to be shut down, an advertising campaign may be wasted, and the reputations or "faces" of all sales and support people along the distribution chain would be damaged.

To export to the Japanese market, you must have exceptional quality control. The cost of freight and duties on products that are rejected when they land is too high to do otherwise. And it is more important to get it right the first time when you have a three-week delivery schedule and you can't quickly or cheaply recall the product or deliver a replacement easily.

WHAT ARE THE REAL KEYS TO SUCCESS?

Patience and persistence combined with flexibility, adaptability, and the ability to listen and learn, to develop connections and long-term business relationships and to work with your partners in Japan for mutual success.

- Have patience. It takes time to research the market, to study the consumer, to identify the trends, and to develop a new product to fit those needs. Give your products time to succeed and be persistent. Take your profits late or on the second product if possible; establish strong roots and distribution links before you extract profits.
- Have persistence. You will be faced with roadblocks at all levels; some will be easy to overcome, others apparently insurmountable. Keep in mind the Japanese proverb: "If you sit upon a rock for three years, it will eventually warm up." If your product is a good one and your partners in Japan see opportunity, they will work to pull it through the system while you push. The end result may not resemble the original product, but you will be doing a good export business regardless.
- Be flexible and adaptable. Listen and make the changes your partners and the market indicate. By bending with the wind the bamboo survives a hurricane, while mighty oaks are blown over. Learn from what is said, what you see and what you experience, and adopt the good and give up the bad or what is no longer relevant.
- Be a partner and an insider. By working closely and tying the success of your firm and products with those of your Japanese partner, you become a mutually supportive team. Become an insider and act as a long-term friend and business partner in all your relations with Japan.
- Expand your business and personal connections and relationships. In Japan, close personal connections in business will smooth the waters of trade and product development. By developing the product in close cooperation with these connections in the marketplace, you can speed the successful introduction of your product or service.
- You must have the corporate desire and will to enter the Japanese market and to stay in that market until you succeed. This corporate will must exist at all levels within your organization over the long term. Certainly, there remain important areas where Japan

still works to limit imports, but more often the main problem is a lack of drive in chasing Japanese business and an unwillingness to adapt products to meet the market's unique needs.

The story of how one U.S. company, JC Foods, succeeded in Japan illustrates all of these points. JC Foods arrived in Japan in 1964 with a novel idea — to market frozen pizza. This was a major challenge for several reasons: There was no consumption of pizzas at that time; customers did not have freezers in which to store the pizzas nor ovens in which to cook them; they did not eat cheese. This did not deter JC Foods, however. The company identified fast food, family-style restaurants as potential clients, and eventually convinced a single chain to try the product. They then modified the product extensively, using a thinner crust and milder cheese, and adding more traditional Japanese toppings such as squid, tuna, and corn.

Gradually the market expanded, but they still could not sell to retail stores. They tried innovative cooking methods to get around the oven problem, recommending that crinkled-up aluminum foil be placed in the bottom of a fry pan, the pizza placed on top, and then covered with a lid to hold in the heat. Admittedly, it didn't work all that well, but sales began to grow. When the toaster oven was introduced in Japan, they reduced the size of their pizzas to fit in a toaster oven and sales took off. The introduction of partially cooked microwave pizzas followed the introduction of microwaves to the market, and again retail sales grew.

In 1986, JC Foods created a new chain of home delivery pizza outlets, introducing the concept of home delivery pizza to compete with Japan's traditional home delivery items: sushi, ramen noodles, and box lunches (bento). They studied consumer concerns with existing home delivery products, specifically that the food arrived cold, it arrived late, and the delivery people were rude and poorly dressed. They developed three-wheeled scooters with heated storage boxes on the back to zoom around traffic jams and guaranteed delivery in less than 30 minutes. They dressed their staff in clean, neatly pressed uniforms and taught them service and customer relations. This new firm, Domino's Japan, has never looked back. JC Foods continues to expand their marketing to other fast food items, to home delivery, retail, and food service products. Just when the chance for success seems bleakest, it is often the time for breakthroughs. Remember, desperation can breed creativity.

I submit to you that your best chance for future success — no, make that survival — is to add value to your exports and to aim for excellence. By moving away from exporting bulk commodity items to more value-added products and production systems, you increase the revenues to your firm. This higher income means more jobs, higher wages, and a more secure future for your company in the global marketplace. By adding value, you distinguish your product from your competitor's, and that insulates you from price competition and creates brand images that foster customer loyalties and steady orders.

I believe the market with the greatest opportunity for these exports in the coming years is, and will continue to be, Japan. Because the Japanese consumer is extremely quality-conscious and the distribution system elaborate and hard to access, success in Japan will mean that the product and the sales team can succeed anywhere. Experience and product development in Japan will train your staff to develop the skills needed to compete in the global marketplace.

You must set yourself the task of delivering world-beating quality to the world's choosiest consumers. By meeting this challenge, you can get the best chunk of their business. It will also give you skills that will distinguish your firm as a world-class, top-quality producer. And as a past president of Unilever Japan said in a speech: "It's tough to be accepted as an insider in Japan — but once you're in, you make an obscene amount of money!"

NOTES

1. *Report of the Canada-Japan Forum 2000, "Partnership Across the Pacific," (December 1992).*
2. *Nigel Austin, "Australia's Beef with the World,"* Marco Polo *(March/April 1992), p. 15.*

CHAPTER TEN

How to Be a Successful Supplier into the Japanese Market

CATHARINE G. JOHNSTON
AND MARK J. DANIEL

第十章

There can be no doubt that Japan is now a world leader in manufacturing in terms of producing high-quality products that are sold in all global markets. Western companies, faced with these Japanese competitors, are increasingly called upon to match their high standards. The Conference Board of Canada, in cooperation with Industry, Science & Technology Canada, has undertaken a series of study tours to examine how the best-managed companies in the world are implementing total quality processes in their own operations. They have now completed eight such tours, three of which have come to Japan. Drawing on what they have observed in top Japanese companies, Catharine Johnston, principal research associate in total quality management, and Dr. Mark Daniel, vice-president of management research, discuss the factors affecting Japanese customer-supplier relationships, and what Western companies need to achieve if they are to become suppliers into the Japanese market.

Increased competition at home and abroad, coupled with worldwide overcapacity, has forced many North American companies to rethink their competitive strategies. In determining what is required to be successful, many have realized that it no longer suffices to be at the forefront of their industry at home. Globalization of commerce has fostered more and better competitors, hungry for both our export and our domestic markets. To prosper, organizations must meet world-class standards in terms of product quality, delivery, and cost.

Recognizing the need to be internationally competitive, many North American companies have begun to explore Japan as a potential market. The Japanese market is one of the toughest to infiltrate, however, and so the decision to compete there — either by exporting or through direct investment — requires a great deal of research and up-front analysis.

Several important considerations may convince Western companies to enter the Japanese market. First, Japan is one of the wealthiest markets in the world, one that many producers cannot afford to leave to their competitors; the potential long-term financial benefits of supplying into this market are immense. Second, affiliation with Japanese companies as a supplier or partner will enable a company to learn valuable techniques about the quality systems that have propelled them to a leadership position in many markets, particularly in manufactured goods. Third, the ability to successfully supply Japanese customers is an excellent credential for entering other international markets: Japanese standards for manufactured goods are among the highest in the world. And finally, many Western companies now have to compete with those high-quality Japanese goods in their own domestic markets and thus cannot afford to ignore the standards they are setting.

For those who have decided to compete directly in the Japanese domestic market, it is necessary to understand what a Japanese customer will expect from a supplier. The stakes are high, and the competition to supply Japanese companies and consumers is fierce. It is, therefore, crucial to understand how Japanese prefer to do business and what in their eyes defines a superior supplier.

Cultural differences and trade barriers are often given as the primary reasons for the difficulties North American organizations experience in breaking into the Japanese market. Although both have an impact on buying decisions, the key reason for the lack of North American success in Japan is an unfamiliarity with the expectations of the Japanese customer — be it the final consumer or an intermediate customer. Potential suppliers must understand and practice the Japanese philosophy of customer satisfaction and embrace many of the organizational systems necessary to ensure the alignment of resources to achieve the goal of satisfying Japanese customers.

Japanese customers are extremely demanding of their suppliers. As the Japanese market has traditionally been relatively closed to non-Japanese companies, what Japanese customers would require of Western suppliers can be determined by studying their relationships with their Japanese suppliers, as well as with their customers. Although there are many things to be learned about working with the Japanese, this chapter will focus on four: What is the nature of business partnerships in Japan? How can you determine what they as a customer want? What are their demands in terms of continuous improvement? How can you demonstrate capability by the use of facts?

PARTNERSHIPS WITH JAPANESE CUSTOMERS

Japanese companies have long recognized that they can succeed only if their suppliers are also successful and vice versa. They believe that "garbage in equals garbage out" and therefore critically analyze their choice of suppliers. Toyota's motto regarding its suppliers is "coexistence and mutual prosperity," as well as "mutual trust." They believe that if their suppliers cannot make a fair profit, then in the long run they will not be successful.

There exists a pact between suppliers and their customers acknowledging that they are working together and so must help each other succeed. Leading companies form alliances with vendors and distributors to ensure the joint continuous improvement of what they offer customers. Suppliers are often selected not on the basis of bids, but rather on the basis of past relationships and a proven record of performance. This "win-win" partnership is relatively foreign to many North American companies, who still pit one supplier against the other, frequently making price the determining factor.

Supplier/customer relationships have emerged quite differently in Japan than in North America. In the automobile industry, for example, Japanese auto producers often outsource from 70 to 75 percent of their supplies, retaining only 25 to 30 percent within the company. (In North America, by contrast, producers tend to manufacture the majority of their supplies in-house.) Out of necessity, the Japanese have had to form strong alliances with their suppliers. Hence, although suppliers and customers may be legally independent, they have formed extremely tight alliances to ensure that they are working together for a common goal. Many companies own shares in their suppliers' companies and vice versa. The extreme form of this type of association are the powerful *keiretsu*, each of which are made up of perhaps twenty major companies. These groupings often include a bank, an insurance company, and a trading company, and are also held together by interlocking equity structures.

In Japan, companies are frequently part of a much larger entity which, in its entirety, is completely integrated, sometimes as far back as the raw material stage up to and including the marketing and sales of the manufactured product, and financing. All of the smaller companies come under the umbrella of a common goal; therefore, the selection of suppliers and the relationships with them are very different than they are in North America.

Unless suppliers are considered "part of the family," Japanese companies claim, they will be part of the problem and not the solution. Although they strongly resist single sourcing, they have considerably fewer suppliers for any one product than is the case in North America. For those products that they do outsource, some estimates say that North American companies have, on average, ten times too many suppliers. Having used the Japanese style of total quality as their template, Florida Power & Light reduced its supplier base by 30 to 40 percent, and after their study of the Japanese system, Milliken reduced its supplier base by 75 percent.

The Japanese believe that they cannot successfully develop close relationships with many different suppliers, and so consciously keep their numbers low. Companies like Komatsu actively work with a few key suppliers in order to bring them into their "family." They explain that they cannot work with a large number of suppliers and still count on the quality of the suppliers' processes and their commitment to Komatsu's end goal of satisfying customers. The integration of effort required to consistently improve the offering to the public requires a close working relationship on the part of everyone involved.

In 1976, to build its partnership with suppliers, Komatsu designed an extremely comprehensive program to ensure that its subcontractors could provide quality parts and service at the price required. It established a Quality Control Award for its subcontractors, who supply approximately 70 percent of the parts it uses. Komatsu stipulates that if a company wants to provide parts to them, it must first apply to be a candidate for the award. If the plant manager from Komatsu decides that the initial application should be considered, a year of counseling begins. During this transition period, technical people from the Komatsu plant work with the potential supplier to ensure that its processes are under control and that its workers have all the necessary skills to solve problems and improve processes.

After one year, if the candidate has satisfied the Komatsu representatives, there is a six-month practice period, at the end of which the vendor is evaluated. The final exam includes a field examination, discussions with its supervisors, and assurance that QC (quality control) circles are up and running, and the company and its employees are enthusiastic about them. After the examination, regardless of the results, the examiners provide a written report for the supplier which highlights the good aspects, and strives to give the company guidance on how it can continue to improve.[1] Only after considerable investment by both parties can a long-term relationship be forged.

There is a regular movement of employees between suppliers and their customers. Frequently, as in the Komatsu example, customers will spend considerable time at their suppliers' companies. One company in Canada was amazed when a potential Japanese customer asked to post a full-time employee in their plant even before the customer had agreed to buy their product. The reverse is also true. Many suppliers in Japan place full-time staff at a customer's operation. In order to stay on top of how a product is functioning and how best it can be improved, both the supplier and customer are anxious to form close, ongoing relationships. At Fuji Xerox, for example, a supplier's employees would blend in completely if not for their uniforms, which are a different color.

Toyota also works very closely with its suppliers and dealers. In 1966, it formed what is now a twelve-company QC liaison with some of its suppliers. The aim of this association is to promote long-term coexistence and mutual prosperity by aggressively promoting study between Toyota staff and the staffs of member companies. There are three subcommittees: quality, cost, and safety.

The liaison promotes research activities that upgrade the level of the member companies in all these areas, sponsors an annual QC convention, has meetings to study QC, and provides training courses and assistance to fellow members. They also have a Toyota Quality Control Award for their suppliers to encourage their self-improvement and a Toyota TQC Prize for dealers. Both suppliers and their customers make considerable investments in these kinds of relationships. Once such a relationship is established, the barriers to change are daunting. Hence, relations tend to be of long duration, and it is extremely difficult, especially for a neophyte to Japan, to penetrate these bonds.

These customer/supplier relations are the backbone of doing business in Japan. They are extremely time-consuming to develop and maintain but the paybacks, if successful, are immense and long term. Many North American newcomers to Japan talk about how long it takes to negotiate a contract. According to the Japanese, the signing of a contract is secondary to the establishment of an enduring relationship based on mutual trust. The difficulties of forming this relationship are compounded when the potential supplier does not speak Japanese. The obligatory socializing takes longer and requires the involvement of the most senior people in the company.

Understanding the nature of the partnerships the Japanese desire is one thing; being able to fill the requirements is quite another. Those wanting to tackle this market must make a conscious commitment to establishing long-term relationships with Japanese companies, and to investing considerable time in doing so.

WHAT JAPANESE CUSTOMERS WANT

To understand what Japanese customers want, it is instructive to understand how the best Japanese companies view their role in society and in serving their own customers. Many Japanese companies profess that the reason organizations exist is to address human concerns. Their continued existence and success, they feel, depends upon how well they meet evolving customer concerns and expectations. They expect the same from their suppliers. Often, they do not define themselves as manufacturing a product (such as cars) but as addressing the needs and concerns of people (for personal transportation). Mr. Yamada, the general manager of the TQC Promotion Department at Toyota, admits that for many years they found themselves in the trap of producing cars rather than giving customers what they wanted.

The former president of Fuji Xerox, Yotaro Kobayashi has stated, "Pursuing efficiency and convenience alone is not sufficient. We must go further and ask ourselves what we can do to make work more humanistic, or better fit for humans." [2]

A number of Japanese companies start their planning by looking at how society might evolve over the next ten to thirty years; what people's needs would be in such an environment; and finally, how they might serve those future needs. Consistently meeting customer expectations is the standard for the Deming Prize-winning companies in Japan. Long-term survival and profits depend upon being better than the competition at understanding and satisfying customer concerns. Matsushita exemplifies the rigorous efforts companies expend to understand their customer concerns and in turn this is what they expect from their suppliers. Their lifestyle research includes answering fundamental value-based questions such as: What is the meaning of products in our society? How could we better use them? And how will they give value to our lives?

In analyzing its customers' concerns, Komatsu, which believes that one of its main businesses is to address the food and shelter concerns of society, foresaw that the demand for its traditional products that scoop and move earth would decline. However, its executives also foresaw a world environment, especially in their major market (Japan), in which there would be overpopulation and land and housing shortages. In this environment, they believe, there will be a need for more underground transit and dwellings. Komatsu is now becoming a leader in underground tunneling technology.

The idea of consistently meeting customer expectations is deceptively simple, but it has taken on a new significance in an increasingly global business environment. The first realization is that quality must be defined by the customer, not by the supplier. Although this appears to be an obvious truth, many companies in North America admit to having chased after targets and measures determined internally, only to have to do an about-face when they finally consulted their customers. Market research was often focused on the product to be sold and not on customers' needs.

Komatsu and Toyota both believe that companies need to practice the "market in" approach — where the demands of their customers drive their processes. They contrast this to a "product out" philosophy, where the goal is to produce products and then sell them in the market. To ensure that their products address the needs of their customers, these organizations spend a good deal of effort translating the customers' requirements into the "language" the people in the company can understand, and then determining which of their processes impacts these needs.

Many of the organizations visited in Japan are developing sophisticated systems to determine their customers' requirements. Methods range from extensive written and telephone surveys to innovative personal contacts. Matsushita, an outstanding example, analyzes its customers' needs with absolute rigor and expects the same from its suppliers. Matsushita has a network system, called QUICS, to collect data on customers and product performance, and ensures that the information is available to everyone in the company. This databank can be accessed directly from personal computers on the network. Matsushita has one thousand people working worldwide on their quality reporting system. This system is designed to monitor the competitive environment, including end-users and retailers of its products, in order to be constantly informed of their opinions.

The Japanese are intolerant of defects and expect these same high standards from their suppliers. Japanese customers, however, do not define total quality only in terms of product. To them, quality is a three-legged stool made up of product quality, price, and delivery (or service). As a supplier into Japan, one must be aware of this and provide a well-balanced offering on all three legs. That the Japanese are uncompromising in quality standards is legendary, and their demand for product quality extends even to the smallest details, such as labeling and packaging.

In an introductory quality control textbook at Matsushita, there is an interview with Arataro Takahashi, a former executive vice-president with the company. Takahashi tells of his experience with a joint venture in the Philippines. On a visit to the factory to view the first products manufactured under the joint venture, he found the finish of the cabinets to be below Matsushita's quality standards. Neither repairs nor retouching would solve the problem. After paying the full amount due, he had the poorly finished cabinets destroyed in front of the president of the supplying company and a number of the joint-venture factory workers. In this way, the commitment of Matsushita to provide only first-class products was effectively brought home.

Japanese firms do not want to incur the costs of inspecting incoming supplies and so must be confident that their suppliers are capable of delivering quality products. They also do not want to keep large, costly inventories on hand and so need to know that the delivery process of their suppliers is equally error free. When the supplies are needed, they will be there — not after and not before. "Just-in-time" delivery of supplies has become such a way of doing business in Japan that the already serious problem of traffic congestion has been exacerbated by the large number of small vehicles supplying goods on a daily basis, or even several times per day.

To the Japanese Deming Prize-winning companies,[3] total quality is about understanding the customers' fundamental concerns and providing products and services that will delight them by addressing those concerns. A good example is Toyota. Only three months after the Lexus was introduced in the United States, Toyota announced a recall of all eight thousand cars sold, on the basis of just two minor incidents. Not only did Toyota check all eight thousand vehicles, but Lexus owners did not even suffer the inconvenience of a trip to their dealer. Within a few weeks, their cars were picked up, fixed, and returned to them. To serve ten Lexus owners in Grand Rapids, Michigan, technicians were flown in from suburban Detroit, 240 kilometers away. They rented garage space, picked up the cars, serviced them, cleaned them, and returned the cars to their owners.

At Toyota in Japan, 70 percent of all the cars sold are sold door-to-door. This personalized selling has helped them gain the first-place market share position in Japan, at 43 percent, and also provides a vital and continuous link with both existing and potential customers. As salespeople visit house after house, they collect valuable intelligence as to what the customers want, like, use, and need, as well as information on the changing economic and family situations of their customers.

When bidding for a contract, Japanese suppliers spend a great deal of time analyzing the job and all the possible scenarios before they bid. Their bids, therefore, tend to be quite accurate and well defined, with little variation once the contract is up and running. This is in keeping with their basic philosophy of doing things right the first time. Japanese customers expect their suppliers to take the time and effort to ensure that their needs are understood and the suppliers processes are capable of consistently meeting those needs before agreeing to any contract.

A COMMITMENT TO CONTINUOUS IMPROVEMENT

Before agreeing to accept a supplier and investing considerable time and resources in them, the customer wants to be assured that the company has potential for the future. Japanese customers gauge a supplier's potential for success beyond the basic financial stability and capacity parameters common in North America. That a supplier can produce a single batch of goods to specification is not enough. They need to ascertain a supplier's capability to consistently meet their requirements. To do this, the customer will not only inspect a supplier's production line and servicing departments, but will also examine how the company is managed. They are looking to establish a long-term relationship and want to know if the management system is strong enough to withstand economic hard times. They will want to ensure that inside the supplier's company everyone is working on continuous process improvement. They want to be assured that the improvement of cross-functional processes leading up to the customers is a priority of senior management, not just the management of the traditional functional silos such as manufacturing, accounting, and marketing.

Japanese companies expect their suppliers to continuously improve the quality of their offering in terms of product, quality, and price. The commitment they seek is more than just words. They expect their suppliers to have structures and systems in place to ensure that their key processes are being constantly questioned, analyzed, strengthened, and improved. Moreover, they expect their suppliers to assist them in their own improvement efforts. This sharing of improvement efforts is facilitated in Japan by a common approach — the Plan, Do, Check, Act cycle (PDCA).[4] To be able to satisfy Japanese customers' concerns for continuous improvement, it will be necessary for North American suppliers to at least understand their system and, even better, be able to apply it within their own organizations.

The PDCA cycle, which was introduced into Japan by Dr. Deming, is one of the basic tenets of their continuous improvement initiative. This is a standard series of steps used by all employees throughout leading organizations in Japan to continuously improve all the processes that either directly or indirectly affect customer satisfaction. According to the Union of Japanese Scientists and Engineers, more than half of Japan's company presidents claim that the cornerstone of total quality in their company is that each and every employee uses this systematic methodology for continuous improvement. Its use enables employees to systematically, logically, and methodically analyze opportunities for improvement, determine root causes of problems, explore potential solutions for improvement, verify the outcomes, and improve and standardize processes.

Senior management also uses the PDCA cycle to select the key objectives on which the organization needs to achieve breakthrough improvements. This ensures that the organization's resources and efforts are aligned with these objectives, and then checks their progress. Senior executives in Japan are fully conversant with the PDCA cycle and in talking amongst themselves, with employees, and with customers and suppliers, the pervasive use of this disciplined framework is evident.

Despite the level of excellence in the companies visited, management was modest about what they had achieved, explaining that the improvement journey is endless and that the challenge to continuously improve is a perpetual success requirement. This discontent with the status quo and a disciplined company-wide approach to improvement are qualities they also demand of their suppliers.

DEMONSTRATING CAPABILITY WITH FACTS

The Japanese are dedicated to the use of measurements and demand the same from their suppliers. They want their suppliers to prove to them, with data, that their processes are capable of producing error-free work every time. Some organizations will expect to see their supplier's control charts along with the shipment.

For the Japanese, accurate and thorough analysis resulting in precise facts is key. Every decision, whether at the policy-making level, in a functional team, or by an individual employee, must be based on substantiated facts in order to be sound and therefore accepted. The foundation of continuous improvement demands that every step taken be based on facts.

The Deming Prize winners are masters of managing by fact. Employees at all levels are expected to present examples of improvement efforts and projects and, at each step, to substantiate their findings with facts that are the result of rigorous analysis. When customers ask for measures of process capability, they expect to see numbers based on statistical facts demonstrating that all the processes for both product quality and service are capable. Anecdotal evidence is not acceptable.

All employees are expected to be capable of collecting the relevant facts (senior staff as well) and analyzing the situation to discover the root cause of an issue. Fact-based decision-making tools such as storyboards are evident throughout the company. Data are displayed in charts on the wall, and are always up-to-date. These companies use facts in discussion with their customers and expect the same from their suppliers. Daihen Corporation, a Deming Prize winner, demands that external suppliers provide them with QC process charts, manufacturing standards, and test reports for all goods supplied. At NEC Kansai, the executive vice-president uses extremely detailed charts to explain what his customers want both inside and outside the organization; there is no guessing or surmising.

There is no doubt that substantial cultural differences exist between Japan and North America. Japanese tend to avoid confrontation, while North Americans relish independent and divergent thinking. It is rare for the Japanese to say "no" or directly refuse to do something. In contrast, in the West we frequently exercise our right of refusal. Teamwork, an established mode of operation in Japanese culture, is weak in many North American organizations. Hierarchy in Japan is well defined and rigid, and employees abide by its often unspoken rules. The presence of women in senior management positions is even more rare in Japan than in North America. It is of course impossible, nor is it the purpose of a business relationship, to alter these differences, but they may be overcome in a successful customer/supplier relationship.

Many non-Japanese businesspeople believe that the key to a successful business relationship with the Japanese is to present themselves as experts in doing business "the Japanese way." This approach is misguided. A newcomer cannot hope to successfully pick up the extremely subtle nuances of doing business "the Japanese way." The Japanese are sophisticated international businesspeople, knowledgeable about Western business practices. They do not expect their non-Japanese suppliers to do business as they do, only to be aware of and respect their customs.

Fortunately, these differences in culture should not preclude any non-Japanese company from doing business in Japan. There are numerous examples of North American suppliers to prove this, both small and large companies. The Japanese have superb business minds which require being, first and foremost, pragmatic. They want to do business with the people who can best supply their needs. Far more important than these cultural differences are the willingness and ability of the supplier to satisfy Japanese customers better than their other suppliers. North American suppliers need to understand that doing business with the Japanese is not about signing contracts, but building long-term relationships based on trust and a belief in mutual success. To establish these partnerships requires knowing the customer's concerns now and for the future; having a philosophy of continuous improvement and being able to demonstrate the capability to achieve it; and making business decisions based on solid facts.

Finally, the Japanese are constantly on the lookout for ways of doing things better, improving on what they already have. One of the aspects of their management system that many willingly admit needs to be improved is their ability to foster independent and creative thinking. According to Mr. Isomura, a senior managing director at Toyota and a member of the board, "If we do nothing but work overtime, we won't be able to produce broad-minded designs and we won't be able to inspire our employees and our business partners." He believes that they need to change their management system in order to foster innovation. The Japanese are seeking ways to achieve this change in their organizations and if they think you can bring this know-how to a partnership, the prospects of doing business together will be enhanced.

NOTES

1. *Kaoru Shimoyamada, "The President's Audit: QC Audits at Komatsu,"* Quality Progress *(January 1987).*
2. *Fuji Xerox instruction booklet.*
3. *Dr. Edwards Deming was one of the world's best-known quality gurus. Since the 1950s, he worked extensively with Japanese manufacturing companies, assisting them in the development of their quality systems. To honor his outstanding contribution, they named their national quality award — one of the most prestigious in the world — after him.*
4. *Plan, Do, Check, Act is the standard methodology used by all Deming Prize-winning companies to control and improve quality throughout their organizations.*

CHAPTER ELEVEN

Demystifying the Japanese Business Environment

JOHN M. POWLES

To the uninitiated, Japanese business practices may appear complex and obscure. Many Western visitors to Japan, overwhelmed by the differences they perceive, quickly become frustrated and dismiss the market as impenetrable. Often, Western attitudes are just as confusing to their Japanese counterparts. The perils inherent in failing to understand and adapt to Japanese business customs can range from simple acts of unintentional rudeness to a collapse in negotiations. In this chapter, John Powles, the manager for Asia of the Council of Forest Industries Canada, sets out some basic rules that will assist you to operate successfully in Japan.

It is hard to imagine a product or service that cannot be sold in Japan today, providing that it is cost-competitive, of suitable quality, and meets local consumer needs. The following comments were directed to a Canadian audience but, with some minor variations, the same can be said of the current marketing efforts by most Western nations in Japan.

> There are many areas of opportunity, including food, software, environmental and other technology, and housing components and complete homes. In fact, almost any sector where products can be custom-designed to fit Japanese needs will find a market. . . . It is vital to Canada's future that more Canadian businesses become aggressive in pursuing those markets which are now open in Japan. Canadian business has been too slow to capitalize on the opportunities. Part of the reason is that previous Japanese restrictions on

> imports have entrenched in Canadian minds the image of a market that is difficult or impossible to penetrate. However, many of these restrictions have largely been loosened or removed, although the perception of an earlier time remains.[1]

The mystique of the Japanese economic success, combined with the image of a closed market, continues to inhibit trade relations with Japan today. Following the Second World War, Japan refined and reapplied elements of the same system which had worked in rapidly industrializing the country in the early twentieth century. Strong central planning and a system of targeted industrial sectors provided for rapid redevelopment of the Japanese industrial base. Initial efforts focused on steel and shipbuilding, automobiles, and, later, electronics. With a few notable postwar exceptions (Sony and Honda being perhaps the best known overseas), many of these industrial groupings were resurrections of the prewar *zaibatsu*.[2]

Japanese industry was allowed to incubate within a protected home market. Long-term planning was encouraged and made possible by programs which favored reinvestment in plant and new technologies, research and development, and technology diffusion.[3] Prices of many goods were (and still are, in some cases) centrally determined. The Japanese government maintained price stabilization through public corporations responsible for controlling the fluctuating prices of raw materials; these corporations stockpiled resources when prices were low and released goods onto the market when prices climbed. Although most market control mechanisms have now been dismantled, some "closed door thinking" remains. With a little effort, it is usually possible to work through these "barriers" today. Many Japanese are not aware of their own market inefficiencies or barriers; the other side of the coin is that many of these same barriers are also effective at preventing intra-Japanese competition, keeping domestic consumer prices high.

The following chapter will give you some pointers in penetrating the "mystery" of Japanese corporate culture. When all is said and done, however, acting naturally and in a way that will leave you comfortable with your own approach is always the best bet.

Rough diamond, or cut and polished — if you act professionally, you should meet with success.

AN INTRODUCTION TO JAPAN

Japanese society is organized as hierarchical communities, posing particular challenges to "outsiders." As a foreigner, you do not face insurmountably greater obstacles in penetrating many of the "communities" of Japan than does a Japanese "from outside the group."

The Japanese corporate world thrives on a system of personal contacts. Japanese business begins with an introduction. The quality of your introduction will have far-reaching impact on the access you achieve in Japan. The best introduction will come from a businessperson with whom you have worked and who has contacts in the Japanese commercial arena. Possibilities include Japanese trading company representatives in your area, banks,[4] the Japan External Trade Organization (JETRO)[5] offices, industry and export associations, boards of trade and chambers of commerce, government agencies,[6] and universities.[7] You may even find Japanese contacts willing to introduce you to competitors. While you may question the impact or value of such an introduction, if this is a first trip, take advantage of whatever leads you get. Do try and get a written copy of your introductions to carry with you. The costs of traveling to and within Japan are substantial, and all efforts should be made to ensure access to the maximum number of contacts before departure.

Having said all this, there is the exception which proves the rule. If you have identified a potential customer but have been unable to arrange a contact, make a cold call. You may arrive on a quiet day and find exactly the person with whom you need to speak. Japanese will tolerate "cold calling" from a foreigner more readily than they would from another Japanese.

CONTACTS AND ASSISTANCE

We have mentioned some of the organizations that can be helpful in arranging introductions to Japanese business. Most levels of government have programs to encourage exports or inbound investment, and you may be able to take advantage of one of these. Besides assistance with business contacts, there are government-led sectoral missions to Japan; for example, JETRO has a program for inviting potential exporters to tour Japan. These programs may not be targeted exactly as you would like, but they do offer a low-cost opportunity to scout out the territory prior to making a commitment. The contacts made will also be a base from which to build your Japanese network.

Trade shows are another avenue, but a word of warning here — large Japanese trade shows tend to be upscale affairs catering as much to a consumer audience as to the trade. Think of them in the context of a North American consumer auto or electronics show. The costs of appearing competitive can be high. Exceptions to this are the small-sector specific shows staged by JETRO and cooperating trade associations, and regional shows hosted by prefectural or city trade associations.

I once found myself manning an industry information booth at one of Japan's largest building products shows. Because the booth was sponsored by the Canadian government, it was given a prestigious location facing the entrance to the show. The booth location was great, but our decoration was "minimalist." I had a few color pictures to put up, odd windows, doors, and kitchen cabinet doors as product samples, and a big "Canada" sign. Immediately opposite was a major Japanese company showing its latest electrically elevated kitchen counter. The counter and surrounding area were decorated with young, bikini-clad attendants. On another side was a Japanese importer of Italian marble with three full-scale "designer rooms." This experience continues to color my view of Japanese trade shows. If you can't be competitive, there are more effective ways to use your limited resources.

If you have been approached by a Japanese buyer and want information on the *bona fides* of the Japanese company, just remember that many consumer services that exist in your own country also exist in Japan. The government agencies noted above may be able to help, but corporate credit-rating organizations such as Dun & Bradstreet also operate in Japan. You can be quite sure that a Japanese buyer will have checked your credentials thoroughly before making an approach. It only makes sense for you to do the same.

While we may be getting ahead of ourselves, another point is to ensure that you (or your product) are not being solicited as a way of keeping you out of the market. Make sure that any exclusive sales or licensing arrangements that you enter into contain performance clauses and sunset provisions. Sad to say, there are some excellent products which will never be sold in Japan because of exclusive rights granted to an agent who turned out to be incapable[8] of or unwilling[9] to market the product.

PLANNING YOUR VISIT

Don't come to Japan without a program and detailed schedule. At worst, you may find yourself arriving in the middle of an extended public holiday — and Japan is an expensive place to vacation.

"Golden Week" is still the most common trap. Beginning in late April (the first official holiday is April 29, but it may start earlier depending on where the 29th falls in the week), this holiday period extends through as late as May 8th. Many offices close or operate with skeleton staff. The interurban transportation system operates at near gridlock. Another period to avoid is from mid- to late August. This *Obon* holiday begins as early as August 12, and many business executives and government officials plan overseas trips during this period which extend through the end of the month. The period from mid-December to mid-January focuses on "year-end" parties; breaks for the New Year's holiday of three to five working days; then opens the year with a series of company New Year's parties. The New Year's period is the most complete holiday in Japan; it can even be difficult to purchase basic necessities around this time. Many Japanese public holidays fall in mid-week, so it is best to consult a Japanese calendar as a first step in planning your trip.

When preparing your program, keep in mind that Japanese meetings take place in a leisurely atmosphere (more on this later) and it will not be possible to accomplish as much in a day as you might in the West. The efficient subway and train system will protect you from fighting through time-consuming and unpredictable traffic snarls in a taxi. If you are traveling on your own to appointments, ask someone at the front desk of your hotel to write out instructions for the taxi or train in Japanese. Allow a little extra time to find your way. Street addresses as we know them are a relatively recent phenomenon in Japan, so a map, faxed from your contact, is a good idea. You may be able to do more in some smaller cities, but three to four appointments a day is the rule of thumb in major centers. It is considered very bad manners to show up late for an appointment, particularly to a first meeting. A last-minute phone call to reconfirm meeting times (or to adjust the time, if necessary) saves traveling across the city for a non-event.

Finally, a word about luggage and clothing. Japanese have a standard business wardrobe consisting of dark blue or gray suits. Sports coats are not common although a blazer and slacks are acceptable. Women should also dress conservatively and not wear a lot of jewelry. You are unlikely to need more than a medium-weight coat in winter. Summers are sticky. If you are going to be traveling around, keep your luggage as simple and light as possible because you will run into stairs everywhere you go. Anyone with restricted mobility will have to be extra careful in planning.

THOSE LITTLE DETAILS

If you forget a toothbrush or your favorite perfume, don't worry; you can buy them in Japan. But there are a few items you should make sure you have. Let us discuss the all-important business card first. You can never have too many business cards in Japan; plan on a minimum of two hundred, and more if you will be staying over two weeks. Adding Japanese on the reverse side of the card is a welcome courtesy, just be careful with the translation. Only your name, title, and company name need to be translated. You may wish to add elements of the address in Japanese, but a letter addressed to you in Japanese would never get delivered in the West, so why not keep it simple.

Titles should be descriptive: not just vice-president, director, manager, or whatever, but they should include some aspect of your responsibilities, such as "exports," "widget production and quality control, Behemoth Factory," etc. The Japanese often joke that everyone is a vice-president when they visit Japan. The nature of your responsibilities will often impress more than your title. Besides, in Japan lofty titles are often accorded those who have been elevated above the working level, or in the worst cases, put out to pasture. A government minister arrived recently with a card describing himself as an "Honorable Minister of Forest Reproduction." The Japanese never add honorifics; the importance of the person will usually be evident from the quality of paper and the type of calligraphy used for the name. Even this can be deceiving, though, as it is considered better to err on the side of humility.

Get a professional to do the translation, then get a second opinion. Too many people are still showing up in Japan with business materials obviously translated by amateurs. Look at this as part of your initial sales pitch, and imagine what your reaction would be to a presentation in fractured English (remember those early Japanese instruction manuals and how funny they were?). More on this later.

While you are getting your business cards (*meishi*) translated, consider getting a corporate profile done in Japanese. One page, to be inserted into your English documents, will go a long way toward showing your seriousness. Ideally, this will include an organization chart which shows where you fit in. A videotape introduction or photo album which you can leave with the customer is also a good tool. Japanese video (NTSC / VHS) is compatible with North American systems.

And lest we forget those personal essentials, be sure to carry any prescription drug requirements with you; the product may not be for sale in Japan. Shoes should be easily removable, presentable (they go on display when you take them off!) and, just for the heck of it, buy some new socks. You will probably have to take your shoes off on occasion, and that hole in your sock could be an embarrassment.

As for money, the key point to remember is that Japan is still a cash society. If you will be doing most of your business within first-class hotels and large restaurants, credit cards will suffice. Step outside and you will find that cash evaporates at an alarming rate. International currency fluctuations make it a mug's game to predict what currency to carry, but a good rule is to limit changing from one currency to another any more than necessary. Virtually all hotels offer foreign exchange desks which give the bank rate. The banks at the airport do not, so change only what you will need to get to your hotel. Traveler's checks, even in yen, can be changed only at hotels, banks, and at some "tax free" stores, so plan your cash needs by the day.

THE JAPANESE MEETING AND WHAT COMES FIRST

Upon arrival, announce yourself by presenting your business card and indicating whom you want to see. Remove your coat before entering the meeting room, and have your business cards ready. You should be introduced to the most senior person first, although a large company may send out a "foreign handler" to get you organized.[10] When all of the introductions and card exchanges have been completed, you will be asked to sit. You will usually be directed to the appropriate place, but if in doubt, ask.

A word on handling business cards and your counterpart's corporate literature. Treat both with respect. Hand out and receive business cards individually; be careful not to shuffle or crumple them. If the business cards are in Japanese only, have someone in your delegation or the interpreter make English notations of the key information on the card. This allows you to refer to it during the meeting. While it is not offensive to write translations on a business card, keep your meeting notes somewhere else. The business card is the main indication of the stature of the person within the company hierarchy. It will be a key ingredient in assessing how seriously you or your proposal are being considered. At the end of a meeting, gather all of the business cards and literature you have received and take them with you. Don't leave anything in the meeting room, even if you don't want it. Take it back to your hotel and dispose of it there.

Japanese meetings are heavy on ceremony and may seem short on content. Be patient. The main purpose of a first meeting is to establish a base from which to arrange future get-togethers. Always start a meeting with pleasantries about the weather, how appreciative you are of this chance for a meeting, how much you have heard about the company you are visiting, and so on. Like people everywhere, Japanese enjoy being flattered. As "corporate persons," good things said about a company reflect well on the individuals concerned. Avoid focusing unnecessary attention on a single individual, which may make them uncomfortable.

NEMAWASHI, "LAYING THE GROUNDWORK"

A Japanese meeting is not a decision-making forum. It can be an information-gathering exercise or, often, it will take place to air a consensus decision. Don't approach a meeting expecting to deliver information and have it acted upon immediately. You will be either frustrated or confused.

What comes before a "decision-making meeting" is key. Begin with a series of courtesy calls (*nemawashi* in Japanese), with individuals as high up as you can get on the corporate ladder. Following a reciprocal round of pleasantries, state clearly the purpose of your visit by introducing the history of your company, its expertise, and why you think this will be of interest to your Japanese contact. You may want to go as far as laying out the objective of your trip, as in: "I plan to spend two weeks in Japan visiting ten different manufacturers in Sapporo, Nagoya, and Hiroshima, and hope to return to my country with a clear expression of interest from two parties. You, Mr. Suzuki, are the fifth visit I have made, and I am very encouraged by the response I have received." Leave it to Suzuki to carry the discussion any further. He may do so on the spot or may indicate the possibility of a follow-up meeting. Leave when you think you have achieved as much as you can, but allow a minimum of thirty minutes to one hour per call. Don't assume that silences mean the end of a discussion, and don't appear rushed. You may want to use your interpreter to signal you when things seem to be winding down. If so, make sure that they know that this is expected of them.

Let us assume that all has gone well and a follow-up meeting is agreed to. Make certain that you know with whom you will be dealing. Delegate working-level meetings to subordinate staff who can discuss substantive information with their Japanese counterparts. Senior staff in Japanese companies function more as advisors than as executives. They will guide the process but they will rarely dictate a course of action, at least not openly. Don't try to drive the process to conform to your own terms. You may force a senior person to appear "executive," but it is probably just a gesture. Decisions announced in such circumstances rarely come to fruition and can be a roadblock to further development of the relationship (particularly if the executive appears to have "lost face" by not being able to deliver on a decision).

If, after a round of meetings or correspondence, things seem to be bogging down, write to the most senior person or go back for another courtesy call at the senior level. Discuss the "status of progress" in general terms. The atmosphere of such a meeting or exchange of correspondence should give you some idea as to whether the slow response is reason for worry. If things are going well, your Japanese customer will appreciate the senior level support your letter or visit lends. If a project (or prospect) has gone off the rails, you will probably find out why, albeit in vaguer terms than you might like. At least you will have a clearer idea of what to do next.

A subtle point and one that often leads to misunderstanding is that Japanese loathe saying "no" in a direct way. You will hear expressions such as "very difficult" or "we must study the matter," which may mean "no" or may simply indicate a very great difficulty brought about by external circumstances. Gentle probing or a working-level social encounter (see below) may be the only way to establish the real meaning of the message.

I have spent over half my life in Japan; I speak and work almost entirely in Japanese. Still, I come out of meetings puzzled as to what, if anything, went on. My Japanese staff may be equally puzzled, so I am pretty sure that I haven't missed some esoteric piece of body language. Dogged but gentle probing is the only way to achieve an understanding of the situation. Making someone feel "cornered" is not going to get you anywhere. You must repeat your own position and request clarification, coming at the issue from different angles. If this still doesn't work, try writing a letter after the meeting, putting your views forward and asking your counterpart if he agrees with your understanding of events. The "distance" achieved by a letter may elicit a clearer response.

Expect the "pre-decision," information-gathering stage of any new contact to take considerably longer than you may be used to. The pace of decision-making has picked up speed in Japan. Nonetheless, it may still appear agonizingly slow. Manufacturers may spend two years or more testing new parts or products before making a purchasing decision. Aside from responding promptly and thoroughly to inquiries and maintaining contact, there is really very little you can do to speed up the process. When responding to requests for technical information, err on the side of plenty. Japanese have a fondness for, and derive comfort from, masses of technical data. You can look forward to a "post-decision" implementation phase that will proceed quickly and with minimum fuss. Look at it as a process of working out the bugs before manufacturing starts.

All of this has assumed that you can delegate part of these duties to subordinate staff. If you can't, you will have to handle both the senior and working-level meetings yourself. While the expense of travel and the availability of staff may preclude a team approach toward the Japanese client, the results may also vary. The Japanese have developed the client meeting ground into a very successful management-training program (see below for details), and it may be worthwhile investing money in some extra support.

KABAN-MOCHI, THE "BRIEFCASE CARRIER"

Japan has developed an apprenticeship form of management-training system. Entry-level employees through junior managers will be assigned to a series of seemingly menial tasks involving little responsibility. If you have ever wondered why there are "twenty of them versus two of us," you are encountering what I call the "*kaban-mochi* system" at work. Each of the junior staff has a function which contributes to the greater whole.

The discussion of the interpreter later in this chapter refers to having extra eyes and ears at the meeting, and this is what your Japanese counterparts are doing. One of the junior staff will be given the task of taking detailed notes; another will be watching the body language of the meeting; a third may be checking interpretation; and others ad infinitum will be arranging taxis, meal reservations, getting coats, or whatever needs to be done to smooth the way and get things done. All are participating and learning about the process, through observation. When their turn comes to conduct meetings or negotiations, they will be skilled at the intricacies of this process. They should be able to score strategic points against someone who has not had this training.

Specialist training programs in Asian Studies or business degrees with an Asian specialty are producing candidates ideally suited to the *kaban-mochi* role. Companies dealing with Japan (and to a great extent all of Asia) will find advantages in adopting aspects of the *kaban-mochi* system.

The worst examples I see of Western management operating in Japan reduce senior management (vice-presidents) to *kaban-mochi* by traveling with no junior staff. A vice-president whose first exposure to Japan has him calling cabs, getting the chairman's coat, or making other menial arrangements, is going to have a difficult time establishing his credibility when he leads the next round of negotiations.

WHO TO BRING TO JAPAN

If you are in manufacturing, consider bringing over a production person and someone from R&D, as well as sales personnel. The ability of your own staff to understand Japanese needs will be enhanced by this approach. Certainly it will work wonders for your credibility. Japanese are innately dubious about individualists, which may slow down their acceptance of your approach, no matter what your track record is. In addition to their own fields of expertise, give each member of your team an additional task, such as observing who is the most forceful person on the opposing team, who is the most open to your presentation, or who seems opposed to the whole process. This may permit you to develop relationships with these individuals, speeding and enhancing your negotiations.

If you have already established business contacts in Japan, you may be met at the airport. Japanese business tends to be conducted from arrival time to departure time, so don't be surprised if your hosts seem to feel you need babysitting. This is considered a simple courtesy to a guest — a sort of door-to-door service. Relax and enjoy, because your protestations probably will not be understood. Should you require time to yourself or to do other work, state this clearly but politely. If you have dietary restrictions or simply don't like the idea of anything raw, make sure this information has been communicated to your hosts, ideally before arrival. Similarly, if you enjoy or wish to sample Japanese cuisine, let them know. Otherwise you may end up eating beef from dawn to dusk.

LANGUAGE AND INTERPRETERS

A decision that you will have to make is whether to engage your own interpreter. Many of the larger Japanese companies will have in-house language expertise or will engage an interpreter on your behalf, but this should be sorted out before your visit. If you are serious about your prospects in this market, get your own interpreter.

Don't assume that just because someone speaks English and Japanese, they will be able to interpret. Even today, more deals fall through and serious misunderstandings occur because of inadequate communications.

As someone who speaks English and Japanese, I have been called upon to interpret and can assess the quality of interpretation. Some people can do it naturally, with experience but little training, but many people never make good interpreters. Using professional line staff to interpret may be a waste of resources because an interpreter can only interpret, and cannot participate in a discussion. If you need line staff engaged in the discussions, hire a professional interpreter. Allow your professional staff to make the most of their training and to back up the interpreter on technical language. That way you will achieve the most professional results.

An interpreter is a major investment. Use him or her wisely. Make sure that the interpreter is well briefed in advance about the nature of your business and specialized vocabulary. You will be operating in a strange environment, so consider making him or her an extra set of eyes and ears to interpret some of the nonverbal dynamics of a meeting. Very often there will be signals that are not translatable, but which add color to the discussion. Make sure that the interpreter knows that you want the color commentary. Schedule debriefing time during meeting breaks or at the end of the day.

Don't expect the interpreter to function as a "gopher" or secretary unless this role has been negotiated. Remember, too, that the interpreter is the facilitator, not the creator of bad news. "Don't shoot the messenger." Never question the interpreter's competence during a meeting. If you feel that you have done an adequate job of briefing but are not satisfied with the interpreter, change interpreters.

There are different levels of interpreters at different costs. If you want someone to get you to meetings and act principally as a guide, request an "escort interpreter." If you are entering serious contractual negotiations, get an "A Class" interpreter, ideally with previous experience in your field. Sticking with one competent person over a period of time is usually more effective than changing interpreters frequently. Make this a condition when you engage the interpreter.

There are many sources of interpreters. Hotel business centers or English "Yellow Pages" found in hotel rooms are two possible starting points. Previous visitors to Japan may be able to direct you to competent freelance operators at a slight cost savings.

When speaking through an interpreter, address yourself to the client, not the interpreter. Speak in short, distinct, and complete thoughts or paragraphs. It is not necessary to speak artificially slowly. The interpreter will stop you if you get too far ahead. Japanese is phrased in the opposite way to English, so it is important to complete your thought before pausing. Forget humor. It doesn't translate easily, is not expected at a business meeting, and may cause confusion if taken literally. If you just have to tell a joke, save it for a social encounter and make sure your interpreter is aware that it is a joke. In the worst case, they can always say, "Mr. Smith has just told an untranslatable joke. Please laugh!"

Given the cost of a good interpreter, you may be tempted to depend on the customer for language assistance. Remember, though, that you'll get half the story while they end up knowing both sides. This doesn't seem like a very smart approach, no matter how honorable your counterpart.

SOCIAL ENCOUNTERS AND NIGHT LIFE

Japanese socializing usually takes place in the evenings. (The exception to this rule is golf, which can just as easily be scheduled for a weekday as a weekend.) Lunch meetings tend to be brief working sessions in contrast to the relaxed pace of evening get-togethers. Like it or not, evening gatherings are an integral part of the "getting to know you" process. As Japanese, generally, will only do business with people they know, make an effort to get to know them. If a daytime meeting has gone particularly well, you may want to sound out your client about getting together for dinner or drinks, or both. If you initiate the proposal, be prepared to pay. This will take a little planning unless your budget is unlimited. The best bet is to tell your hotel what your budget is, and get them to recommend a restaurant at which to start off. Have the name and location communicated to your client.

Japanese evenings tend to involve alcohol in large quantity. Actually, though, many Japanese do not or would prefer not to drink. If you do not want to make alcohol the central part of the evening, let your counterparts know that you do not drink. Do not try to escape with "not drinking much." You will find that non-drinking get-togethers put more emphasis on the quality of the food and evenings tend to end earlier. It may take a while longer to establish the peculiar bonds so easily wrought by alcohol because Japanese use alcohol as the principal escape mechanism from their strict social patterns. This allows underlings to tell bosses off with impunity, and buyers and sellers to deal with sticky points without the interference of normal "diplomatic niceties."

Evenings start early in Japan; 6:30 p.m. is a safe time to

suggest. Be there early to greet your guest, who will arrive promptly if not a few minutes early. If your Japanese guest knows some English, dispense with the interpreter. Use the evening as a purely social encounter — the purpose is to establish a personal relationship which will further the professional bond. Keep the approach light. If the discussion strays to work, talk about your personal aspirations and experience. Expect what may seem like a grilling on your age, family life, wife, children, etc. Counter with the same sort of small talk. Dinner probably won't take more than an hour and a half. If things are going well, your guest may suggest moving on to a watering hole. Unless you have planned for this, leave it up to your guest to make a suggestion; he probably has a regular spot. At this point it may be a good idea to clarify who will be hosting the second round: "Of course I would like to visit your regular spot, but please remember you are my guest tonight." If he insists that it is his turn, let him pay.

Even if this first evening has gone well, your guest may not want to make it a late night. Don't take this as a slight. Most Japanese have a long commute to get home, and Mr. Suzuki may have had a late night the night before. Just as in the business meeting, never try to rush the development of the relationship. If you and Mr. Suzuki do carry on, remember that, the next time you meet, no reference needs to be made to the occasion (especially your "misdeeds") beyond a thank you. Work is work and play is play. One contributes to the other, but there is very little discussion of the gory details of play in the work context.

Another purpose of the social evening can be to work out problems which have come up in the course of the work day. The subtle signals of difficulty that you (or your staff) have been picking up can be dealt with in a more direct atmosphere after a few drinks. This type of "working out the bugs" is best left to the working level unless the situation has reached a total impasse. Only then will you want to invite your senior counterpart for a "problem-solving evening" (never expressed so bluntly). The danger of moving too quickly up the corporate ladder is that you may find yourself left without further recourse. Ideally, your staff will be able to achieve a consensus with their Japanese social partners. Then you and the boss will be able to go and celebrate the solution.

WOMEN IN THE WORKPLACE

Westerners coming to Japan will have heard that "this is a man's world" and may assume that women staff can play no role here. We are all outsiders, however, and gender should not be a determining factor in planning the business trip. Don't make an issue of the issue. While still rare, Japanese women are advancing rapidly up the corporate ladder of some companies today. Japanese business is awakening to the fact that many household financial decisions are made by the woman. If you are in the consumer products, food, education, housing, or advertising fields, there may be an added advantage to tapping female resources, both Western and Japanese.

On the other hand, if you are traveling with a spouse, don't expect the spouse to have much of a role to play either during the working day or in the socializing at night. If you want an accompanying husband or wife to be included in the social encounters, make this point to your counterparts early. This will not usually be a problem. Don't expect to socialize with Japanese couples. The Japanese wife will usually opt to stay clear of business-related social gatherings. If the "significant other" is a male, he is probably occupied with his own professional socializing. It is easier to break down this barrier with Japanese traveling or working abroad. If you have an established relationship with a Japanese couple who were living in your country, you may be able to continue this pattern when visiting Japan. Make your expectations known and then accept whatever happens.

THE EXCHANGE OF GIFTS

Like the old joke about never winning at strip poker with a kimono-clad lady (the kimono has endless layers and accessories), you will never win a gift-giving match with a Japanese. Travel with a small supply of gift-wrapped, good-quality corporate mementos. Remember that your meetings in Japan will probably involve larger numbers of people than you are used to and plan accordingly. If someone has been particularly helpful to you, or you have received an elaborate gift, consider reciprocating after the fact, or when the person visits you. Do it on your own terms and don't try to compete. It is really the thought that counts. Picking something unusual but representative of your country will get you out of the value game.

REPRESENTATION IN JAPAN

When you reach the point of determining representation in the Japanese marketplace, there are a number of factors to consider. I believe in the value of having someone from your own company/ country/culture (in that order) do the representing.

If time permits, the ideal is to recruit a home country national with Japanese-language capability. This is not as difficult as it once was. The recruit should spend some time at the head office or a principal production facility learning about your needs and corporate culture. Should your operation in Japan be a joint venture, your representative should have a clear reporting line back to you. This should be set up in a way that avoids any appearance of having to "go behind the back" of the Japanese joint venture partners, who may be in charge of the operation overall. Just as with an interpreter, a language-proficient non-Japanese will be able to provide head office with local color that might not be apparent nor seem important to a Japanese.

What sort of home country national should you post to Japan? Start with the assumption that you will eventually get more from someone working in Japan who can speak Japanese. There are many valid operational reasons why this may not be possible, but there are even more excuses bandied about for avoiding this course of action. Remember that, just as a Japanese without English would have trouble penetrating the Western market, the very same ultimately holds true in Japan.

Apart from language ability, you want to post someone who has an "open approach" and who will accept ("bend to" may be a better analogy), not fight, the differences inherent in doing business in Japan. If the post demands the presence of a senior company employee with long experience, consider appointing a younger bilingual staff person as an assistant or to a desk job.

Having two non-Japanese on the job will be planning for the future, and should ensure that the senior person does not get isolated from the Japanese staff.

There are many Westerners living and working in Japan. A relatively small proportion has a working ability in Japanese, but this is changing rapidly. Our universities and colleges are graduating several hundred students a year who have language training. Many of these people are pursuing business degrees with specialized Asian business courses. Many are forced to pursue careers outside of their own country because there are few jobs at home.

Quite by accident, I recently discovered two fluently bilingual Canadian mechanical engineers working for Japanese financial institutions in Japan. One still hears "complaints" from the corporate world that non-Japanese who speak Japanese "don't have any other expertise." This is an out-of-date generalization and also overlooks the fact that acquiring the technical expertise may be easier than learning Japanese!

Advertising in Japan, requesting informal assistance from your government offices, or contacting business associates in Japan are all ways to track down qualified candidates. Some of the foreign chambers of commerce in Japan maintain referral services. Universities and colleges maintain alumni records and may be of assistance. For the time being, though, word of mouth seems to be the primary tool used in identifying qualified candidates.

Finally, never make assumptions about language ability. Always use professional resources to test the level of ability. Many universities offer this service and some private language schools may also be able to undertake this task. Based on the candidate's language assessment, you should consider making on-the-job specialized language tutoring part of the employment package. Look at it as an investment in professional training that should pay handsome dividends over the years.

JAPANESE RECRUITS

There are many good books available on the challenges and methods of recruiting Japanese nationals for foreign firms, so I will not explore this area in depth. However, besides all the usual recruiting requirements, there is an aspect of hiring Japanese that should be left to professionals in Japan. This is the determination of the candidates' ability to function vis-à-vis other Japanese. You yourself can make this judgment when it comes to your home country staff, but Japanese who mix easily with "foreigners" do not always have the same ability when it comes to associating with other Japanese. They may have spent so much time abroad that they have lost the link to their own culture, or they may want to work for a foreign company because they do not like the Japanese corporate world. Whatever the reason, there are personnel recruitment agencies which specialize in this field. Leave it to the professionals, and do not make your decision based solely on language ability. Consider broadening recruitment to Japanese who do not speak English but express a willingness to learn. You may get a more interesting cross section of candidates from which to recruit; language training can be offered as part of the employment package.

When it comes right down to it, doing business in Japan is not all that different from doing business in any other foreign country. It may take a bit more preparation to get started, but approach it professionally and you should garner good results. Entry into Asia through a successful venture in Japan may also provide you with a springboard to other interesting opportunities in the region. Wherever you go in this part of the world, you will find people pursuing their destiny with pride. The way they approach life may be a little different from what you are used to, but didn't someone famous once say: "Variety is the spice of life?" Quoting from the president of the American Chamber of Commerce in Japan:

> It's Business 101 — just as important here as in the U.S. It's about long-term relations, sensitivity to customers' needs, and gaining recognition for commitment to the market. . . . The greatest grade on anyone's report card is that follow-on order; you do things right at the first stage and you get invited back to the party.[11]

NOTES

1. *Report of the Canada-Japan Forum 2000, "Partnership Across the Pacific," (December 1992).*
2. *The* zaibatsu *were family-directed conglomerates, many of which were begun as state enterprises; the state enterprise was privatized when it was deemed to be viable commercially and turned over to a noble or samurai family. Today's* keiretsu *are their successors, although ownership has often passed out of private hands (to banks), and the web of suppliers may have no direct ownership links to the hub companies.*
3. *Japanese copyright, trademark, and patent protection is still philosophically aimed at achieving technology diffusion. If you have any questions about your level of protection, get professional advice before entering the market.*
4. *Banks are usually at the center of Japanese* keiretsu, *or corporate groupings. An introduction from a Japanese bank or to a Japanese bank from a foreign correspondent institution can be useful in getting inside the* keiretsu *wall.*
5. *JETRO was originally established by the Japanese government to promote Japanese exports abroad. It has now been given a parallel mandate to promote exports to Japan. JETRO offices are also called "Japan Trade Centers" in some cities.*
6. *Depending on your area of interest, government agencies may open the most doors. Japan tends to be a bureaucratically driven society, so being introduced by a government official is an effective entry point. If you have to go through a regulatory framework, try and get the regulators to introduce you to Japanese companies in the field.*
7. *Many Western universities and colleges now have programs which train specialists and place them in internship programs with Japanese companies. Most of these programs are less than five years old, but their breadth of contacts is expanding rapidly, and should be explored as part of your information gathering.*
8. *First-time visitors are often inclined to deal with someone who speaks English; it makes things so much easier. Language ability is only one of the qualifications for a good representative — make sure you have someone who can do the job, not just tell you about it!*
9. *The Japanese corporate world can be very competitive and Japanese manufacturers or other members of a* keiretsu *may attempt to gain control of a potential import for the express purpose of keeping it out of the country.*
10. *The foreign handler or "*gaijin *greeter" can be both useful and a hindrance.*

He or she will usually be an older person who speaks English and on whom bothersome visitors can be palmed off. While often able and very sociable, this person can rarely lead you to real business opportunities.

11. *Richard Johannessen, Jr., president of Rockwell International Japan Co., and of the ACCJ, quoted in the* Nikkei Weekly *(February 15, 1993).*

CHAPTER TWELVE

In Search of Investment Capital from Japan

RUSSELL T. MARK

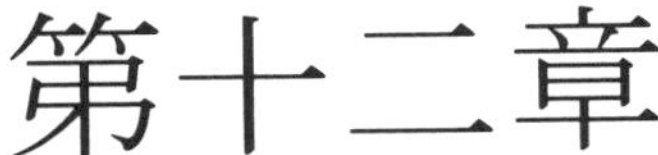

In previous chapters, we have examined the strategies and skills that must be developed in order to sell your products or services into the Japanese market. Many companies also come to Japan seeking investment funds for their domestic operations. Russell Mark, senior manager and director of Japanese practice for KPMG Peat Marwick Thorne in Vancouver, examines the recent trends in Japanese foreign direct investment, and outlines the critical steps a Western company must take in order to successfully obtain Japanese investment for its projects.

As the world grows smaller, businesses have more options for outside financing than ever before. Media reports of Japanese mega-deals have become commonplace: Sony's purchase of Columbia Pictures, Matsushita's buyout of MCA, and Bridgestone's acquisition of Firestone Tire and Rubber Company, not to mention high-profile real estate transactions such as Mitsubishi Estate's purchase of an interest in the Rockefeller Center, Daiichi America Real Estate's acquisition of the Tiffany Building, and Minoru Isutani's purchase of the Pebble Beach Company (including the famed Pebble Beach Golf Course). It seems only natural, then, that when reviewing alternatives for potential sources of investment, Japan quickly comes to mind. Before you approach the Japanese, there are a few things you should consider.

THE BACKGROUND

After seven years of dynamic growth to the end of fiscal year 1989,[1] Japan's direct investment overseas has been waning. Indeed, the pace set in the latter half of the 1980s would have been difficult to sustain. In the four and a half years between the Plaza Accord of 1985 and the end of 1989, virtually one-half of all Japanese overseas direct investment since 1951 occurred. Despite the lower amounts registered in 1990, 1991, and 1992, the flows for these three years alone represented over one-third of the total recorded.

Japanese direct investment overseas first surpassed $10 billion in 1984, peaking at $67.5 billion in 1989, aided by an appreciating yen from 1985. Japanese direct investment overseas during this period was not restricted to "brand name" or major Japanese corporations. In 1985, firms employing less than three hundred people accounted for less than one-quarter of Japanese investment overseas; by 1990, companies of this size were responsible for more than 60 percent of the total.

The increasingly protectionist trade policies of major trading partners made it attractive for Japanese companies to establish or acquire operations abroad in order to maintain their market share, and the prospect of a unified Europe added urgency to the need to invest in that "new" marketplace. At home, spiraling land and stock prices, and the easy-credit bank policies that resulted from this asset inflation (the so-called "bubble economy"), abetted this spending spree — as did substantial differences in production costs between Japan and neighboring Asian countries.

Some of these same factors came into play in the recent downturn in overseas investment. Growth in the Japanese economy reached a virtual standstill in early 1992 and languishes there (although signs of a long-awaited recovery continue to be reported); land prices are off some 20 percent from their peak; and the Nikkei stock index reached almost one-third of its December 1989 peak before it rebounded to just short of 20,000 in late March 1993 and fell again to the 16,000 range in late November 1993. The combination of these factors has created a tighter credit environment in Japan. In addition, many enterprises posted substantial declines in earnings as the economy slowed, and investment spending abroad was slashed as a result. Some felt that they had already completed the process of establishing themselves overseas (although others have indicated that they need to continue to invest overseas to counter trade friction and the threat, perceived or otherwise, of protectionism), and the domestic and global recession dampened the urge to acquire new assets abroad. Instead of making new investments, many companies were struggling to find a way to shed poorly performing overseas assets. Some of the same trading companies and financial institutions that developed profitable activities advising on corporate mergers and acquisitions for production bases in North America, more specifically in the United States, now find themselves assisting clients in restructuring or withdrawing smoothly, minimizing costs and friction with local communities.

Domestic demand for investment was growing concurrently, as severe labor shortages necessitated productivity-enhancing, labor-saving capital investment. (From mid-1988 to the end of 1992, the Japanese unemployment rate was below 2.5 percent and the ratio of job offers to applicants was in excess of one, indicating more jobs than applicants to fill them.) Demands for improved quality of life mean that capital which could have gone abroad will likely be invested in infrastructure projects at home instead.

While the effects of the slowdown in Japanese investment were felt around the world, new investment slipped dramatically in North America, where it was down by 57 percent from 1989 (to $14.6 billion)[2] in fiscal 1992, primarily as a result of the North American and global recessions. Europe, which showed tremendous growth in the closing years of the 1980s, fared similarly, with direct investment declining by 52 percent (to $7.1 billion), likely as a result of a combination of recessionary pressures and the completion of investment strategies in preparation for the creation of the European Community in 1992. Japanese investment in Asia dipped a mere 22 percent (to $6.4 billion). Japan's Asian neighbors, virtually all with growth rates in excess of 5 percent per annum, are the newest markets that Japanese companies wish to tap. Total decline in Japanese direct investment overseas in fiscal 1991 was 18 percent — following 27 and 16 percent declines in 1991 and 1990 respectively.

Indeed, these declines might have been due to rising awareness that some Japanese investments overseas have not been as successful as originally envisaged. Recent data available from the Ministry of International Trade and Industry indicates that the ratio of pretax profits to sales for manufacturers' overseas subsidiaries in fiscal 1991 (fiscal 1990 figures in brackets) registered 3.3 percent (5.0 percent) in Asia, 0.0 percent (3.2 percent) in Europe, and −0.6 percent (−0.9 percent) in North America. Because of this experience, Japanese investors are becoming much more selective.

WHAT HAVE THE JAPANESE INVESTED IN?

Despite the announcement of several major investments in the forestry sector in Canada, and, of course, the Japanese automobile "transplant" operations in North America, major greenfield investments have been rare. Instead, there has been a proliferation of Japanese acquisitions (of entire companies, or of operating divisions), participation in strategic alliances (including minority cross-shareholdings), and equity purchases.

Without attempting to unduly oversimplify the intentions of Japanese investors in North America, it appears that outright ownership or majority interest are the preferred forms of investment in natural resource and manufacturing operations — as are partnerships, joint ventures, and other forms of alliance in knowledge-intensive industries. Typically, these forms of investment allow returns on a much shorter time frame than greenfield investments. This is especially true in the high technology and information industries, where an in-depth understanding of competitors, current technological advancements, and changing markets — as well as access to key intellectual resources — are all so important. Taking Canada and the United States as a whole, by number of cases reported, the most popular investments have been in computers, chemicals, health and health care, financial services, mining and metals, commercial and leisure properties, and electrical machinery.

The Japanese strategy in Asia has been quite different. Initially, it was a strategy to secure access to resource-rich neighbors. By the late 1980s, a strengthening yen and rising labor costs at home forced Japanese companies to scour Asia for low-cost labor. Now Japanese investors are investing in Asia less to establish low-cost export bases, but more to service the rapidly growing local markets. Given the variety of languages and cultures in Asia, joint ventures are the most popular form of accessing Asian markets.

WHAT THIS MEANS TO YOU

The recent downward trends do not mean that Japanese foreign direct investment globally or in North America will cease. The Ministry of Finance's International Finance Bureau predicts that direct overseas investment will return to a growth trend, albeit exhibiting slower growth than seen in the late 1980s. Clearly, the move toward globalization cannot be abandoned or ignored. For now, though, it has peaked, and that means that there is much more competition for any and every available yen — from inside the potential investor's own organization, from domestic investment alternatives, and from any number of international businesses seeking access to the same pool of capital.

If you are to be successful in accessing potential Japanese investors, you must differentiate yourself from the competition to vie for those same investment yen funds. A first step, and one that is often forgotten or passed over lightly, is to identify your own objectives and what you ultimately seek to achieve from any investor, including one from Japan. A realistic assessment of your own financial expectations will also go far in saving time and effort in targeting, and negotiating with, an appropriate investor for your project. To reach an agreement with an investor, you must develop a financing structure and determine how participation in the project will be priced. This process involves the estimated future value of the project proposed and is, of course, highly subjective.

FINANCIAL RETURN AND STRATEGIC ADVANTAGE

Western culture may be seen as individual-centered, encouraging the development of community to serve individual needs. In contrast, Japan may be viewed as a community-centered culture that encourages the development of individual strengths to keep the community healthy. These different viewpoints are also evident in business thinking. Ask North Americans for whom they think corporations exist, and the answer is likely to be "the shareholders" and "management." Ask Japanese the same question, and the answer is most likely to be "the employees" and "society" as a whole. The fact that corporations exist in both cultures indicates no difference in the way of thinking, but the answers to the question reflect different standards of reference.

When presenting an investment opportunity, remember that the vast majority of business proposals which Japanese investors see will show credible financial returns (long or short term) to the investor; these are expected as a given. To differentiate yourself from your competitors, you should clearly identify the strategic (rather than financial) advantage to be gained by the potential investor from making an investment in the project described in your proposal.

Financial returns are important, but potential Japanese investors will also look to the strategic advantages offered in a proposal, most especially those which will assist them in achieving their own corporate objectives over the long term. They will look for answers to basic questions such as: "What's in it for the investor?" or "Why should the investor be interested in the proposal?" Try to present answers to these questions in clear, straightforward language.

While every investment proposal will offer different strategic advantages to potential investors, the following provides a general listing of strategic objectives to which Japanese investors may be receptive (in order of priority from the highest):

- *Access to new markets*. Nippon Sheet Glass, a major sheet glass manufacturer, which exports approximately 6 percent of its production, purchased a significant share of Libby-Owens-Ford, an American glass manufacturer, in order to gain experience in and access to the major glass market in the United States.
- *Maintenance of or increase in market share*. A consortium led by Mitsubishi Corporation constructed a pulp mill in Alberta.

With plans to construct a paper mill, they thus secured the supply of pulp and paper for sale or use by consortium members in Japan.

- *Access to new technologies/products.* Green Cross, an Osaka-based pharmaceutical company, invested $40 million in Viagene of San Diego, California, in return for worldwide marketing rights to a drug under development to combat the AIDS virus.
- *Joint new product development (shared risks, reduced R&D outlays, increased flexibility and shortened lead times).* NTT and Moli Energy of Burnaby, British Columbia, formed a joint venture to further develop Moli's proprietary molybdenum lithium battery technologies for use in NTT's communications products.
- *New distribution channels.* Sunstar, a Japanese soap, cosmetic, and personal care product manufacturer, acquired John O. Butler (an American oral hygiene product manufacturer), gaining a valuable distribution network for its compatible products.
- *Unique management talents and skills.* Matsushita purchased Geffen Records in order to secure the talents of executive David Geffen, who was touted to take the top management position at (newly acquired) MCA.
- *Increased manufacturing capacity.* Onoda Cement, a leading Japanese manufacturer, whose own domestic plants were running at full capacity, acquired the largest cement producer in California, with 21 percent of the market, using the acquired plant's excess capacity to service export clients of Onoda, thus alleviating stress on domestic operations.
- *Access to manufacturing know-how.* Komatsu, one of the world's largest construction machinery companies, purchased a significant share of Husky Injection Molding of Canada in order to gain access to Husky's quality injection molding machinery manufacturing processes.
- *Entry into a new industry.* Nippon Mining acquired Gould, an American metals company, in order to capitalize on the computer-related potential of its key technologies: copper foil, circuit protectors, and optical electronic components.

TARGETING POTENTIAL INVESTORS

Most successful companies stay in businesses that they understand, and preferably in businesses they know. Prudent foreign investors will not likely stray far from their traditional lines of business in search of new opportunities. Knowledgeable investors contribute more to a business transaction when they actually understand the industry because they can bring more than money to the deal, including marketing and manufacturing understanding and experience. They also are in a significantly better position to evaluate the financial aspects of the transaction and the potential synergies which might develop.

You must deliberate upon the types of companies that might be interested in your proposal and specifically target them. Look to companies in the same business, or related industries/companies which would benefit from your (identified) strategic advantages. Then determine who within these organizations might read your proposal (a senior executive with a mandate to search for new opportunities, someone introduced by a mutual acquaintance, or a long-standing contact in an organization with whom you have done extensive business); what they might already know about you and your organization; what more they might want to know; and how they might intend to use the information they will find in your proposal. With these questions considered and explored, you are ready to begin preparing a detailed proposal.

Objectively review your own network of contacts for possible relationships with Japan which might be useful; prior business relationships, friends, acquaintances, industrial associations, chambers of commerce, and possible contact generators such as sister-city relationships and sports and school exchanges could be followed up. Relationships are the foundation of doing business in Japan. The value of any existing relationships with or personal introductions to organizations you might be targeting cannot be understated.

For assistance in targeting actual companies, consider contacting organizations with representation in Japan, or representatives of Japanese organizations in North America: major domestic and Japanese financial institutions, appropriate agencies and departments of the federal and provincial or state governments, industry associations, the Japanese Embassy, JETRO, and major trading companies. Do not overlook lawyers and accountants, many of whom have developed relationships or have affiliates in Japan. Research any potential target companies to ensure that they are viable targets. This research pays off in many ways, by determining the *bona fides* of a target company, by allowing you to "customize" your proposal to the particular circumstances of the target, and by revealing possible commonalities on which a potential relationship might commence or develop. (Valuable research resources would include the services of a major credit rating organization such as Teikoku Data Bank or Dun & Bradstreet.)

If at all possible, you should select a mentor from your network of contacts. This individual would likely be an experienced businessperson, consultant, banker, professional advisor, or diplomat, with a deep appreciation and understanding of how business is done in Japan. The mentor's role would be to get to know your project, and to provide you with advice and guidance on the presentation of your project proposal, including a critical review of the likelihood of successfully attracting interest in Japan. Your mentor may have several contacts in Japan (possibly working in sectors outside your targets), who would be in a position to provide their own comments. Based on the feedback received from your mentor (and his contacts), your proposal can be refined and further "fine-tuned."

Bear in mind that if you can identify one potential investor in Japan, you can likely identify a number of others. Identify as many as possible, conduct preliminary research to identify the "best" candidates, conduct further research on these, then prioritize. If you have confidence in your understanding of the targeted companies' goals and objectives, you may wish to approach a number of companies at the same time. Alternatively, you may wish to restrict your initial approach to only two or three companies, using them as test cases to learn more about the actual issues and concerns most affecting investment decisions in your sector. Whichever method you choose, seek to maintain confidentiality; the desirability of a proposal seems to diminish disproportionately as the number of organizations approached increases and becomes known.

WHERE DOES THIS LEAD?

The primary factors critical to establishing a successful dialogue with a potential investor include a thorough introduction of the principals of the project, a complete description of the organization (company or companies) involved, and an equally thorough introduction of the key members of the project's management team and their relevant experience and skills. In short, provide all the information necessary to accelerate the creation or further development of a relationship.

The next stage involves the identification of what the principals are offering the potential investor. Obviously, the proposal has to have merit in the investor's eyes; it must fit into the strategic and operational goals of the investor; and it must project a high probability of success.

This information should be presented in a credible, articulate, well-organized and detailed business proposal, accompanied by an Executive Summary and a covering letter. If you have targeted a potential investor who may receive many such proposals, bear in mind that the reviewer may not get past the Executive Summary. It must therefore give the reader an overall understanding of your business, and answer that most pressing of all questions: "What's in this proposal for the investor?"

These basic requirements are not exclusive to Japanese investors; North American investors would demand similar information. However, the normally conservative (and recently, selective) nature of Japanese investors, combined with the often lengthy decision-making process in Japan and the care with which projects are scrutinized, dictates that proposals have to be written in considerably more detail than proposals presented in North America. As noted above, the proposal also must refer specifically to strategic advantages beyond mere financial reward.

STRUCTURING A DETAILED BUSINESS PROPOSAL

Generally speaking, a detailed proposal (or business plan) would focus upon:

- Company description: a complete description of the company, its products, and industry.
- Market analysis: including believable, reasonable, and obtainable projections pertaining to the size of the potential market, market share, competition, potential customers, and pricing. This section should also clearly demonstrate that there is a market need for the company's product or service, that management understands this need, and that it can be sold at a profit.
- Marketing and sales activities: including discussions of specific marketing techniques, pricing plans, planned sales force, customer base, customer service, and advertising and promotion. This section should adequately describe an efficient approach to potential customers.
- Products and services: including the extent of invention or development required to make the product market-ready, the track record of key technical people in developing other similar products, the proprietary aspects of the technology, and how the company's product is more advanced than existing products on the market. This section should emphasize the positive aspects of the product's ability to meet existing market needs and the company's ability to satisfy the needs of the marketplace.
- Operations: including plans for operations such as facilities, work force by major job categories, extent of subcontracting, sources of supply, warranty and service strategies, and economies of scale.
- Management team: including details of team members' experience and talents in the most important management disciplines, such as research and development, marketing and sales, manufacturing, and finance. This section should introduce members of the management team, highlight their experience and skills, and indicate how these are relevant to the venture and will contribute to the success of the project. Companies succeed not because of their products, but principally through the skills of the people who make the entire operation work.
- Financial summary: including summaries of income statements, cash flow analyses, balance sheets, and projections based on prospective scenarios. Detailed financial information

and forecasts should likely appear in an appendix. Basic information with respect to rates of return (and alternative exit strategies if venture financing is being sought) should be found here.

Remember to take nothing for granted about what the readers of your business plan might know about you, your company, or your country. Points about geography, weather, and transportation that are obvious to you may be missed completely by a potential investor. (How familiar are you with Yamanashi Prefecture — headquarters of Fanuc Ltd., the world's leading manufacturer of numerical control equipment?) If your project is not located in a major population center, consider including a map and other relevant details.

THE EXECUTIVE SUMMARY

You could be sending your proposal to a potential investor who reviews many of them on a regular basis. More often than not, they do not have the time to get past the covering letter and the Executive Summary of the proposals they receive. Between them, these two documents must therefore give the reader a useful understanding of your proposal. The covering letter should also answer the basic question: "What's in the proposal for the investor?"

The Executive Summary usually does not exceed two to three pages, and should include a brief discussion of:

- The Team. The management team's talents and skills are some of the few truly unique aspects of any project. This section must indicate why they are a part of your organization's distinctive competence that cannot easily be replicated by your competition, and how they will make the project successful. These individuals should possess an unqualified commitment to the project, a strong will to succeed, an understanding of the key strategic issues, and the ability to implement highly focused action plans.
- The Vehicle. The product, service, or technology proposed must have unique or proprietary elements that will provide a lasting competitive edge.

- The Potential. The venture must have the potential to grow significantly. This growth capability is usually a result of the company being in a dynamic or expanding market, identifying a new segment of a more stable market, or being capable of outperforming competitors.
- The Deal. The financial participation alternatives for a potential investor and how this participation might be structured provide the remaining essential facet for a potential investor to judge preliminary interest in the proposal.

UNDERTAKING FOLLOW-UP

Now you have a viable project; you have identified possible target organizations, and have explored commonalities and relationships which might be useful. You have invested time and money in the development of an articulate and credible business proposal, Executive Summary, and covering letter.

In your covering letter, you should indicate that if you do not hear directly from the target organization within a fixed length of time, you will follow up by fax — but remember to allow sufficient time for adequate review of your proposal. Two weeks would not be unreasonable.

Unless you know the target organization well and the individuals within it, and are confident of your mutual ability to communicate, avoid the urge to follow up by telephone. Verbal miscommunications may be fatal to your proposal. (Most Japanese companies have the capability of reading English and can prepare at least rudimentary responses in English, but their verbal abilities are generally limited.)

The responses you receive will dictate your next course of action, be it further refinement of your proposal, selection of more (or other) target organizations, a visit to Japan or receiving visitors from Japan, or any combination of these.

Whatever the course of action, bear in mind that Japanese investment will serve to transfer business resources, perhaps including technology and management know-how, together with capital, to your company. The development of ongoing relationships with potential investors may be fundamental to the success of your proposal. After all, potential investors may also be potential trading partners.

APPENDIX: BACKGROUND QUESTIONS INVESTORS MIGHT ASK

REGULATORY CONTROLS

- Are there restrictions imposed by the various levels of government on the level of foreign ownership in business entities or industrial sectors? Are there any foreign investment controls affecting the establishment of new businesses and acquisitions which might affect participation in the proposal?
- Are there restrictions imposed by the various levels of government on exchange of funds, repatriation of profits or dividends, or on borrowing by foreign affiliated entities?
- Are there any immigration and labor regulations which might restrict the transfer of management and employees to actively participate in the proposed project?
- Are there any other regulations which might affect or limit foreign participation in the proposal?
- Do the various levels of government offer investment incentives? If so, in what form and in what amounts?

GENERAL

- How was the potential investor targeted? Were domestic investors canvassed? What were the reasons for their lack of interest?
- How much time has passed since the proposal was first presented to a potential investor? Have other investors investigated the proposal and declined?
- Why will this proposal be successful? What critical success factors have been identified and incorporated into the proposal?

PROPOSAL-SPECIFIC

- What is the history of the organization presenting the proposal, assuming that it is not an initial (start-up) venture? Who are the major shareholders and do they participate in the business? Who are the directors?

- In what lines of business does the organization participate? Where are major business offices? How many employees are on the payroll? What are the business results of the past five years?
- What are current conditions in the industry and what is the future growth potential of existing business lines?
- Are there existing important managerial and technical contracts in place such as licensing and other agreements?
- What is the current image and reputation of the organization, its products, and services compared to industry leaders?
- What are recent trends in market share of the organization in its main business lines? What are major developments among competitors which may affect this market share?
- What is the extent of government regulation under which the organization operates?
- Are there any significant external or internal developments which will affect the organization, such as general positive (or negative) economic outlook, industry cyclical factors, labor negotiations, contracts or leases near expiration, capital commitments, current or potential litigation, and other pertinent factors?
- Does the organization possess special skills and advantages, such as unique technical position, established market, new product success, goodwill, excellent labor management relations, and so on?

NOTES

1. *Fiscal year 1989 refers to the year ended March 31, 1990, during which peak direct investment flows from Japan, of $67.5 billion, were registered. Annual investment flow figures refer to the corresponding fiscal year, i.e., 1990 represents the year ended March 31, 1991.*
2. *The investment figures and statistics in this paragraph are contained in a Japanese Ministry of Finance report on overseas investment, which details, on a notification basis, annual flows of investment capital from Japan, but not necessarily covering all transactions made.*

CHAPTER THIRTEEN

Technology and Business: Forging Relationships with Japan for the Twenty-first Century

GERALDINE KENNEY-WALLACE

第十三章

The field of science and technology may determine a company's opportunities in Japan for two reasons: S&T offers a valuable avenue for entry into the Japanese market in terms of partnerships with Japanese companies in the development of new technology; secondly, with the increasing importance of value-added products in the mix of Japanese imports, S&T allows foreign companies to upgrade their offerings to the Japanese market. Dr. Geraldine Kenney-Wallace, president and vice-chancellor of McMaster University and vice-chairman of the Canada-Japan Forum 2000, delineates the main opportunities in science and technology in Japan, and offers advice on how to maximize upon them.

Science and technology are agents of socioeconomic and cultural change, both globally and locally. This chapter explores some of the entry points into Japan, where technology is seen as a natural advantage in any trade or business relationship or venture, and science and technology projects are considered key to cooperative international relationships. Technology and trade, already inextricably bound, will become increasingly so, shifting the focus and dynamics of competitive advantage away from traditional resource-based economies.

The benefits of liberalized trade do not simply flow to the older, scale-based economies. New technologies and science-based innovation require an emphasis on creative and critical thinking, flexibility, economies of scope, and the indigenous technological capacity of a country to be both a smart importer and a smart exporter. The 1992 research and development expenditures, or spending as a ratio of GDP (GERD) in the United States was 2.8 percent, 1.46 percent in Canada, and 3 percent in Japan. Across a range of economies, correlations between the investment in research and development (R&D) and investment in the technological capacity of the work force reveal interesting trends with respect to a nation's output. It has been well documented for both industrialized and newly developing countries that regardless of the size or nature of the economy, the higher the investment in R&D, the higher the GDP; and the higher the number of scientists and engineers per thousand in the population (as an indication of the technological capacity of the work force), the higher the component of manufacturing contributing toward the GDP.[1] Japan holds a leading position in both investment and technological personnel.

What we trade, how we trade, and with whom we trade reveal a markedly different world in 1994 than that of even a decade ago, when many businesspeople of today gained their experience or finished their M.B.A. The impact of technology, from fax machines to foundries for semiconductors, has already moved the competitive goal posts and changed the formal rules of the trading game. Ongoing science-based innovation will have a similar and substantive impact on tradable goods and services by 2010. Business managers need to be "re-tuned" to the demands and needs of trade in a different geopolitical reality.

As trading nations, the United States and Canada seem to prefer domestic markets where, culturally, it is easier to do business. Although our neighboring economies have long been dominated by cross-border trade, we are now witnessing a growing two-way trade with Japan which, in magnitude, is becoming more important than that traditionally conducted with Europe. We must do more with Japan, and science and technology provide an attractive route for those seeking to add value to their output, whether by upgrading current resource-based exports or by targeting new advanced materials such as photoactive medical drugs or environmental products, to name two key growth areas. Because trade and technology are inevitably interlinked, the international currency in constant demand is that of new ideas for new markets, based upon technology, innovation, and value-added strategies for all kinds of products and processes. Americans and Canadians have no choice but to be aggressive international market players, and the purpose of this chapter is to offer guidance to those who wish to become strong performers in Japan and thus to secure a beachhead within the greater Pacific Rim.

Both Canada and the United States have signed bilateral science and technology agreements with Japan, which include relatively detailed appendices of areas of science and technology, and which are reviewed on a regular basis. The Canada-Japan Agreement also allows for private sector activity, not just government to government projects, which is unusual. The Canada-Japan Complementarity Study (1989) was the basis for the latest agreement on enhanced R&D opportunities signed in 1990, and contains specific science and technology areas as examples of international cooperation. The 1992 Canada-Japan Forum 2000 report is a wide-ranging agreement based on the work of a strictly private sector "wise-persons" group commissioned by the prime ministers of the two nations. It contains explicit sections on business, investment, and trade, including dispute resolution recommendations and environmental and technology projects. The U.S.-Japan panel discussions are even more focused on science and technology. Over all, it is clear that technology pervades these developing bilateral relationships, and is a lever for future trade and broader relationships. Through bilateral and multilateral negotiations, mechanisms and institutions have been established to encourage scientific exchanges and to increase joint activities. Detailed information on existing agreements may be obtained through your country's embassy in Japan or through national research agencies in your home country. National research agencies can provide valuable information on both the framework of the agreements and priority sectors, as well as advice on funding and grants.

While science and technology are key instruments in an innovation strategy, and research and development are vitally important to the development of new products and processes, R&D alone is not sufficient to meet competitiveness targets. Clearly, the cost of capital, interest rates, access to financing, management of technology, manufacturing quality, international marketing savvy, the pool of creative and qualified people, and strategic infrastructure (including land costs, energy, transportation, taxes, and the regulatory framework) all enter into the business equation. Science and technology must be viewed as an essential set of foundation stones upon which the business enterprise can be built, with employees who view continuous innovation as a natural state of mind.

Not that science lacks intrinsic value; research and knowledge fuel our imagination and curiosity. Research may even be described as a tithe for enlightenment, but in times of fiscal constraint, selling enlightenment is difficult. Despite the significant contributions of science and technology over millennia to medicine, the arts, modern communications, and the improvement of the environment, there persists a residual belief within the business community that S&T is someone else's problem. On the contrary, science is everyone's business, from those in the laboratory to those in the marketplace. Nowhere is this more vividly demonstrated than in Japan and in the other Pacific nations such as Taiwan, Singapore, Vietnam, and Korea that have experienced remarkable recent growth. It is interesting to note that many of their technological and business leaders were educated in U.S. and Canadian universities on international aid programs a quarter of a century ago.

EMERGING SCIENCE AND TECHNOLOGY OPPORTUNITIES IN JAPAN

Japan is a country in transition, with major contemporary discussions focusing on topics as diverse as the role of peacekeeping for the Japanese military, the ethical definition of brain death, and the role of women in society. Science and technology, as powerful agents of change, have long been accepted by Japanese society. In turn, traditional culture and changing societal norms profoundly influence the way S&T projects and business ventures are carried out in Japan. In responding to demands for an improved quality of life, the government has tried to transform Japan from an economic superpower (*keizai taikoku*) into a lifestyle superpower (*seikatsu taikoku*), which means, first of all, a significant increase in the disposable income of Japanese families. The Japanese must focus on technology and economic objectives to achieve this social goal, and this leads to new opportunities in terms of the business context for existing technology, such as computer technology for the disabled and visually impaired and products for the aging population in general.

Technology engines driving the new economy include the health and medical industries, the environmental industry, telecommunications, the optical industry, and continuing developments in electronics as the new generations of semiconductor chips, computers, and interactive computer/television modules begin to have a powerful impact on, for example, education and electronic classroom learning.

Ethical issues in the realm of health sciences and biomedical ventures must be carefully examined in a society whose demographic profile makes gerontology and topics of practical needs for an aging society key items in the stated objectives of the science and technology councils of Japan. Clearly, this profile will describe market needs and niches. As an illustration, in the absence of an accepted definition of brain death in Japan, certain types of biomedical R&D and business initiatives, which would be the accompanying infrastructure of, for example, open-heart surgery, simply have not existed. These circumstances are changing; in the areas of health, biotechnology, genetic engineering, cosmetics, pharmaceuticals, and so forth, it is critical to keep track of the current debates in Japan and recent changes in legislation in order to fully understand the constraints on opportunities, and hence the attitudes of your Japanese partners. Recently, for example, the Japanese Science and Technology Agency (STA) released goals for future technology and time scales of development which predicted that, by 2001, Japan would have the same frequency of organ transplants as the United States and Europe had in 1991. Future opportunities in the health sciences are extremely attractive for S&T-based ventures, particularly as they relate to the needs of an aging society.

Peacekeeping in the post-Gulf War world has taken on a high profile. The Japanese are now involved in their first experiences as peacekeepers, against the backdrop of a military budget capped since the Second World War at 1 percent of GDP, which now exceeds $30 billion. Sponsored by these funds, substantive efforts have been made for R&D and manufacturing in civilian-linked consumer industries such as microelectronics, aerospace, satellites, fine ceramics, optoelectronics, and in advanced urban and marine transportation, including magnetically levitated trains, energy-related materials, and so forth. As nations worldwide share a heightened peacekeeping role through the United Nations, it would not be surprising to see new strategic defense and "military" initiatives reshaped into a push on environmental technologies and technology transfer during the 1990s. North American and Japanese defense groups are already discussing such options. As economic interdependence begins to include global environmental factors, and notions of a "sustainable economy" become part of trade negotiators' parlance for any comprehensive security agreement, so applied R&D will shift emphasis again. What was once R&D linked to military and defense may reappear linked to peacekeeping initiatives. As Agenda 21 of the United Nations Conference on Economic Development (held in Rio in June 1992) somewhat slowly but inevitably becomes the new paradigm for the development of harmonious bilateral, regional, and multilateral trade, a spin-off corps of engineers functioning as an "environmental peacekeeping corps" may come into existence.

Following the G7 Tokyo summit in July 1993, it became clear that international financial stability and comprehensive global security arrangements will directly benefit from new technology, such as earth observation satellites for monitoring environmental needs. Trade, aid, technology, mobility of people, and the preservation of the environment are all part of the equation of international competitiveness and global stewardship for the future.

Planners of future ventures in Japan should watch these trends, because new environmental standards and regulatory practices will also begin to appear. Discussion and analysis of exactly how this should be accomplished will be a lengthy process, but action, when it occurs, will be swift. This is a critical transition period in which to become part of the consensus-making process. Environmental technologies, for example, are expected to be a major driver for small and medium-sized enterprises over the next two decades. Japan has already established a hundred-year "green plan," and the Keidanren (Federation of Economic Organizations) has issued a business charter for sustainable development. There is a strong argument for businesspeople, scientists, and engineers to become involved in determining reasonable, feasible, and scientifically sound practices for sustainability before somewhat arbitrary procedures are imposed by government policy.

As Pacific Rim nations, the United States and Canada will find information on new opportunities in the area of environmental science and technology in the February 1993 report from Japanese Pacific Climate Studies, part of the R&D group at the STA. The Pacific Ocean plays an important, but as yet unresolved, role in the exchange of heat, moisture, and energy (momentum) between the ocean and the atmosphere. To promote further study, there are cooperative scientific projects between Japan and the United States, Canada, and Australia, which lead to both the sharing of locales for joint experimentation and the sharing of data. From the atmosphere to surface shipping to deep oceans, business should not underestimate the economic potential of the engineering, materials, and instrumentation needs — whether computers, interactive video/computer simulations, or new processes for resolving pollution problems, such as designing biodegradable plastic for the fishing industry (one of the major debris problems in the oceans being plastic netting). The integration of satellite, ship, buoy, and submarine communications and data transmission systems for comprehensive data collection, analysis, and problem diagnosis will be in demand in markets worldwide.

For over two decades we have witnessed the increasing impact of molecular biology on applications in fields as diverse as aquaculture and agriculture to the fermentation industry and pharmaceuticals. Biotechnology is an "enabling technology," cutting across traditional scientific disciplines and industrial sectors, and Japan is particularly responsive to opportunities to expand bio-industries. The Ministry of International Trade and Industry (MITI) is launching R&D projects on the availability and usefulness of tropical-based microorganisms toward enhancing the genetic database and gene selection characteristics. This could have a direct impact on, for example, food, drugs, pharmaceuticals, research on genetic-based diseases, sterilization, and health care products, or environmental cleanups for oil, mining, and agribusiness companies. With market growth rates in the region of 40 percent annually, this area of biotechnology is positioning to mature in the 2010 to 2020 period, in the process becoming analogous to the role computers now occupy as a ubiquitous and enabling information technology in the 1990s.

In Japan, serious attention is being placed on the generation, transformation, and encapsulation of carbon dioxide by major conglomerate companies such as Mitsubishi, which is not only heavily involved in aerospace, radar, and satellites, but also in developing novel technology for disposal strategies in the deep ocean. The Japan Marine Science and Technology Center (JAMSTEC) is a consortium of over 160 companies involved in ocean-related science and technology. It plays an active role in the commercialization of technology and the deployment of prototypes through the extensive R&D linkages it supports. Mitsui Engineering and Shipbuilding company and its many affiliates, for example, have been active in building robots for these R&D projects on the commercial side, and in promoting deep sea exploration for minerals, new plant forms, and pharmaceutical resources. Mitsubishi and Kawasaki are also heavily involved in the development of Kaiko, the deep sea robot, and Shinkai 6,500, the world's deepest-diving submersible. Following the 1989 Montreal protocol on regulating chlorofluorocarbons (CFCs), an enormous effort has been put into the development of substitutes or alternatives. This area offers business opportunities, from consumer personal products all the way to commercial refrigerants and new air-conditioning techniques.

Other environmental activities currently enjoying special focus in Japan concern innovative ways to deal with urban pollution — using architectural designs to create wind flows within a city to ameliorate auto exhaust pollution, and planting selected trees to act as local sinks for noxious gases in high-density areas, to name two specific plans. In the future, the development of satellites in Japan will be for "niche" observational purposes, not only to gather astrophysical cosmic UV data, but also to collect data on fish, to assemble geographic information resources, and for the remote sensing of tropical precipitation or destruction of rain forests. All of this new technology brings with it important scientific, technological, and commercial opportunities, including lidar monitoring of CFCs in particular, and of wind direction and velocity in general. Weather forecasting, improved prediction of natural catastrophes, and environmental stewardship are other areas with enormous potential for business opportunities with Japanese interests. Science and technology is usually seen as the critical entry point for foreign partners to these new ventures.

SCIENCE AND TECHNOLOGY: INFRASTRUCTURE AND ACCESS

With the current recession in Japan, companies are undergoing a certain amount of necessary restructuring. Companies that are no longer internationally competitive are having to downsize, and there is an erosion of lifetime employment. While recent articles in the Japanese press indicate that there is a fall in R&D investment from the peaks experienced during the "bubble economy" of the late 1980s, it is unlikely that the general emphasis on new technology or R&D investment will be diminished, and, in relative terms, it will remain significant. In times of crisis, Japan usually emphasizes the need for long-term R&D investment in order to generate a pool of business opportunities. Similar events occurred during the yen shock of 1987, and the subsequent restructuring of certain major industrial sectors led to a successful period of business innovation.

In view of the fact that Japan funds over 10 percent of the world's scientific and technological research, international attention must be directed to how it is funded, to whom the results are available, and the economic consequences of that situation. There is a massive science and technology infrastructure in Japan, of which only the essential components will be mentioned here as practical knowledge needed for potential S&T ventures.

In Japan, the government funds high-risk research requiring major facilities, basic research with long-term horizons (ten years), research with major public welfare or safety components (such as atomic energy, space, and oceans), and basic research toward the development of strategic technologies. Many agencies are involved, and a hierarchy has developed as ministries have competed for prestige projects over the past four decades. Furthermore, since some ministries have different missions but require similar technology, duplications of institutes and laboratories have occurred. The wary businessperson, scientist, or engineer must examine exactly which route is most productive before entering the S&T maze. A Japanese partner can help to negotiate the regulatory framework applicable to your particular business venture.

The private sector contributes vigorously to the R&D effort in Japan, running impressive frontier research laboratories with an acceptance of the protracted time scales needed before prototypes and practical results appear. Their financial resources and positive attitude toward "patient" capital, and their willingness to accept small but regular dividends on an investment, contrast starkly with the typical North American short-term view, characterized by the need to see a minimum double-digit return within the year. As a result, over the 1980s Japanese firms pulled ahead in technology-intensive areas in the production of automobiles, marine transportation and robots, heavy electrical technology and electronics, and precision machinery, and began to move into optoelectronics, biotechnology, and health sciences as preludes to twenty-first-century business opportunities. A company such as Toshiba illustrates this dual strategy when, as a major integrated company, it invests over 7.5 percent of sales in R&D and begins to focus on new opportunities in bio-membranes with a long-term view, at the same time as it is perfecting high-definition television for the market in competition with the United States and Europe.

Every major Japanese company, as part of a group of affiliated companies (*keiretsu*), drives its global R&D agenda with focus and aggression, not to mention a full range of resources, including the relatively low cost of capital. The Japanese private sector contributes a far higher percentage of the nation's R&D than other nations, typically over 60 percent, compared with about 40 percent in the United States. In Canada, because government laboratories have played a major role in R&D for over a century, and now comprise about 50 percent of the S&T

national activity, the private sector role is limited, accounting for only about 27 percent of the total effort. Universities in Canada also play a large role, representing about 23 percent of the R&D effort in comparison to about 20 percent in Japan and about 18 percent in the United States.

Universities in Japan fall into several categories; we will discuss only the research institutions that are competitive with their North American counterparts. In Canada, with eighty-nine degree-granting institutions for 27 million people, fourteen universities undertake about 75 percent of all the research funded by the government, various foundations, and private sector contracts. In the United States, there is a similar class of research-intensive universities selected from the over three thousand educational institutions involved in post-secondary teaching. In Japan, the thirteen former "Imperial" universities (including the Tokyo Institute of Technology) are the equivalent grouping, led by the University of Tokyo and the University of Kyoto. The University of Tsukuba, as the core of Science City (near Tokyo), offers the most S&T human resources in one locale. Both public and private major universities claim research excellence in selected areas. University research budgets have been notably increased in the past two years (over 10 percent per year), reflecting the high priority given to fundamental, long-range research, despite current economic pressures felt by Japan.

As the Educational Reform Bill and other legislation of the later 1980s is implemented in Japan, programs are becoming more international, new interdisciplinary institutes are being established, and opportunities are expanding for university-industry R&D exchange which could not have existed under the law five years ago. Foreign companies and international students are now playing increasingly important roles, and professional industrial employees are being accepted at major university laboratories as part of "joint venture" activities.

In both the United States and Canada there have been notable increases in exchanges with Japan of both university researchers and projects, and many universities have formal agreements with Japanese counterparts, as do technical and trade associations. Business schools are certainly urged to do more in terms of linking into specific Japanese firms for work-term experience. In turn, businesses in North America are encouraged to hire these young students or take advantage of their skills by using them as part of a field team for particular R&D projects.

What are the areas of research to which Japanese R&D is directed? Table 1 illustrates the results of a poll conducted by the Science and Technology Agency among leading Japanese researchers to define R&D activities between now and 2020. The STA has set the development of the national economy and improvements of national life through science and technology as its primary mission, and oversees national large-scale projects on space, oceans, and nuclear energy. The STA also has a central coordinating function for all other departments in S&T, and presents and argues for the S&T envelope in the Diet.

From a business perspective, in terms of close contacts with the private sector and regulatory approval, the most critical ministry for commercial R&D is the Ministry of International Trade and Industry and MITI's Agency of Industrial Science and Technology (AIST). All government and industry projects, big science activities for R&D or industrial restructuring, energy and trade policies with industrial impact (including impact on the environment), and long-range research policies fall within AIST's mandate. National projects are regularly updated or reshaped at MITI's laboratories, and when research endeavors are of such a magnitude to require partnerships, either the private sector is given a contract (for full-cost funding) or a consortium of firms is put together to share risks, costs, and the resulting technologies. Thus, for short periods of time, antitrust laws do not apply to cooperative R&D activities. Two recent examples are an optoelectronics project and the Fuzzy Logic Engineering Laboratory; there are also the well-known High Speed Computer projects, which include supercomputer developments, and a number of dedicated national energy and materials laboratories. There are increasing opportunities for foreign companies to become involved, such as with the recently established Information Technologies consortium.

The pattern of consortia and active cooperation on pre-competitive research is long established in Japan; more recently, foreign companies have also been invited to play a role in consortia.

Table 1 Chronology of Future Technologies As projected in 1991 by Policy Research at the Japanese Science and Technology Agency (STA)

YEAR	TECHNOLOGY EXPECTED TO BE REALIZED
2001	• An economical means to select, separate, and recover valuable materials from urban wastes will be in practical use. • The implantation of internal organs (the kidney, heart, liver, etc.) will be conducted as frequently in Japan as in Europe and America in 1991.
2002	• An ultra-LSI memory chip, with 1 giga-bit memory or more, will be in practical use. • The formation, variation, and elimination of the ozone layer will be elucidated. • The breeding of crops (for volume, resistance to drought, salt, cold, or disease, etc.) by gene manipulation will be in practical use.
2003	• A technological system to automatically divide general wastes into inflammables, metals, glass, etc. will be in general use in Japan. • A four-dimensional aircraft control system by position and time will be developed to cope with high-density flight operations and the need to improve safety. • An early detection system for cancer will be completed, and over 70 percent of all cancer patients will live at least five years. • A system will be in practical use whereby an individual's health can be checked and diagnosed at home. • With the progress of television, telephones, on-line systems, fax machines, etc., general office work, with the exception of interviews and negotiations, will be done at home. • A multipurpose nursing robot will be in practical use which can properly take care of the handicapped and bedridden.
2004	• The precise mechanisms for generating and removing carbon dioxide in the atmosphere will be made clear. • Micro-machines will be in use in a variety of operations in wide-ranging areas such as biochemistry, microprocessing and assembling, manufacturing of semiconductors, etc. • A waste recycling technology, which may reduce urban wastes by half, will be developed. • Because of the development of a battery with sufficient capacity for commuting use, electric automobiles which can run in city traffic will be in general use.
2005	• Water purification technology will be in practical use and will contribute to improving the environment. • Rises in the sea surface due to global warming will be predicted precisely. • Two types of artificial kidney — partial refit and total implantation — will be developed to replace dialysis machines.
2006	• The prediction of volcanic eruptions a few days in advance will become possible. • A treatment for AIDS will be established.

Table I (continued)

YEAR	TECHNOLOGY EXPECTED TO BE REALIZED
2007	• Solar cells will be in general use to supply electricity to residential homes. • Telephone numbers responding to individual use will be achieved, and international personal mobile phones will be in practical use. • A linear-motor car, with a maximum speed of about 500 kilometers per hour, will be in practical use. • An effective method of treating antisclerosis will be developed.
2008	• Electric machines for industrial purposes using superconductive materials (which have a critical temperature higher than that of liquid nitrogen) will be in general use. • A portable particle accelerator to repair ozone holes, which can be loaded onto an aircraft, will be developed. • An automatic, real-time interpreting telephone (Japanese/English) will be developed. • A three-dimensional picture display device, which can be used at home without special glasses, will be in practical use. • Regional disaster-prevention systems for predicting earthquakes, landslides, etc. will be in general use.
2009	• Technology for biochemical conversion, storage, etc. of solar energy will be in practical use. • An approach to mental health will be developed that will enable the prevention of problems due to stress.
2010	• Intelligent materials incorporating sensor programming and effector functions will be developed. • The mechanisms of human memory, recognition, and learning will be made clear and will be modelled to the extent capable of being applied to computer science. • All DNA base-pairs of the human chromosomes will be determined. • Technology will be developed with which one can predict several days in advance the occurrence of earthquakes of magnitude 7 or more. • The mechanism of carcinogenesis will be clarified for almost all cancers.
2011	• Pictures of the movement and storage of carbon dioxide across whole sections of the atmosphere, oceans, and seabed will be clarified; technology to maintain a balance between the use of fossil fuels and the preservation of the earth's environment will be developed. • A passenger plane will be developed with a speed of Mach 4, passenger capacity of 300, and that can fly across the Pacific Ocean in three hours. • An effective method to prevent Alzheimer-type dementia will be developed.
2012	• A superconductive-electromagnetic ship will be in practical use.

Table I (continued)

YEAR	TECHNOLOGY EXPECTED TO BE REALIZED
2013	• A medication to prevent carcinogenesis will be developed. • The mechanism of aging will be elucidated. • A space factory that uses the spatial environment to produce semiconductors, medications, etc. on a commercial basis will be built. • A space plane operating aircraft between the ground and a space station will be in practical use.
2014	• The process of the generation and growth of the brain will be elucidated on a molecular level.
2015	• A permanently manned base will be built on the moon for space observation. • World emissions of carbon dioxide will be reduced to 20 percent of 1991 levels. • An ultrahigh building (with a height of 1,000 meters or more) will be constructed with comfortable dwelling spaces.
2016	• Gene therapy will be in practical use for many diseases caused by gene defects.
2017	• A superconductor will be developed which has a shifting superconductivity point of room temperature. • A fast-breeder reactor (FBR) system, including the full nuclear fuel cycle, will be in practical use.
2018	• A long-term (10–20 years) forecast of variations in major fishery resources will become possible; a production-adjustment system for controlling resources will be developed.
2019	• A superconductive energy storage system, with a capacity comparable to a pumping-up power plant, will be in practical use.
2020	• A method to preserve a living body, by using hibernation or other means, will be developed.

The continuous consultation process ensures that when R&D results approach market potential, the firms quickly move independently and in competition for the market, with an understanding of the probable size of their eventual market share. Japan's Research and Development Corporation (JRDC), with headquarters in Tokyo, can advise on opportunities and eligibility for such private sector involvement. What criteria are invoked depends very much on the specific R&D venture, with a good match in needed expertise and project demands as a necessary beginning. Databases are available through JRDC, and inquiries can be made at a local JETRO office in North America. JRDC may also direct you to a more appropriate agency, whether for financing, such as the New Energy and Industrial Technology Development Organization (NEDO), or for collaboration on national consortium projects, via the research-based ERATO program, now accessible to foreign members.

The consortia model is also well established in Canada. Paprican was founded in 1926 as a research consortium for the pulp and paper industry; one of the more recently established is PRECARN (1986), which focuses on robotics and artificial intelligence. A company interested in consortia in Japan could examine these models as a preparatory step for the kinds of business and technology decisions which may have to be explored. North American businesses can prepare for Japan by pursuing the ERATO model in particular, a brilliant scheme involving frontier commercial opportunities such as Superbug and pharmaceuticals, or Nanomover and miniaturization in manufacturing. These are based on "matching fund" concepts. Not all models work, and not all may be a good match for your business.

In the United States, private sector consortia are a recent development. A consortium was attempted for semiconductor manufacturing (Sematech) in the 1980s. Present policy discussions in the States have shifted to new consortia models for the 1990s. While the American private sector traditionally prefers collaborations with universities, not with other corporations, R&D imperatives for future technologies and the development of new international business may require a fundamental shift in attitude among business managers. For this to be possible, government policies and antitrust laws will also have to be reviewed.

In Japan, business can now collaborate with the universities. Historically, attitudes and legislation have led to very different patterns than in North America. Until very recently, university professors at the national universities were regarded as civil servants; thus, technology transfer and patenting with commercial partners were not common at Japanese universities. Researchers sometimes had to move into the private sector to pursue R&D projects. On the other hand, private sector laboratories offer tremendous resources to research faculty at universities in certain areas, such as semiconductors, where computers or electronic devices can be designed and tested quite freely.

If your attention turns to a university project within consortia such as the ERATO project, supported by the JRDC, then the point of entry for potential projects and approval is also the JRDC. If the project is confined to a university institute or laboratory, then the Ministry of Education, Science, and Culture (Monbusho) should be your first call as a source of information on international opportunities; the International Science Division deals with both project and personnel exchange opportunities. Up-to-date brochures in English are available from all R&D organizations, which provide a valuable source of information on the research base in Japan and its priorities. Furthermore, as in North America, professors maintain contact with their former students in industry and can provide another source of intelligence on who is doing what and where.

Should space science and technology be your particular interest, then the National Space Development Agency of Japan (NASDA) under the auspices of the Science and Technology Agency is of prime importance to you. Other space-related activities occur in many different locations, a premier institute being the Institute of Space and Aeronautical Science (IASA), which has become a national research institute for joint use by universities, shifting from its origins as the University of Tokyo's center for nonmilitary rocket research. Monbusho thus supports the design and launch of purely scientific satellites. It is not possible to list all the institutes, space commissions, and government coordinating activities here, but the Canadian Space Agency and NASA are essential contact points, since bilateral and multilateral agreements exist that cover space activities.

RIKEN, the major national institute for physical and chemical research outside Tokyo, is an interdisciplinary set of laboratories closely associated with national standards and national research councils, and with an international mandate and potential for commercial collaboration. The Electrotechnical Laboratory and Geological Survey of Japan are under the auspices of MITI's research wing and are often involved in commercial development integrated into their basic R&D functions. Medical R&D usually falls under the Ministry of Health and Welfare in Japan, while industrial health is covered under the Ministry of Labor. The Ocean Research Institute operated by the University of Tokyo is an entry point for marine-based R&D activities, and the National Institute of Polar Research for polar and ice-based engineering and environmental technologies. Electronic instrumentation and detector equipment is not only extensively used by, but also developed in collaboration with, foreign groups at KEK, the National Laboratory for High Energy Physics at Tsukuba Science City.

Environmental research is being undertaken at literally hundreds of research institutes in Japan at the national and prefectural levels, as well as in private research centers. Much of this activity is linked to national projects, which tend to be longer-term, fundamental research, but research with short-term applications is also extremely active. A number of the national research institutes have been restructured to facilitate the interdisciplinary nature of environmental issues. Institutes have been established, including STA's National Institute for Environmental Science (NIES), where traffic pollution and architectural simulations in real time are observed, as well as laser ozone and experimental tree projects. MITI recently established the Research Institute of Innovative Technology for the Earth (RITE). RITE was established as a private and public sector initiative, with a strong international mandate. Each year, RITE calls for submissions, and accepts several international proposals.

Over the past decade, surveys have shown a dramatic increase in the amount of private sector R&D activity conducted in Japan by North American firms. The area of growth most notable in the 1990s is environmental technology, as demonstrated by the thousands of attendees at the Globe '90, '92 and now Globe '94 International Trade and Environment Expositions. Environmental and trade R&D clearly transcend single departments, but the Environmental Agency is responsible for both global environmental planning as well as research projects in Japan. A project involving, for example, environmental R&D activities on the North Pacific Ocean, a region of great interest to Canada, Japan, and the United States, could involve as many as nine ministries. All such S&T activity, if government plays a central role, would have to be launched through the auspices of the Ministry of Foreign Affairs (Gaimusho), whose director general is responsible for North America and for the bilateral science and technology agreements. If you wish to consult or give a presentation to many ministries at the same time, this S&T desk is the appropriate host, and embassy staff can assist in setting up such a meeting, once objectives are clearly understood by all parties.

In summary, a proposed R&D project may have many players and overlapping opportunities for interest and support in Japan. The first step is to become knowledgeable and map out the overlapping opportunities, because the latter are also usually accompanied by constraints. When a project is begun by STA, for example, it will not necessarily be supported by MITI if this is not negotiated ahead of time. All Japanese partners must be at the table during the formulation of a proposal. The prestige of ministries, and thus of desirable projects, certainly influences the strategic pathways through which the project can be funded or supported in other ways. An incorrect or ill-considered entry into the S&T infrastructure maze can lead to immense delay and frustration. As with any North American project, it is important to identify a champion. This is a slow and careful process in Japan, but once the champion is in place, progress occurs with pleasing speed and real results.

MARKET ENTRY AND PARTNERSHIPS

As a company president or strategist, you will be faced with some practical questions if you have a new technology to develop, market, or position in the Japanese business sector. Your opportunities

Table 2 Business Technology Matrix for North America: Japan Opportunities

NORTH AMERICAN FIRM PROFILE	JAPANESE PARTNER OR VENTURE MCH	MCL	TCA	NTS	ETN
MCH	X X	JV JV	JV / MA JV	JV / TJV MA	JV JV
MCL	JV / TJV JV / TJV	JV JV	MA JV	SUB JV / TJV	JV JV
TCA	MA MA	MA MA	X X	X X	MA MA
NTS	X SUB / JV	JV SUB / JV	MA X	JV JV	JV JV
ETN	X SUB	JV SUB	JV / MA JV	JV JV	JV JV

NOTE: In each box, the upper line represents North American ventures into Japan and the lower line, Japanese ventures into North America.

PARTNERSHIPS:
MCH Major corporation/existing division and products
MCL Major corporation/new initiative upon established track record
TCA Trading company or affiliate of corporation, "umbrella"
NTS New technology/start-up company/frontier venture
ETN Established technology niche

MECHANISMS:
X Rare interactions
JV Joint venture (50/50) preferred interactions
TJV Trilateral joint ventures, financed accordingly
SUB Subsidiary formation, wholly owned
MA Marketing agreements

will depend on the scope and scale of your business and that of potential partners in Japan. How does one identify which companies or agencies might be involved?

Table 2 is a matrix designed to give you a "rough cut" on the answer to the question of partnerships. Consider examples of major corporations with existing technology or products, those with new initiatives, trading companies or affiliates, start-up companies with new technology, or firms or individuals operating in an established technology niche. How do you approach the equivalent Japanese organization? Is it going to be fruitful as a first step? And how could the Japanese approach you?

Based on extensive experience of technology-based firms, Table 2 shows the most probable interactions, ranging from "rare" through to joint ventures, marketing agreements, or the acquisition or formation of a subsidiary. Joint ventures can often involve trilateral partnerships, cross-licensing, and so on. In using Table 2 to see what strategy would work best for your campaign in Japan, first consider the sector in which your business falls. Electronics, for example, is frequently a standards-driven business, while food products are more market-controlled in terms of culture and task. At the present time, engineering construction is governed more by Japanese business practices and market access, while drugs and noninvasive medical treatments are strongly influenced by clinical standards, hospital practices, and societal mores.

Next, the analysis of your core technology business will help determine which of the many strategic issues in your mind will be the critical ones for joint research and commercialization of R&D. In general, cross-licensing agreements are appropriate for global technology markets and for new technologies with a world-product mandate. However, experience has shown that it is not always productive to fight the Japanese view of the pre-eminence of Japanese technology products, particularly if your Japanese CEO or partner believes his products already satisfy world demand.

Should one approach a government agency first or the private sector — or a nongovernmental organization (NGO) involved in R&D? Again, the answer is sector-specific. In aerospace, government linkages are vital, while in electronics a private sector linkage can be established more quickly as a first step, because very often governmental processes are too slow in comparison to the product shelf-life and the market window. New materials and biotechnology also invite immediate private sector linkages, although Japanese R&D in MITI government laboratories is quite extensive. Telecommunications and software both have a strong private sector, but also a regulatory, character. There is no single blueprint. Environmental technologies have enjoyed much success in Japan over the past two decades, but this is only the beginning — and many products will require an "environmental assessment" by a Japanese government agency. Current European business practices are closer to those in Japan than are North American protocols, in terms of accepting the uncertainties of, for example, "polluting materials," whether in inks for printing or in lead solder on electronic boards. There is a different sensitivity to chemicals, and ethnocultural allergies, like differences in diet or population health, cannot be ignored. One well-known example is the sensitivity of Asians to enzymes (lactose) in milk, a condition much less common among Westerners.

Historically, the time frames are long for obtaining government approvals, if they are needed. But once the first approval has been given, further applications move much faster. Learning to deal with a particular person in the agency and identifying a champion is the most practical advice, because personal relationships within the bureaucracy can accelerate professional responses. Patience is required, with persistent follow-through and thorough documentation.

The major funding decisions on government and related programs must all be concluded in August of each year by the Ministry of Finance, so new ventures requiring R&D seed funding for support should be coordinated with the next business cycle of the Japanese government. The private sector has its own cycle of technology funding programs and must be dealt with on an individual basis — of increasing importance is the "matching funds approach," usually fifty-fifty in a two-partner venture. The private sector often has access to much lower-cost capital than do U.S. or Canadian firms. If the Japanese partner chooses to pursue market share and long-term capital gains, be prepared to consider similar strategies: Japanese companies expect profitable ventures from their foreign partnerships and are prepared for a long-term relationship built upon expertise, trust, and a willingness to fix problems promptly when they inevitably arise in any new and bold venture.

I would like to offer an example of an activity that occurred over the course of a decade, and that has led to successful market penetration in the highly competitive world of modern telecommunications. The chairman and CEO of Northern Telecom made a strategic "market-opening" visit to Japan in 1982, armed with a long-term corporate commitment. By setting up Tokyo offices, meeting high-level government and private sector opinion leaders, and becoming familiar with market niche opportunities, the groundwork was carefully laid. He built relationships with NTT (Nippon Telegraph and Telephone) that eventually resulted in a pilot central office telecommunications switch being installed in 1983. As the first technology ever provided by a non-Japanese vendor, the switch was competitive with the best in the world, but by NTT standards in Japan (where even a tiny dent is a defect), it was originally unsatisfactory. To some, such extraordinary high standards are typical of nontariff barriers.

Companies presuming that "best price and best technology" will win the deal are frustrated by what they perceive as "structural" barriers to markets, and often complain that meeting such standards adds too much expense. In contrast, Northern Telecom did not walk away, but worked to understand the requirements of the Japanese client, modified manufacturing and support processes, and vastly improved the quality of its DMS-10 switch to the point where it is now a global leader among switches. By 1988, the quality push had resulted in Nortel being a primary supplier of rural switches to NTT, and since then business has grown tenfold, with a new agreement signed in 1993 and R&D partnerships created to work on the next generation of switches. With annual 10 percent growth rates being the tangible result of building partnerships and listening to Japanese customer quality needs, this company is now poised to move deeper into Asia, with a long-term view for the year 2000 and beyond.

In order to be tuned to reality, going to Japan requires planning that includes a grasp of the culture, language, human resources issues, and the level of work-force training, as well as the R&D business venture and financing, which naturally dominates a business plan. Basic business etiquette, such as keeping appointments and punctuality, goes a long way toward building strong relationships in Japan. Many universities and colleges in Canada and the United States now offer resources of great value to the potential traveler in terms of language programs, R&D project experience, and business seminars. Increasingly, research faculty have links to the chambers of commerce in Japan. Why not take advantage of these linkages? By sponsoring a student for a year in Japan, your company may not only acquire eyes and ears "on-the-spot," but also have in place a person whose networking skills may prove invaluable in the future.

Throughout this process of forging new relationships with Japan, it is essential that North American companies recognize that cultural differences will affect a product's success in Japan.

Furthermore, some technologies are accepted more rapidly in Japan than in North America. For example, rapid developments in cosmetics in Japan offer opportunities to biotechnology pharmaceuticals (and to the study of the physical chemistry of complexions), but the types of complexions and the norms of beauty are different in Japan. Food products, beer, and other beverages rely on basic principles of biochemistry, food technology, and fermentation, but the preferred degree of sweetness or dryness is a cultural matter. The color of flour for cookies, the degree of gloss in cosmetics, or the texture of a hand cream are related to the science and technology of bleaching, oil-based versus water-based materials, and the viscosity of polyaromatic substrates, respectively. Even the age-old art of packaging has experienced a renaissance driven by space-age materials and the rising demand for environmentally friendly and recycled materials. All these factors influence the design and choice of technology for Japan.

ON INTELLECTUAL PROPERTY: INNOVATE OR LITIGATE?

In this new era of globalization driven by technological innovation, it is clear that economic development and expanding international trade will make smoother progress if these activities are coupled with an acceptance of intellectual property rights (IPR) as part of the competitiveness and business equation. This, in turn, implies an acceptance of a minimum standard of protection and enforcement of IPR. The culture of innovation, rather than litigation, is far more familiar to the Japanese, where the number of scientists and engineers notably exceeds the number of lawyers, and over 75 percent of private sector CEOs have a sciences and engineering background. In contrast to other jurisdictions, however, the Japanese readily file patents, promote a multiplicity of applications, and focus on incremental improvements, which often lead to an operational nontariff barrier if not well understood by North American visitors or negotiators.

As a businessperson with new products or processes, or a lawyer about to negotiate a new business deal, you may not have included or conceived of IPR as a comparative market advantage or indeed as a potential vulnerability. As a scientist or engineer, your knowledge of IPR should be an essential part of R&D. This need for prior knowledge has become more important over the past decade, R&D has increased markedly. University, research institute, or government policies, when applied to grants and contracts, will determine the degree of freedom and incentives available to any individual on the collectivity of IPR, which includes: patents, copyright trademarks, licensing agreements, industrial designs, plant-breeders' rights, software copyright, protection of integrated circuits, and specific sector legislation, such as the U.S. Semi-Conductor Chip Protection Act or the Canadian Pharmaceutical Patent Act.

Thus, whatever your background, if you are involved in any technology-based venture or science-based innovation, it is prudent to have the answers to the following questions before any agreement is finalized or project formally proposed:

- Who owns the R&D, product, or process that is being discussed?
- What IPR issues should be considered? The list may involve several topics.
- If patents are involved, what patent conventions are to be followed (discovery, First-to-File, First-to-Invent)? Who initiates?
- What dispute resolution mechanisms are or should be in place?
- What enforcement mechanisms (against piracy or other violations of IPR) are in place?
- How long will it take to obtain the patent, and for how long is the IPR protection in place?
- What is the start-up and annual cost of IPR protection?
- What are the consequences of a deliberate decision not to pursue IPR? In Japan, this is generally a sector-specific question, because in some cases the process of obtaining IPR is so slow in comparison with changing market pressures that legal processes can adversely hold up business decisions to launch a new product.

The last question may be surprising, but in cases of fundamental scientific research, very often the answer is to publish the results freely and communicate widely among the international community. Once the novel scientific or technical results are published in the journal literature, the degree of public knowledge is such that no one can patent the results anywhere else. That in itself is a degree of protection, because another's patent might well unexpectedly impede your own particular R&D project. Furthermore, in areas such as microelectronics and optoelectronics, patents cannot keep pace with the rapidly evolving market, where new products or processes appear practically every month.

Canada (since 1989) and Japan now both follow the convention of First-to-File for patent credit, as do the U.K. and members of the EC. The United States has consistently followed the First-to-Invent approach, where annotated notebooks play a major role, even for prior invention/art arguments on another's patent application. Thus, there exists between Canada and Japan a harmony on patent practice (but not on patent culture, as discussed below), while the United States and Japan stand in stark contrast. The ongoing litigation in the Sony/Kodak dispute on magnetic recording head technology is a classic example of the clash of two patent systems and cultures.

In the United States, the operating IPR philosophy yields a single patent for a given technology, a bold strike disciplined by a rigorous first patent discovery and examiner step, and language that includes all spin-offs for its genre. In Japan, the operating IPR philosophy promotes a flood of patent applications, often with only minimal variations on the same technology, encouraged by a relatively easy first patent examiner step, and much later rigorous proof. Every improvement triggers a new patent. Thus, American patents appear more general but are potentially also more inclusive. Japanese patents appear too detailed, and are thus restrictive.

It is not surprising, therefore, that there is often a ten-fold difference in patent applications in a given technology area between the United States or North America and Japan. In Canada, patent culture is less aggressive but comparably as rigorous as in the United States, while the U.K. and Europe fall in between. The final difference in patent culture, to which one should be alert, is in published information. Until patents are approved, and thus published, in the United States, all information is strictly confidential. In Japan, eighteen months after filing, all is published; Canada and Europe are comparably open.

IPR should be part of any business strategy. Cross-licensing can be strategic for international projects involving consortia of several firms or R&D laboratories. Indeed, in the enormously important area of magnetic and optical data storage, the production of the early compact discs in the 1980s involved such an approach. Philips worked with Sony, Sharp, and a Japanese consortium, in which the mandatory cross-licensing of any new technology to the other partners provided an effective motivator to produce all the components as fast and inexpensively as possible. The goal was to capture the world market and to set world specifications in a new realm of CD technology with enormous growth potential. We are now seeing (and hearing) the results in an increasingly digital world of information technology.

In summary, when proposing to work in Japan, answer the IPR questions posed above in order to create a framework for response, and preferred options for action. I will conclude with a few more practical words of advice.

First of all, prepare all business presentations in clear and unambiguous English, with a minimum of jargon. Although we can assume that the Japanese businessperson or scientist reads English, language can be an accidental nontariff barrier. Often our business communications are garbled with jargon or colloquialisms. Jargon builds barriers, which can become excuses for "misunderstanding" at a later stage. Scrupulously avoid jargon and you will maximize understanding. Clarifying the meaning is sensible diplomacy and saves face for everyone. When IPR is involved, this is crucial.

Secondly, if patents have already been issued in North America or Europe, this makes a substantial impact on the project or deal in Japan. Bring proof of having received a patent. It is much more difficult to make a case on a "patent pending" basis.

Thirdly, the Japanese are very "hands-on" by temperament. Bring, if possible, a well-designed prototype available for a demonstration and/or have one available if a Japanese team visits your laboratory or firm. A video is an acceptable alternative, and has the advantage of presenting an activity in context or the device in a real-world situation. The accompanying technical description should be reviewed by a Japanese speaker (preferably an engineer or technically literate person) in order to remove linguistic ambiguities, which inevitably exist, and to clarify any issues which can arise as much from cultural as from scientific reasons. If you leave devices behind, be prepared for "reverse engineering," and do not through naiveté invite confidentiality problems.

Fourthly, be patient and never give in to the temptation to be scientifically or technologically arrogant. The Japanese, in questioning you, will show polite ignorance. The Japanese are short on generalists and long on technical experts, and may test you by repeated questions to see if you say the same thing over and over again accurately. Nor is this a matter for impatience — your confidence is being tested, not to mention your business or scientific poise under pressure. The Japanese themselves are open to answering scientific or technical questions and will welcome your interest. It is wise to ensure a technical expert is part of your team.

Fifthly, as a businessperson, it is often very difficult to get a good and quick assessment of the level of technological skills in the groups of Japanese people you meet. However, if you are not a scientist or engineer yourself but bring a technological consultant with you who is also a professor in Canada or the States, the Japanese will be very pleased to open up all for you to view. Professors, teachers, education, and research, and knowledge in general enjoy high status in Japanese society.

Finally, when establishing an R&D project or new business or new product/process for Japan assessment, the key question posed will be: "Who is the competition?" or "Why is this project or product so unique?" It is possible that the deal or agreement could collapse on the failure to address this question well ahead of time. In North America a patent search would reveal technological uniqueness, but in Japan this can be somewhat frustrating since vaguely worded disclosures leave much uncertainty. A thorough and costly study could be launched, but a rapid assessment is very difficult. If your project or product has already been established elsewhere, it is easier to make the case for uniqueness, but often you will meet arguments summed up by the phrase: "Things are different in Japan." That is culturally true and should not be taken as a negative, but rather as a challenge to continue to build relationships with your partners and seek to understand the differences.

For example, to trigger funding in Japan for an R&D project, the partners must first agree on all the project details — what, who, how, when — before fiscal resources can be allocated to the project. In North America, however, projects usually appear in response to an announcement of funds being allocated to a program: big science projects are usually line items in government budgets. Thus, within the Canada-Japan Complementarity Study (1989), which established the subsequent Japan Science and Technology Fund (JSTF), wording was chosen to ensure that funds could be allocated for projects and programs in the two countries in accordance with existing mechanisms and cultural norms. As another example, in the United States, negotiations often start from an opening assumption that 100 percent of the project design belongs to the American partner, while the foreign partner will contribute 50 percent to be part of implementation. Final positions depend on the merit of the case.

As in any other activity, for a truly successful venture you need to identify a sponsor as well as a champion in the Japanese government, the private sector, or a university research department. This person must then be very carefully and frequently briefed. Incremental improvement is part of the business culture, and continuous innovation part of the impressive success. This implies a continuous update for the information base shared with your partner. Building relationships works more effectively this way as trust is built.

Complacency is a mistake, even for successful ventures. Beware the culture of continuous improvement. You too must have a constant flow of improvements, because otherwise someone else will copy and innovate, and soon a Japanese product will compete in the marketplace. But the more patiently and fully developed your IPR or patent(s) are, the less likely that anyone will do an end run or steal your designs. Visiting space research laboratories in Japan and seeing smaller replicas of Canada's Space Arm, or seeing biotechnology at work in miniature bovines, DNA-bred for small free-roaming spaces in Japan based on Canadian medical scientific research, are healthy reminders of the commercial impact of IPR, and the return on investment from R&D conducted decades ago.

In Japan, where the number of science and technology professionals per thousand people is 8.1, in comparison to 4.3 in Canada and 6.6 in the United States, it is clear there is a larger technological capacity to produce innovations. Calls for more scientific and engineering literacy in Canada and the United States are often repeated by those who have worked successfully in Japan and seen the "miracle" at work. By successfully steering through the S&T infrastructure and IPR challenges, you will have undergone an immersion course in S&T and the new business literacy. Technology and business offer an exciting new set of partnerships for economic relations with Japan. It is preferable to innovate, rather than to litigate; but be prepared to protect your IPR when the game gets rough. Such strength is admired in Japan — but only when based on substance, overall quality, and the sparkle of excellence.

NOTES

1. *These trends are examined in detail in G.A. Kenney-Wallace, "Science and Technology and Linkages to Contemporary Business: Distraction or Destiny?"* Business in the Contemporary World *(Autumn 1990).*

DR. KENNETH COURTIS is first vice-president and senior economist and strategist at Deutsche Bank Research in Japan, responsible for economic public policy and investment research on the principal economies of East Asia. He began his academic career at the University of Toronto, and completed post-graduate degrees at the University of Sussex, INSEAD and the Institute of Economic and Political Studies in Paris. He is currently a visiting professor of international finance and economic policy at Keio and Tokyo Universities. Dr. Courtis is widely published and is a member of several advisory boards, including the International Policy Study Group of the Japanese Ministry of International Trade and Industry.

JAMES M. LAMBERT is first secretary (economic) at the Canadian Embassy in Tokyo, covering macro-economic developments in Japan and their impact on third countries. Mr. Lambert is a graduate of Queen's University and studied international relations at the Norman Paterson School of International Affairs at Carleton University. He has served at various posts with the Department of Foreign Affairs and International Trade, including Nigeria and Costa Rica.

GREGORY CLARK has been a professor in the Japanese Studies Department of the Faculty of Comparative Culture at Sophia University in Tokyo since 1979 and chancellor of the Institute of Developing Economies Advanced School since 1990. A graduate of Oxford University, Mr. Clark worked in the Australian Department of External Affairs, serving in Hong Kong and Moscow. He then undertook research at Australian National University and Hitotsubashi University and Institute of Developing Economies, before heading up the Tokyo Bureau of *The Australian*. Mr. Clark has published several books in both English and Japanese, including *The Japanese: Origins of Uniqueness* and *Understanding the Japanese*. He has served on numerous Japanese government committees, his most recent appointment being as a Special Member of the Economic Council of the Economic Planning Agency.

DR. JAMES ABEGGLEN is currently chairman of Gemini Consulting (Japan), chairman of Asia Advisory Services K.K. and professor of international business in the Faculty of Comparative Culture at Sophia University. Dr. Abegglen received his doctorate from the University of Chicago and after post-doctoral work at Harvard University taught at the University of Chicago and Massachusetts Institute of Technology. Dr. Abegglen has worked as a management consultant for over thirty years, and was a founding officer of Boston Consulting Group, establishing the group's Tokyo office as well as directing its London and Paris offices. Dr. Abegglen lectures frequently at international meetings and has authored ten books, including *Kaisha, The Japanese Corporation* and his most recent, *Sea Change: Pacific Asia as the New World Industrial Center*.

GEORGE FIELDS is the former chairman and C.E.O. of ASI Market Research Japan, which he helped establish in 1966 and which became the leading cross-cultural market research group in Japan. In 1992, he became its chairman in Japan and left the group in 1993 to become Visiting Professor in Marketing at the Wharton School of the University of Pennsylvania. He has authored eight books in Japanese and two in English — *From Bonsai to Levi's* and *The Japanese Market Culture*. He is a regular contributor to the Japanese broadcast and print media and is currently a weekly columnist, in Japanese, for the Sunday

Mainichi. He is active as a consultant and serves on several public and private bodies, including as Councillor for International Broadcasting for NHK (the Japanese Broadcasting Corporation) and advisor to the American Management Association in Japan.

DR. KIRK PATTERSON is the president of Gavin Anderson & Company (Japan) Inc., a public relations consultancy. An eleven-year resident of Japan, Dr. Patterson has extensive experience in Japanese corporate communications, working as a senior associate with IBI, a leading Tokyo agency, and as a co-founder and director of IR Japan, the first and largest investor relations consultancy in Japan. A graduate of University of Victoria, he obtained post-graduate degrees at Queen's University and the Fletcher School of Law and Diplomacy, Tufts University. Dr. Patterson is a member of the planning committee of the newly created Japan Investor Relations Association.

MICHAEL LESLIE is the president of Nakodo Consulting Inc., a Calgary-based consultancy specializing in product development for export to the far Eastern markets. A graduate of the University of Manitoba, he began his career with Alberta Agriculture specializing in marketing agricultural products and became a Trade Director in the Japanese market development division. This included a secondment to The Seiyu, Ltd., Japan's third-largest grocery chain. Mr. Leslie then worked with the Canada Beef Export Federation as the director responsible for Japan and Pacific Asia, before returning to Canada.

CATHARINE G. JOHNSTON is a principal research associate at The Conference Board of Canada, responsible for total quality management. Since 1990, she has co-chaired with Mark Daniel three International Executive Study Tours to Europe, the United States and Japan to study some of the best total quality initiatives. Three reports have been published on the findings of the study tours: *Customer Satisfaction Through Quality: An International Perspective, The Integrated PDCA Approach to Continuous Improvement* and *Setting the Direction: Management by Planning*. Both papers were co-authored with Dr. Mark Daniel. Ms. Johnston holds a post-graduate degree in business from McGill University.

DR. MARK J. DANIEL is the vice-president in charge of organizational effectiveness and the management of total quality with The Conference Board of Canada. He has co-chaired, with Catharine Johnston, three International Executive Study Tours to Europe, the United States and Japan and co-authored the resulting reports. A graduate of the University of Maryland, he also holds a post-graduate degree from the University of Minnesota. Dr. Daniel has held positions with the government of Canada as an economist and with Canada Post in industrial relations.

JOHN POWLES, a thirty-year resident of Japan, is manager, Asia for the Council of Forest Industries Canada (COFI). COFI is responsible for ensuring market access for forest products in Japan, the largest sector of Canadian trade with Japan. Mr. Powles was raised in Japan by his missionary parents, and studied at the University of British Columbia. He joined the Canadian federal government in 1969 and held a variety of positions in the fields of public affairs and expositions. From 1978 to 1987, he directed Canada's participation in international expositions. He is Canada's representative to the Japanese prime minister's

Import Advisory Board and is the current president of the Canadian Chamber of Commerce in Japan.

RUSSELL T. MARK is senior manager and director of the Japanese practice for KPMG Peat Marwick Thorne in Vancouver. Prior to his return to Canada in 1993, Mr. Mark had worked for over ten years in Tokyo, as a public accountant, senior provincial government representative and most recently as the Canadian embassy's special adviser (investment). He has now returned to the accounting profession, where he continues his active involvement in Japanese business affairs. Mr. Mark graduated from the University of British Columbia.

KEVIN K. JONES is a vice-president of Booz-Allen & Hamilton in Hong Kong, responsible for North Asia, including Hong Kong, China, Taiwan and South Korea. Prior to moving to Hong Kong in 1992, Mr. Jones worked for over nine years in Japan, where he was a partner of McKinsey & Co. While there he worked with both Japanese and foreign companies, focusing on integrating Japan into the global organization and on regional strategies. Mr. Jones was educated in England and completed an MBA at INSEAD. He has published many articles and is a contributing author in *Collaborating to Compete*, on global alliances. He has a forthcoming book on foreign business in Japan.

TODD NEWFIELD is the president of FACT Communications, a database marketing and interactive telemedia bureau based in Tokyo. He graduated from the University of Calgary and holds a master's in Japanese Business from a joint program sponsored by the Japanese–American Institute of Management Science. In Japan, Mr. Newfield has worked for a Japanese securities house promoting their international investment banking services and for Gifco Marketing, one of Japan's largest sales promotion agencies, where he developed their interactive media services. He has also worked as a consultant for various governmental organizations, advertising agencies and marketers on introducing consumer products to the Japanese market.

DR. GERALDINE KENNEY-WALLACE was appointed president and vice-chancellor of McMaster University in 1990. Educated in Oxford and London, she completed her doctoral work at the University of British Columbia in chemical physics. She held post-doctoral fellowships at U.B.C. and Notre Dame, joined the chemistry faculty at Yale in 1972 and moved as assistant professor to the University of Toronto in 1974–75, becoming full professor in physics and chemistry by 1980. Dr. Kenney-Wallace has received several national and international awards for her laser research and has served on numerous advisory councils, including the CIDA National Advisory Panel on Centers of Excellence in International Development, and the Science Council of Canada (where she was chairman from 1987 to 1990). Most recently she chaired a Canada–Japan Complementarity Study (1989) on enhanced cooperation in the field of science and technology, was vice-chair of the 1992 Canada–Japan Forum 2000 Panel and has been appointed to the panel that will monitor the follow-up to its recommendations. She sits on the boards of several multinational companies.

DR. ROBERT J. BALLON is professor emeritus of Sophia University (Tokyo) and doctor "honoris causa" of the Catholic University of Cordoba in Argentina. He first came to Japan in 1948 and he is the founder and director of the International Management Development Seminars held at Sophia University since

1964, which focus on business with and in Japan. His many publications include: *Doing Business in Japan, Joint Ventures and Japan, The Japanese Employee, Foreign Investment and Japan, Marketing in Japan, Financial Reporting in Japan, The Financial Behavior of Japanese Corporations* and *Foreign Competition in Japan: Human Resource Strategies*. Dr. Ballon graduated from the University of Louvain (Belgium) and the Catholic University of America.

JANE WITHEY coordinated and edited this book. Educated at Queen's University, she worked as a solicitor in Toronto, before moving to London, England, to take a master's degree in business. She worked in corporate finance at James Capel & Co. After moving to Tokyo, she became the director of publications for the Canadian Chamber of Commerce in Japan.

Chapter One: Japan in the 1990s

Aoki, Masahiko. *Information, Incentives, and Bargaining in the Japanese Economy*. Cambridge: Cambridge University Press, 1988.
Written by one of the foremost Japanese experts in the field, this micro-analysis of the Japanese economy goes beyond narrow, market-oriented notions of industrial organization. Though aimed at economists, it offers the businessperson valuable insights on the capital and information structure of firms, incentive schemes, industrial groupings, innovation, and more.

Ito, Takatoshi. *The Japanese Economy*. Cambridge, MA: MIT Press, 1992.
A highly commendable introduction to the macro side of Japan's economy, using standard economic concepts enlightened by comparison with the United States (performance, institutions, and government policies). Relevant aspects of history, culture, and politics are presented briefly.

Komiya, Ryutaro. *The Japanese Economy: Trade, Industry, and Government*. Tokyo: University of Tokyo Press, 1990.
A distinguished economist and advisor to various government agencies provides a thoughtful analysis of Japan's trade and investment practices, in particular with and in the United States.

Tokunaga, Shojiro, ed. *Japan's Foreign Investment and Asian Economic Interdependence: Production, Trade, and Financial Systems*. Tokyo: University of Tokyo Press, 1992.
From a regional and local perspective, Japanese and Chinese economists provide detailed insight into the economic interdependence (in terms of production, investment, trade, finance, information, and transportation) that blossomed in the region during the decade of the 1980s. Their findings are confirmed by three case studies: Malaysia, Thailand, and China.

Yamamura, Kozo, ed. *Japan's Economic Structure: Should It Change?* Seattle: Society of Japanese Studies, 1990.
If Japan's economic structure is in need of change, why and how? The question is forcefully argued by American and Japanese economists and lawyers, with a concluding chapter providing a European viewpoint. The discussion is academic, but most enlightening to the businessperson in that it gets "behind" the arguments used in international trade negotiations and journalistic reviews.

Yamashita, Shoichi, ed. *Transfer of Japanese Technology and Management to the ASEAN Countries*. Tokyo: University of Tokyo Press, 1991.
Economists from Japan and several ASEAN nations report on how local industries and enterprises are affected by the sudden increase after 1985 of Japanese investment, and the local reactions to Japanese management and technology transfer.

Stanford University Press has published three volumes written by American and Japanese specialists addressing the general public. They constitute a state-of-the-art analysis of the economic rise, society, and place in contemporary world affairs of postwar Japan (especially after 1973). The papers are future-oriented.

Yamamura, Kozo, and Yasukichi Yasuba, eds. *The Political Economy of Japan. Volume 1: The Domestic Transformation*. 1987.

Inoguchi, Takashi, and Daniel I. Okimoto, eds. *The Political Economy of Japan. Volume 2: The Changing International Context*. 1988.

Kumon, Shumpei, and Henry Rosovsky, eds. *The Political Economy of Japan. Volume 3: Cultural and Social Dynamics*. 1992.

Chapter Two: Japan's Changing Marketplace

Hayashi, Kichiro, ed. *The U.S.–Japanese Economic Relationship: Can It Be Improved?* New York: New York University Press, 1989.
Contributions by American and Japanese experts and mutual comments.

Oppenheim, Phillip. *Trade Wars: Japan vs. the West*. London: Weidenfeld and Nicolson, 1992.
Trading relationships between Japan, Europe, and North America are analyzed and numerous examples provided. Tensions are worsening because Japanese competitiveness is growing, and to its own detriment, the West is turning more and more to protectionism, using supposedly "unfair" Japanese trade practices as an excuse.

Stern, Robert M., ed. *Trade and Investment Relations Among the United States, Canada, and Japan*. Chicago: University of Chicago Press, 1989.
American, Canadian, and Japanese contributions, each followed by comments of the participants at a conference held in 1987, focusing on fundamentals rather than short-term issues.

Thurrow, Lester. *Head to Head: The Coming Economic Battle Among Japan, Europe, and America*. New York: William Morrow, 1992.
This book offers a balanced perspective on the three actors, focusing on the 1990s in terms of what is called "the new competition." It stresses the "new way" of thinking and acting that international values and practices are forcing on the participants, be it about human resources, material resources, or key industries. The "battle" will see many losers, and winners will owe their survival to effective cooperation with their main competitors.

Chapter Three: Japanese Culture and Society

Doi, Takeo. *The Anatomy of Dependence*. Tokyo: Kodansha International, 1973.
A classic, this book by a Japanese psychiatrist offers profound insights into the Japanese character by analyzing key concepts, particularly the concept of *amae*, which means, literally, "indulgent love" but is used to describe the dependency relationships through which Japanese society functions.

Dore, Ronald P., and Mari Sako. *How the Japanese Learn to Work*. London: Routledge, 1989.
This book covers the full spectrum from primary education to company training, from vocational education to informal training in factories and offices. It answers such questions as: What should you expect from trainers? How do you instill pride in a job well done? What should you expect from job classifications? How do you promote training among colleagues?

Inohara, H. *Human Resource Development in Japanese Companies*. Tokyo: Asian Productivity Organization, 1990.
This book reviews in detail all pertinent practices, supported by effective use of

statistics. It includes human resource development in small and medium-sized enterprises, and sheds light on transferability abroad. In Japan, human resources are not so much managed as developed. Japanese terminology, easily misinterpreted in translation, is used and carefully explained.

Nakane, Chie. *Japanese Society*. Berkeley: University of California Press, 1970.
A seminal study providing indispensable insight into Japan's social structure. It describes the continuity of group dynamics that characterizes individual behavior and interpersonal relations, from village to corporation, in government, in the universities and in religious organizations.

Rohlen, Thomas P. *For Harmony and Strength: Japanese White-Collar Organization in Anthropological Perspective*. Berkeley: University of California Press, 1974.
Using the observer-participant approach, a cultural anthropologist describes vividly the "inside" of a local bank employing three thousand people. Personnel administration, daily interaction, company ideology, dormitory life, family and outside commitments are presented in a sensitive and penetrating manner. This book is most helpful in understanding the practices of managing a white-collar work force.

Yoshino, Kosaku. *Cultural Nationalism in Contemporary Japan: A Sociological Enquiry*. London: Routledge, 1992.
This book analyzes the perception of "uniqueness" among Japanese intellectuals, educators, and, particularly, businessmen. A comparative perspective of history and sociology clarifies the value of nationalism. This represents a helpful contribution to an understanding of international business, its negotiations and operations.

Chapter Four: The Japanese Market and its Consumers

Fields, George. *From Bonsai to Levi's*. New York: Macmillan, 1983.
A survey of Japanese culture through anecdotes and facts, this book examines the Japanese consumer through the eyes of a practicing market researcher.

Fields, George. *Gucci on the Ginza*. New York: Kodansha International, 1989.
This book provides observations of the social dilemmas posed in the confrontation between Japanese culture and the broadly sweeping currents of "internationalization."

Hakuhodo Institute of Life & Living (Tokyo).
Detailed descriptions of Japanese consumer values and behavior, based on interviews and mail questionnaires.

Hitonami: Keeping up with the Satos. 1983.
Japanese Women in Turmoil. 1984.
Young Adults in Japan: New Attitudes Creating New Lifestyles. 1985.
Japanese Seniors: Pioneers in the Era of Aging Populations. 1987.
From Family Ties to Financial Ties: Shifting Values in the Japanese Family. 1989.
Japanese Salariimen at the Crossroads. 1991.

March, Robert M. *The Honourable Customer: Marketing and Selling to the Japanese in the 1990s*. London: Pitman, 1990.

This book describes Japanese customers, their values, attitudes and assumptions, what and who influence them, and what criteria they use for decisions on buying.

Chapter Five: The Nature of the Japanese Corporation

Abegglen, James C., and George Stalk, Jr. *Kaisha: The Japanese Corporation.* New York: Basic Books, 1985.
This remains the classic analysis of the Japanese corporation's dynamism. Specific cases raise fundamental questions about management and competition. Based on intimate knowledge and practical information, it offers careful analysis and expert advice.

Chalmers, Norma J. *Industrial Relations in Japan: The Peripheral Workforce.* London: Routledge, 1989.
"Peripheral" here means workers in small and medium-sized enterprises as well as non-regular employees in large firms — the majority of the Japanese labor force too little considered in Western literature. The study limits itself to the manufacturing sector. The description of institutional aspects of industrial relations is most helpful.

Choi, Frederick D. S., and Kazuo Hiramatsu. *Accounting and Financial Reporting in Japan.* London: Van Nostrand and Reinhold, 1988.
A comprehensive and detailed survey by native Japanese contributors that is an indispensable reference tool for investors and businesspeople. International business communication can be hazardous without knowledge of these essential practices.

Dore, Ronald, Jean Bounine-Cabale, and Kari Tapiola. *Japan at Work: Markets, Management, and Flexibility.* Paris: OECD, 1989.
This book describes the long-term and dynamic process whereby organizations and workers adapt to new technologies, changing markets, and other factors, particularly the promotion of and response to endless change. The well-known "lifetime commitment" pattern of employment is seen as facilitating adaptability.

Friedman, David. *The Misunderstood Miracle: Industrial Development and Political Change in Japan.* Ithaca: Cornell University Press, 1988.
Flexible (as opposed to mass) production, if adopted on a large scale, permits rapid product innovation and product competition in global markets. A detailed analysis of the machine tool industry demonstrates that small firms are vital participants, while strengthening themselves by regional cooperation.

Fruin, W. Mark. *The Japanese Enterprise System: Competitive Strategies and Cooperative Structures.* Oxford: Clarendon, 1992.
A thorough analysis of prewar and postwar Japan's industrial structure. Emphasis is on lesser-known micro aspects, in particular how managers have responded to and shaped rapid technological and economic change through "competitive strategies and cooperative structures." The book traces the historical evolution of major companies such as Matsushita and Toshiba and their related firms.

Gerlach, Michael L. *Alliance Capitalism: The Social Organization of Japanese Business.* Berkeley: University of California Press, 1992.
This book focuses on the innovative and increasingly pervasive practice in post-

war Japan of bringing together a cluster of affiliated companies that extends across a broad range of markets, stressing its effectiveness for handling complexity and rapid change and making useful distinctions between Japanese and American practices.

Hirschmeier, J., and T. Yui. *The Development of Japanese Business, 1600–1980*. (2nd Edition). London: Allen & Unwin, 1981.
This describes Japanese management of "big business," from merchants in the Tokugawa era (1600–1868) to entrepreneurs (1868–1895), college graduates (1895–1945) and postwar organizers. Indispensable background reading, its Japanese translation has been used as a textbook in many universities.

Kang, T. W. Gaishi: *The Foreign Company in Japan*. New York: Basic Books, 1990.
An experienced insider (born in Korea, educated in Japan and the U.S., worked for INTEL Japan, and has now established his own consulting firm) describes Japanese business culture. More effective strategies in product development, sales, recruitment, training, cross-cultural partnerships, etc. are vividly illustrated. "Competing in the Japanese market and competing globally against the Japanese are two sides of the same coin."

Kojima, Kiyoshi, and Terutomo Ozawa. *Japan's General Trading Companies: Merchants of Economic Development*. Paris: OECD, 1984.
Sponsored by the OECD as part of research on new forms (minority ownership and non-equity type) of investment in developing countries. Analyzes these companies as major institutions of Japan's postwar economy and their role in international trade and overseas investment.

Odagiri, Hiroyuki. *Growth through Competition, Competition through Growth: Strategic Management and the Economy in Japan*. Oxford: Clarendon, 1992.
Japanese management is characterized by the pursuit of growth (by internal investment) and intense competition within and between firms. This is possible through an efficient and flexible internal labor system, and its consequent impact on industry and the economy at large is profound.

Chapter Six: Routes into Japan

Bleak, J., and D. Ernst, eds. *Collaborating to Compete: Using Strategic Alliances and Acquisitions in the Global Marketplace*. New York: John Wiley, 1993.
This is a strategic and operational guide to designing and managing cross-border alliances. Various authors contribute chapters based on their experiences of alliances forged by multinationals around the world, including two on Japan contributed by Kevin Jones.

Kevin Jones has written a series of articles for the *McKinsey Quarterly* which are of interest to Western businesspeople operating in the Japanese market:

Jones, Kevin. "The FAC Dilemma: Surviving Middle Age in Japan." (Winter 1990).

Jones, Kevin, and Tatsuo Ohbora. "Managing the Heretical Company." (No. 3, 1990).

Jones, Kevin, and W. E. Shill. "Allying for Advantage." (No. 3, 1991).

Jones, Kevin. "Competing to Learn in Japan." (No. 1, 1992).

Chapter Seven: Public Relations in Japan

Hall, Edward T., and Mildred Reed Hall. *Hidden Differences: Doing Business with the Japanese*. New York: Anchor, 1987.
What are the hidden cultural traps of East-West communications for the Western business executive? Patterns of thought and behavior determine vital business information on both sides of the Pacific.

Nihon Shimbun Kyokai (The Japan Newspaper Publishers and Editors Association). *The Japanese Press*. Tokyo, 1992.
This is an annual survey of trends in the newspaper industry in Japan, covering editorial issues, reporting, production, management, sales and circulation, and advertising. It also includes a directory of Japanese newspapers, news agencies, broadcasting stations, and Japanese correspondents overseas.

Vogel, Ezra. *Modern Japanese Organization and Decision-Making*. Berkeley: University of California Press, 1975.
The section by Nathaniel Thayer ("Competition and Conformity: An Inquiry into the Structure of the Japanese Newspapers") is most relevant to this chapter.

Chapter Eight: Advertising, Sales Promotion, and Direct Marketing in Japan

Dentsu Inc. *Japan 1994 Marketing and Advertising Yearbook*. Tokyo, 1993.
An overview of the year's advertising award-winners, advertising trends, and listings of advertising agencies, public relations firms, market research firms, and media.

Dodwell Marketing Consultants. *Direct Marketing in Japan*. Tokyo, 1990.
An overview of the history and characteristics of direct marketing in Japan, together with a summary of the activities of major direct marketers.

JETRO. *Japanese Consumer Handbook 1992: A Businessman's Guide to the Japanese Consumer Market*. Tokyo, 1992.

Tobin, Joseph J., ed. *Re-Made in Japan: Everyday Life and Consumer Taste in a Changing Society*. New Haven: Yale University Press, 1992.
Anthropologists present Japanese consumer behavior in regard to the introduction of Western products and practices, such as haute couture, Tokyo Disneyland, nouvelle cuisine, and the Argentinian tango, which have been "domesticated" to suit Japanese culture and consumption.

Chapter Nine: Marketing Value-Added Products to Japan

Batzer, Erich, and Helmut Laumer. *Marketing Strategies and Distribution Channels for Foreign Companies in Japan*. Boulder: Westview, 1989.
Based on the experiences of German manufacturing companies and trading firms, this book describes the complexities of marketing in Japan, and points to the failure of many foreign firms to understand how the system works and hence to find suitable marketing channels for their products.

Czinkota, Michael R., and Masaaki Kotabe, eds. *The Japanese Distribution System: Opportunities and Obstacles, Structures and Practices*. Chicago: Probus, 1993.
A helpful set of papers by Japanese and non-Japanese experts, presented at a

conference sponsored by the American Marketing Association. Besides pertinent observations about the nature of the distribution system, it looks at wholesale, retail, and market entry. The set concludes with four case studies: U.S. Air Express, Kodak vs. Fuji, the auto aftermarket industry, and fish distribution. Bibliographies offer additional sources of information.

Dodwell Marketing Consultants. *Industrial Goods Distribution in Japan*. 2nd edition. Tokyo, 1991.
Marketing consultants describe business practices in Japan such as purchasing decision, delivery, financing, joint development, leasing, etc., and then focuses on eleven markets where foreign companies are most active. Includes a list of major importers by industry and a list of trade associations.

Dodwell Marketing Consultants. *Retail Distribution in Japan*. 4th edition. Tokyo, 1991.
This describes the characteristics of the distribution system and import trends (practices and participants), major retailers and retail groups, and wholesalers by industry, together with a list of trade associations.

Lynn, Leonard H., and Timothy J. McKeown. *Organizing Business: Trade Associations in America and Japan*. Washington DC: American Enterprise Institute for Public Policy Research, 1988.
This book provides valuable information on the workings of Japanese trade associations, in particular in the iron, steel, and machine-tools sectors.

Maurer, P. Reed. *Competing in Japan*. Tokyo: *The Japan Times*, 1989.
This book reflects the writer's experiences in Japan's pharmaceutical industry and market, and describes the challenges, but also the opportunities: "A one per cent market share (in 1987) translates into a 260-million-dollar business."

Morgan, James C., and J. Jeffrey Morgan. *Cracking the Japanese Market: Strategies for Success in the New Global Economy*. New York and Toronto: Free Press, 1991.
A broad review of what American companies have achieved in Japan in the 1980s as seen by two businessmen, father and son, in the light of what they experienced in establishing and developing Applied Materials Japan, a semiconductor equipment maker. With help from the Japan Development Bank, their enterprise included a Technology Center. Japan provided to them and others like them an indispensable fulcrum for becoming a world-class competitor.

Chapter Ten: How to Be a Successful Supplier into the Japanese Market

Gitlow, Howard S., et al. *Tools and Methods for the Improvement of Quality*. Homewood, IL: Dow Jones–Irwin, 1989.
This book provides a comprehensive approach to Deming's philosophy of improvement for quality, productivity, and competitive position. The PDCA cycle is described as a method that can aid management in pursuing continuous improvement.

Imai, Masaaki. *Kaizen: The Key to Japan's Competitive Success*. New York: Random House, 1987.
This book introduces the Japanese concept of *kaizen* (continuous improve-

ment), which is at the root of the ability to adapt manufacturing processes to rapidly changing requirements. With the help of examples, cases, and graphs, the author explains how *kaizen* is established and works.

Shingo, Shigeo. *A Study of the Toyota Production System*. Cambridge, MA: Productivity Press, 1989.
A clear and specific study by an engineer who played a major role in developing the Toyota system by applying common sense to the production line, its people, and equipment. Toyota discovered that of the four aspects of production — processing, moving, storing, and inspecting — only processing adds value, and consequently the other three should be reduced or eliminated.

Smitka, Michael J. *Competitive Ties: Subcontracting in the Japanese Automotive Industry*. New York: Columbia University Press, 1991.
The author argues that a heavy reliance on outside suppliers is the key to the success of Japanese cars in world markets. By developing cooperative relationships, suppliers are turned into a competitive resource because costs are held in check and rapid technical change and improved product design are promoted.

Trevor, Malcolm, and Ian Christie. *Manufacturers and Suppliers in Britain and Japan*. London: Policy Studies Institute, 1988.
A major competitive advantage of Japanese manufacturers appears to be its close management of the buyer-supplier relationship in terms of quality, delivery, and cost. The contrast with standard practices in the U.K. is striking. This book is required reading for any firm aspiring to supply a Japanese buyer.

Walton, Mary. *Deming Management at Work*. New York: Putnam, 1990.
This excellent book describes the PDCA cycle at work in the Florida Power & Light Company and the Hospital Corporation of America. In its literature, Florida Power & Light notes, "The PDCA cycle is a concept that can be applied to any process. It is also the concept that underlies the Quality Management Story — plan for improvement, institute improvement, check the results, and act to further improve or standardize. It helps us keep on track as we solve problems and make continuous improvement."

Womack, J. P., D. T. Jones, and D. Ross. *The Machine that Changed the World*. New York: Rawson, 1990.
Based on the worldwide Massachusetts Institute of Technology study on the future of the automobile industry, this book looks at the evolution in the industry from mass production to "lean" production, the latter inspired by Japan. Recombining the activities of managers, workers, suppliers, and dealers, lean production permits almost instantaneous response to ever-changing customer demands. Other industries are following.

Chapter Eleven: Demystifying the Japanese Business Environment

American Chamber of Commerce in Japan. *Setting Up an Office in Japan*. Tokyo, 1993.

Ballon, Robert J. *Foreign Competition in Japan: Human Resource Strategies*. London: Routledge, 1992.
This book focuses on how human resources are organized and motivated in Japanese corporations, the problems this creates for foreign firms, and the

strategies to adopt in order to survive in the Japanese market. The work environment is reviewed in detail.

Business Traveller's Guides: Japan. London: *The Economist*, 1987.
This guide gives short but incisive descriptions of the industrial, political, and business scene. The required awareness of business and social practices is then described in succinct form. Finally, major cities are profiled and helpful hints provided.

Graham, John L., and Yoshihiro Sano. *Smart Bargaining: Doing Business with the Japanese*. Cambridge, MA: Ballinger, 1984.
Based on field observations, interviews, and techniques of behavioral science, this book explains how propriety and social conventions are different and suggests that some simple preparatory steps and sharper attention to nuance and detail will secure better communications and stronger agreements.

Huddleston, Jackson N., Jr. *Gaijin Kaisha: Running a Foreign Business in Japan*. Armonk, NY: M.E. Sharpe, 1990.
A long-term American business executive in Japan, the author relates his and colleagues' experiences. There is no one way to do business in Japan, but helpful descriptions and prescriptions are provided about daily problems, and how to obtain support from the home office and assistance from the Japanese community.

JETRO. *Setting Up a Business in Japan: A Manual*. Tokyo, 1991.

March, Robert M. *The Japanese Negotiator: Subtlety and Strategy Beyond Western Logic*. Tokyo: Kodansha International, 1988.
Business and cultural factors influence negotiations. This book gives several cases of both effective and ineffective negotiations, providing insight into Japanese tactics as well as Western "grand" strategies. In conclusion, valuable guidelines are described.

Taylor, Jared. *Shadows of the Rising Sun: A Critical View of the "Japanese Miracle."* New York: William Morrow, 1983.
Taylor grew up in Japan, spending his youth living and being educated "as a Japanese." Returning as a working adult, Taylor analyzes many aspects of Japanese society with a humorous clarity that can only be achieved from knowing the inside story. If you read one book on what makes the Japanese tick, this should be it.

Whiting, Robert. *You Gotta Have Wa*. New York: Macmillan, 1989.
The author is renowned for his books on Japan and sports, the sport of baseball in particular. This book, nominated for a Pulitzer Prize, has become required reading in many Japanese Studies programs in North American universities because of its insights into the philosophy of management in the business world.

Zimmerman, Mark. *How to Do Business with the Japanese: A Strategy for Success*. New York: Random House, 1985.
This book debunks the myth that business in Tokyo is not that much different from business in New York. Practical advice is offered on "succeeding" in Japan: general values and attitudes, negotiations and decision making, competing for market share, and cooperating with the Japanese.

Chapter Twelve: In Search of Investment Capital from Japan

Dunning, John H. *Japanese Participation in British Industry*. London: Croom Helm, 1986.
Written by a foremost British expert in direct foreign investment and based on original field research, this book gives special attention to the extent to which direct investment by Japanese multinationals has aided the transfer of Japanese management styles and technology to the U.K. economy, and identifies both the incentives and obstacles to these transfers.

JETRO. *White Paper on Foreign Direct Investment 1993*. Tokyo, 1993.
An annual overview of trends in Japanese foreign direct investment.

Kester, W. Carl. *Japanese Takeovers: The Global Contest for Corporate Control*. Boston: Harvard Business School Press, 1991.
The author argues that Japan has not had an active market for corporate control because it has not needed one. Companies prefer building and managing long-term relationships with other firms, even overseas, where Japanese takeovers are often triggered by the need to defend a valuable relationship.

Trevor, Malcolm. *Toshiba's New British Company: Competitiveness through Innovation in Industry*. London: Policy Studies Institute, 1988.
The author describes in great detail Toshiba's experiences as the company implemented a new integrated production and marketing system, as well as a new approach to employee relations, which resulted in better quality of goods and services and a more motivated work force.

Chapter Thirteen: Technology and Business

Anderson, Alvin M., and Jon Sigurdson. *Science and Technology in Japan*. Revised edition. Harlow, Essex: Longman Group Ltd., 1991.
First published in 1984, this is the first book to comprehensively describe the science and technology infrastructure in Japan with respect to government partnerships with industry, university programs, and research institutes. Although written over a decade ago, this material still serves as a valuable template upon which to build modern organizational know-how and linkages.

Arrison, Thomas S., et al., eds. *Japan's Growing Technological Capability: Implications for the U.S. Economy*. Washington, DC: National Academy Press, 1992.
This book assesses in detail the strengths and weaknesses on both sides and concludes that Japan's challenge is formidable and growing. The American, Japanese, and European contributors are experts in technology and in the economics of technological innovation.

Cusumano, Michael A. *Japan's Software Factories: A Challenge to U.S. Management*. New York: Oxford University Press, 1991.
An in-depth study of how leading Japanese companies (Hitachi, Toshiba, NEC, and Fujitsu) organize and manage the process of developing software by a factory-like approach, namely, through routinized tasks, controlled work flows, and standardized design, procedures, and tools. The book shows how not to crush the creativity and motivation of hundreds of programmers, and the surprising results of persistence.

Fransman, Martin. *The Market and Beyond: Cooperation and Competition in Information Technology in the Japanese System*. Cambridge: Cambridge University Press, 1990.
This book details how the Japanese government aided industry to confront IBM while maintaining fierce competition among the member firms. This thorough analysis of the industrial electronics sector shows that the firms prefer in-house research, but the government supports joint research.

Golden, William T., ed. *Worldwide Science and Technology Advice to the Highest Levels of Government*. New York: Pergamon Press, Inc. 1991.
An authority on policy formulation and a science and technology advisor to Washington from President Truman in 1950 onwards, William Golden has assembled succinct essays by senior advisors from some thirty-five countries, including the United States, Canada, Japan, and other major industrialized countries, as well as the rapidly developing countries. This book offers a fascinating glimpse at science and technology policy issues and programs worldwide, and underscores the complexities of adding the necessary social and economic dimensions to policies that originate from purely scientific judgments. Many of the present advisory structures have been built up over the past decade in response to the pressures of international competitiveness, big science issues, and radical transformation of the economy by the major enabling technologies.

Kenney-Wallace, G. A., "Science and Technology and Linkages to Contemporary Business: Distraction or Destiny?" *Business in the Contemporary World* (Autumn 1990).
In this special issue on Canada-U.S. business relations, the author focuses on science and technology as a business strategy for international competitiveness and presents arguments linking investment in R&D and the technological capacity of the work force to enhanced GDP over several different types of national economies, including Japan.

Kirton, John, and Sarah Richardson, eds. *Trade, Environment, and Competitiveness*. Ottawa: National Round Table on Environment and Economy, 1992.
Based on papers presented at an international conference in Toronto in November 1991, this book covers environmental, world trade, and legal issues, including relationships between Canada, the United States, and Japan. With almost 400 pages of text and references, this volume is a valuable introduction to the issues and opportunities inherent in the concept of "sustainable economies."

Smith, Murray G., ed. *Global Rivalry and Intellectual Property*. Ottawa: Institute for Research on Public Policy, 1991.
A series of essays and practical examples on intellectual property issues by notable experts in trade, technology, private sector, and government policy from the United States, Canada, Japan, Europe, and South America.

Tyson, Laura. *Who's Bashing Whom? Trade Conflict in High-Technology Industries*. Berkeley: Institute for International Economics, 1993.
The chief White House economist has just published a book on managing trade conflicts in high-technology industries.

Whittaker, D. H. *Managing Innovation: A Study of British and Japanese Factories*. Cambridge: Cambridge University Press, 1990.

The author compares the use of innovative technology, concentrating on computerized machine tools, in nine British and nine Japanese firms. He contrasts the British craftsman approach and the Japanese technician approach, focusing on employee relations, the introduction of machines, operator training, and work-load distribution.

Canadian readers in particular may be interested in the following government reports, available from the Asia-Pacific Foundation of Canada:

Canada-Japan Forum 2000 (December 1992) *Joint Report to the Prime Ministers of Canada and Japan.*

Canada-Japan Complementarity Study (July 1989) *Joint Report to the Prime Ministers of Canada and Japan.*

Directories

Dodwell Marketing Consultants. *Industrial Groupings in Japan.* 10th edition. Tokyo, 1992.

This key source outlines the eight horizontally connected and thirty-seven vertically integrated industrial groups. Over three thousand companies are presented by group affiliation. In addition, group strength by industry is described.

Japan Chamber of Commerce and Industry. *Standard Trade Index of Japan 1992–1993.* 36th edition. Tokyo 1992.

JETRO. *Japan Trade Directory 1992–1993.* 11th edition. Tokyo, 1992.

JETRO. *STEP: The Facts and Figures of Doing Business with Japan.* Tokyo, 1990.

This manual provides background information about the Japanese market, as well as a bibliography of JETRO publications and videos, and listings of Japanese trade associations, foreign trade representative offices, media, financial organizations, lawyers, accountants, research organizations, and office help companies.

Kompass Japan. *Japan Company Information 1992.* Tokyo, 1991.

Nikkei Weekly. Japan Economic Almanac 1993. Tokyo, 1993.

Tokyo Foreign Trade Association. *Buyer's Guide of Tokyo 1992–1993.* Tokyo, 1992.

Toyo Keizai Inc. *Japan Company Handbook.* Tokyo, 1993.

INDEX

PRINTED IN CANADA